T0183875

Lecture Notes in Computer Science   11293

Commenced Publication in 1973
Founding and Former Series Editors:
Gerhard Goos, Juris Hartmanis, and Jan van Leeuwen

More information about this series at http://www.springer.com/series/7408

Lei Bu · Yingfei Xiong (Eds.)

Software Analysis, Testing, and Evolution

8th International Conference, SATE 2018
Shenzhen, Guangdong, China, November 23–24, 2018
Proceedings

 Springer

Editors
Lei Bu (ID)
Nanjing University
Nanjing, China

Yingfei Xiong (ID)
Peking University
Peking, China

ISSN 0302-9743   ISSN 1611-3349 (electronic)
Lecture Notes in Computer Science
ISBN 978-3-030-04271-4   ISBN 978-3-030-04272-1 (eBook)
https://doi.org/10.1007/978-3-030-04272-1

Library of Congress Control Number: 2018961173

LNCS Sublibrary: SL2 – Programming and Software Engineering

This Springer imprint is published by the registered company Springer Nature Switzerland AG
The registered company address is: Gewerbestrasse 11, 6330 Cham, Switzerland

Preface

The Annual Conference on Software Analysis, Testing and Evolution (SATE) is organized by the Technical Committee of Software Engineering (TCSE), the Technical Committee of System Software (TCSS), and the Technical Committee of Information System (TCIS) of the China Computer Federation (CCF) with a focus on software analysis, testing, and evolution. SATE provides a premier forum for software engineering researchers, professional software analysts, testers and developers to present research findings, share practical experience, and exchange academic ideas.

SATE solicits high-quality submissions describing significant and original results related to software analysis, testing, and evolution, including theoretical research, empirical studies, new technology, case studies, and industrial practice. This year, we received 34 submissions. All submissions were reviewed by at least three members of the Program Committee and were thoroughly discussed online. Finally, the Program Committee selected 13 submissions to be included in the English proceedings, making an acceptance rate of 38.2%. We would like to thank all the 43 Program Committee members from different countries for their effort with the paper reviewing and online discussion.

This year SATE was co-located with the National Software Application Conference (NASAC 2018) in Shenzhen, Guangdong, China, on November 23. Besides paper presentation, SATE 2018 also included invited talks from top researchers in software analysis, testing, and evolution. We invite academic researchers and industrial practitioners from software engineering and other related areas to participate and exchange ideas about research and practical issues in connection with software analysis, testing and evolution.

October 2018

Baowen Xu
Lei Bu
Yingfei Xiong

Organization

Program Committee

Lei Bu	Nanjing University, China
Yan Cai	Institute of Software, Chinese Academy of Sciences, China
Junjie Chen	Peking University, China
Lin Chen	Nanjing University, China
Liqian Chen	National University of Defense Technology, China
Yuting Chen	Shanghai Jiao Tong University, China
Zhenbang Chen	National University of Defense Technology, China
Wei Dong	National University of Defense Technology, China
Wensheng Dou	Institute of Software, Chinese Academy of Sciences, China
Chunrong Fang	Nanjing University, China
Xinyu Feng	Nanjing University, China
Yang Feng	University of California, Irvine, USA
Qing Gao	Peking University, China
Jeff Huang	Texas A&M University, USA
He Jiang	Dalian University of Technology, China
Yanyan Jiang	Nanjing University, China
Yu Jiang	University of Illinois at Urbana-Champaign, USA
Ding Li	NEC Labs America, USA
Guoqiang Li	Shanghai Jiao Tong University, China
Li Li	Monash University, Australia
Hui Liu	Beijing Institute of Technology, China
Yang Liu	Nanyang Technological University, Singapore
Yepang Liu	Southern University of Science and Technology, China
David Lo	Singapore Management University, Singapore
Xin Peng	Fudan University, China
Xiaokang Qiu	Purdue University, USA
Yulei Sui	University of Technology, Sydney, Australia
Jun Sun	Singapore University of Technology and Design, Singapore
Cong Tian	Xidian University, China
Song Wang	University of Waterloo, Canada
Xiaoyin Wang	University of Texas at San Antonio, USA
Xin Xia	Monash University
Xiaoyuan Xie	Wuhan University, China
Yingfei Xiong	Peking University, China
Chang Xu	Nanjing University, China
Jifeng Xuan	Wuhan University, China
Zijiang Yang	Western Michigan University, USA
Tingting Yu	University of Kentucky, USA

Danfeng Zhang   The Pennsylvania State University, USA
Hongyu Zhang   The University of Newcastle, Australia
Lingming Zhang   The University of Texas at Dallas, USA
Lu Zhang   Peking University, China
Xin Zhang   Massachusetts Institute of Technology, USA
Jianjun Zhao   Kyushu University, Japan
Hao Zhong   Shanghai Jiao Tong University, China

Additional Reviewers

Chen, Lingchao   Xu, Chuanqi
Chen, Yuqi   Xu, Luhang
Hu, Chi   Xue, Jianxin
Jiang, Yanyan   Yu, Hengbiao
Li, Jiaying   Yu, Runze
Li, Leping   Zha, Junpeng
Li, Yanze   Zhang, Haitao
Shi, Hao   Zhang, Yufeng
Xiao, Siyang

Contents

Testing and Monitoring

Program Repair

Which Defect Should Be Fixed First? Semantic Prioritization of Static Analysis Report

Han Wang$^{(\boxtimes)}$, Min Zhou, Xi Cheng, Guang Chen, and Ming Gu

School of Software, Tsinghua University, Beijing, China
h-wang16@mails.tsinghua.edu.cn

Abstract. The usability of static analyzers is plagued by excessive false alarms. It is laborious yet error-prone to manually examine the spuriousness of defect reports. Moreover, the inability to preclude overwhelming false alarms deters user's confidence on such tools and severely limits their adoption in development cycles. In this paper, we propose a semantic approach for prioritizing defect reports emitted by static analysis. Our approach evaluates the importance of defect reports by their fatality and priorities defects by their affection to critical functions. Compared to the existing approaches that prioritize defect reports by analyzing external attributes, ours substantially utilizes semantic information derived by static analysis to measure the severity of defect reports more precisely. We have implemented a prototype which is evaluated to real-world code bases, and the results show that our approach can effectively evaluate the severity of defects.

Keywords: Defect prioritization · Static analysis
Defect propagation analysis

1 Introduction

Software analysis tools such as static analyzers are broadly adopted in real-world development cycles to eliminate possible defects which may hinder the safety and security of the subject software system.

Static analyzers are almost doomed to emit false alarms due to the imprecision of analysis algorithms and the lack of external environment specifications. Manually precluding false alarms is time-consuming and error-prone, so it is desirable to automate such a process. According to the observation that the severity of a defect report is associated with the lexical and semantic information of relevant program code, we evaluate the importance of defect reports by leveraging static analysis to help users focus on the most possibly severe defect reports and suppress false alarms.

On the other hand, many software systems have a strict plan for release, or the development is limited by the resources. In that case, not all defects could

© Springer Nature Switzerland AG 2018
L. Bu and Y. Xiong (Eds.): SATE 2018, LNCS 11293, pp. 3–19, 2018.
https://doi.org/10.1007/978-3-030-04272-1_1

be fixed. Developers need to decide which defect should be fixed first, so defect prioritization should be adopted.

Some solutions have been proposed to prioritize defects automatically using statistical or machine learning methods. Ruthruff *et al.* [13] use logistic regression models to predict accurate and actionable static analysis warnings. Lamkanfi *et al.* [11] use Naive Bayes classifier to predict the severity of a reported bug. These kinds of approaches can learn hidden expert knowledge of defects and classify defects into different categories. But these approaches require large amounts of labeled data to gain satisfying accuracy and only analyze external attributes of defects such as severity, category, reporter, etc. Existing approaches have limited capability to measure the influencing scope of a certain defect, which hinders the semantic prioritization of defect reports.

We propose an automatic approach to prioritize software defects by leveraging static analysis in this paper. Our contribution includes: (1) Extensible static data propagation analysis framework. (2) Hybrid analysis on the affection domain of defects (control flow analysis, data flow analysis, global variable analysis, etc.). (3) Defect fatality measurement tool implementation and application.

The paper is organized as follows. Section 2 surveys the related work. Section 3 introduces preliminaries for our method. Section 4 describes the defect prioritization based on static analysis. Section 5 implements our algorithm. Section 6 demonstrates the experimental results. Section 7 discusses threats to our algorithm's validity and future work. Finally, Sect. 8 concludes this paper.

2 Related Work

Kaushik *et al.* [9] believe that there are two research directions in defect prioritization, multi-objective defect prioritization and utilizing software artifact traceability links. Uddin *et al.* [14] give a small theoretical study of bug reports and summarize existing work on bug prioritization and some possible problems in working with bug prioritization.

Statistical approaches utilize the powerful statistical model to represent the properties of defects, which facilitates mining of knowledge on the priority of defect reports. Kremenek *et al.* [10] use a statistical model to rank error reports emitted by static analyzers. Guo *et al.* [5] use a statistical model to predict the probability of an incoming bug to be fixed. Recent research interest in machine learning grows substantially, and some approaches leveraging machine learning techniques have emerged. Abdelmoez *et al.* [1] use Naive Bayes classifier to predict time cost of bug fixing. Kanwal *et al.* [8] use support vector machine (SVM) to develop a bug priority predictor.

The mainstream machine learning based approaches require a large amount of labeled data to achieve satisfying accuracy and analyze only external attributes of defects. Some approaches attempt to improve defect prioritization accuracy by enriching program context information. Jeong *et al.* [6] improve bug triage by utilizing bug tossing history with Markov chains. Liang *et al.* [12] improve defect detection and warning prioritization by introducing a novel Expressive Defect Pattern Specification Notation.

All of these works focus on analyzing external attributes of defects such as severity, category, reporter, etc. Our method uses static analysis to track the propagation of defects, which takes context information of defects into consideration. But because our method uses static analysis, our method need the source code of defects to be provided.

3   Preliminaries

Control-flow Automaton (CFA). CFA is a graph representation of the program which consists of control locations and control-flow edges [2]. Control locations model the domain of program counter *pc*. There are two kinds of edges in CFA, one is instruction edge, the other is assumption edge. Assumption edge is labeled with a condition expression which is the guard condition for the edge to be taken. On the other hand, instruction edge is labeled with an action that is performed when the edge is taken. For example in Fig. 1, edge N9 → N11 and edge N9 → N10 are assumption edges, edge N11 → N12 and N10 → N13 are instruction edges. Static analysis algorithms rely upon traversal on CFA.

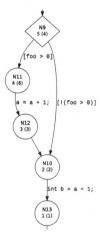

Fig. 1. Control-flow automaton.

Access Path. It is an abstract representation of physical memory locations. The abstract representation describes how a variable can be accessed from an initial variable in a store-less model. We use the same access path as Cheng et al. [3] in our approach to conduct basic pointer analysis and abstract memory model. For example, the access path of $b[1]$ at line 3 would be $a.4\_8$ in Fig. 2. It represents the corresponding memory location which is allocated for the local variable a and the offset is $[4, 8)$.

Control Dependency. An instruction Y has a control dependence on a control instruction X if only X determines whether Y executes. Consider the previous

```
1 ║   int a[10];
2 ║   int* b = a;
3 ║   b[1] = 1;
```

Fig. 2. An example for the access path.

example in Fig. 1, instruction $a = a+1$ (edge N11 → N12) has control dependence on instruction $foo > 0$ (edge N9 → N11). Basically, if we have a branch, all subsequent instructions have control dependence on the branch. With the knowledge of control dependencies, we can easily tell if an instruction can be affected by some branch instructions. But whether the subsequent instructions outside of the branches will be executed will not be determined by branch instructions. This information is very important for our following defect propagation algorithm.

Critical Functions. Critical functions are a set of functions which is considered to be crucial to program security. Critical functions are ones that (1) perform critical operations such as memory allocation, (2) have a large number of callers. Also, critical functions can also be manually specified by the program analyst. If poisoned values of defects are propagated to critical functions, the subject program would be vulnerable to external attacks. Some strategies have been proposed in Sect. 4.3 to identify critical functions. After defect propagation analysis, we will check if a defect will affect critical functions. In general, a defect that affects critical functions has higher priority.

4 Defect Prioritization

As presented in Fig. 3, our defect prioritization approach contains three major phases: *Pre-process Phase* (**PP Phase**), *Defect Propagation Analysis Phase* (**DPA Phase**) and *Defect Prioritization Phase* (**DP Phase**). The input of our approach is a C program and reported defects in the C program by a static analyzer (such as clang's *scan-build*), while its output is the prioritized defects.

PP Phase pre-processes the program to be analyzed. Given a C program, we first capture compilation commands for each executable and mutate the arguments of compilation commands that generate .o files to produce LLVM assembly files (.ll files). Then we use clang-linker to link all LLVM assembly files into one LLVM file. Next, the single LLVM file is parsed into CFA, which is one of the infrastructures for our analysis algorithm. Our following algorithms are implemented based on that CFA.

DPA Phase analyzes the propagation of each defect. Defects that are memory related and assigned to variables can apply to our defect prioritization analysis. First of all, variables used by defected expressions are labeled as affected. Then we assign those variables a default score 1 called **fatality score** initially and propagate the score during the analyzing process. Our analysis starts at the node right after the defect and propagates fatality score to all reachable nodes. The defect propagation is performed with respect to specific rules represented in Algorithm 1 in detail. During the process of defect propagation, we

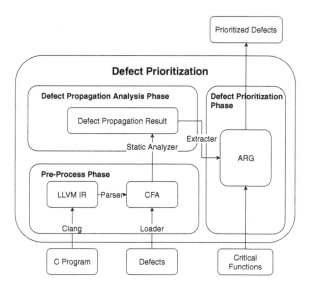

Fig. 3. Defect prioritization.

store each CFA node and its corresponding fatality score into a data structure called abstract reachability graph (ARG). ARG is a stateful CFA and describes the reachability of each CFA node.

DP Phase collects propagation results of defects stored in ARG from *DPA Phase*. Critical functions can be specified by users. If not, a heuristic approach is employed to automatically derive critical functions from source code (**Critical Function Set** in Sect. 4.3). According to the selected critical functions, we compute the weighted sum of variable fatality scores in the entry nodes of critical functions with Eq. (1) and take it as the fatality score of the defect. The reason for choosing the entry nodes of critical functions instead of the exit nodes is that the defect has affects the critical function, and skipping the analysis of function body can speed up the process of defect prioritization.

$$s = \sum_{f}^{CFS} p_f S_f \tag{1}$$

In Eq. (1), s is the fatality score of the defect, CFS is a set of critical functions, p_i is the critical coefficient of function i and S_i is fatality score for the entry node of function i. After all defects are analyzed by *DPA Phase* and *DP Phase*, we can get the fatality score for each defect. Then we prioritize these defects according to the defect fatality score.

4.1 Data Propagation Rules

In our analysis, we abstract all instructions in LLVM into 3 types of edges on CFA: *operation edges, function call/return edges* and *assumption edges. Opera-*

tion edges abstract operations such as binary instructions and memory related instructions in LLVM. *Function call/return edges* abstract function calls/returns. *Assumption edges* abstract branch assumptions and switch assumptions. We define global variable set as G and fatality score of the variable v as $I(v)$. Based on that, we analyze the propagation of a defect according to rules in Table 1:

Table 1. Fatality score propagation rules

Statement	Fatality score propagation rules
$y = op(x_1, \ldots, x_n), y \notin G$	$I(y) = \max\{I(y), \max\limits_{i=1\ldots n}\{I(x_i)\}\}$
$g = op, g \in G$	$I(g) = \max\{I(g), \frac{I(op)}{n}\}$
Function call/return	Pass parameters
Branch instruction	Propagate in controlled instructions
Merge statement	$I(y) = \max\{I(y), \max\limits_{i=1\ldots n}\{I(y_i)\}\}$

Instruction Rule. We only deal with instructions with the form $y = op(x_1, x_2, \ldots, x_n)$, where op can be compound or expression statements. Because an operation can propagate poisoned data if and only if it assigns some values to memory locations.

For assignment operations, fatality score will pass from right-hand side (RHS) to left-hand side (LHS). If the LHS of the assignment operation is not a global variable, the fatality score of the LHS is updated as that of the RHS. Formally, if we have $y = x, y \notin G$, then $I(y)$ is assigned with $\max\{I(y), I(x)\}$.

For other operations, the fatality score of operations is the maximum score of all operands. Formally, if we have operation with the form of $y = op(x_1, x_2, \ldots, x_n)$, $y \notin G$, then $I(y)$ is assigned with $\max\limits_{i=1\ldots n}\{I(x_i)\}$. Although both *max* and *sum* can be applied to the fatality score update, we choose the *max* function for two reasons: the influence degree of different variables should not be equal and the use of *max* will make the variable have a smaller value for convenience calculation.

If we write a global variable somewhere, it will affect some instructions which read the global variable. If a defect is propagated to a global variable, instructions which read the global variable before the defect will not be affected, while instructions which read the global variable after the defect may be affected by the defect. Our approach is as follows: propagating the fatality score of global variables to all instructions which read the global variable with a loss parameter p. Currently we define the loss parameter p as $\frac{1}{n}$. Formally, if we have $g = op, g \in G$, $I(g)$ is updated as $\max\{I(g), \frac{I(op)}{n}\}$.

In order to propagate fatality score from a global variable to all instructions which read it, we need to build connections from its reads to its writes, which can be expensive. If we want to build connections from a global variable's reads to its writes, we need to find writes of the variable in all source code. Our approach works from the opposite direction: build connections from the writes of a global to its reads. In this way, we just need to check if a global variable has been propagated by defects whenever we reach the writes of the variable.

If a global variable is propagated from some defects, we record the specific variable and store its fatality score into memory. Whenever a global variable is read, we check if it has been recorded, if so, take fatality score of the variable from memory, otherwise, set fatality score of the variable to 0.

Function Call/Return Rule. Defect propagation analysis is an interprocedural analysis. So we handle function calls/returns by passing parameters from actual parameters to formal parameters.

If we have function $void\ foo(n_1, \ldots, n_n)$ defined, we get $I(n_i) = I(a_i), \forall a_i \in \{a_1, \ldots, a_n\}, n_i \in \{n_1, \ldots, n_n\}$ when we call $foo(a_1, \ldots, a_n)$. If we have function $int\ foo()$ with return statement as $return\ bar$, we get $I(y) = \max(I(y), I(bar))$ when we call $y = foo()$.

Assumption Rule. If a defect is propagated to an assumption edge, it will affect the result of condition statement on the assumption edge, then affect which branch will be taken in the following instructions. That means all instructions in the branch will be affected by the defect.

```
1 ||    if ( condition statement ) {
2 ||        //code block 1
3 ||    } else {
4 ||        //code block 2
5 ||    }
6 ||    //code block 3
```

Fig. 4. The assumption rule example.

For example, if the condition statement in Fig. 4 is propagated from a defect, whether instructions in code block 1 and 2 will be executed will be affected. Since all instructions in code block 1 and 2 will be affected by the defect in the condition statement, the propagation is different from normal propagation. The defect will be propagated to all instructions in code block 1 and 2. This mode of propagation ends at code block 3 because not all instructions in code block 3 will be affected by the defect.

During analysis, if condition statement is affected by a defect, only the instructions inside the scopes of branching statements are propagated. Since in general multiple branches are possibly reachable while only one branch is reached in a concrete execution, the propagation inside each branch should be weakened. Consider the example in Fig. 4, if the condition statement is propagated by fatality score $I(c)$, instructions in code block 1 and 2 will be propagated by fatality score $\frac{I(c)}{2}$. For code block 3, however, not all instructions in it will be propagated. So this mode of propagation ends at code block 3.

4.2   Defect Prioritization Algorithm

Our defect prioritization algorithm is shown in Algorithm 1. The input of our algorithm is (1) the source files, (2) defects D, (3) the set of critical functions S labeled with their weight. Our algorithm performs a traversal on the CFA. It employs a flow-sensitive, field-sensitive, path-insensitive pointer analysis based on access path. During the process, we maintain the alias information and handle propagation of defects on various types of transitions. Each memory location (presented as access path) is labeled with a fatality score. Then prioritization is performed based on the fatality score.

Algorithm 1. Defect Prioritization Algorithm

Input: CFA of source files
defects D
critical functions S
Output: Prioritized defects D'

DEFECT-PRIORITIZATION(S)

1   **for** $d_i \in D$
2   DEFECT-PROPAGATION(d_i)
3   FATALITY-SCORE-CALCULATION(S)
4   $D' = sort(D)$
5   **return** D'

DEFECT-PROPAGATION(d)

1   $waitlist = \{nodes\ directly\ affected\ by\ d\}$
2   **while** $!waitlist.isEmpty()$
3       $cur = waitlist.pop()$
4   **for** $e \in outEdges(cur)$
5   **if** e is $InstructionEdge$
6   apply **Instruction Rule**
7   **elseif** e is $functionCallEdge$ or $functionReturnEdge$
8   apply **Function Call/Return Rule**
9   **elseif** e is $assumeEdge$
10   apply **Assumption Rule**
11      $currentNode = merge(currentNode, prevNode)$
12      $waitlist.push(currentNode)$

FATALITY-SCORE-CALCULATION(S)

1   $score = 0$
2   **for** $e \in CFA.EntryNodes()$
3   **if** $e \in S$
4           $score\ += w_i * I(e)$
5   **return** score

We first apply *instruction rule* (line 6), *function call/return edge* (line 8) and *assumption edge* (line 10) to prioritize defects in Algorithm 1. Then we use *merge* function at line 11 of function DEFECT-PROPAGATION to merge and update the fatality scores. Merge operation combines multiple propagation states when a join point of program paths is encountered. For each variable, we just compare the fatality scores stored in both of the nodes and take the maximum to be the fatality score. For example, if node 1 stores variable-fatality score map $\{(a, 1.0), (b, 0.5)\}$, node 2 stores $\{(b, 1.0), (c, 0.5)\}$, then their merging result is $\{(a, 1.0), (b, 1.0), (c, 0.5)\}$

We give an illustrating example to show how our algorithm works in Fig. 5. Given critical function `memoryOperation`, if variable a is affected by some defect at line 15, which taints the value of variable a. Our algorithm will be able to detect that variables b, c, d will be affected by our defect propagation algorithm and evaluate the defect priority by the observation that it affects critical function `memoryOperation`.

```
1    int G;
2
3    void memoryOperation(int n) {
4        // critical function
5        int* var = malloc(sizeof(int) * n);
6        ...
7    }
8
9    int foo() {
10       return G;
11   }
12
13   int bar() {
14       int a, b, c, d;
15       a = defect();
16       G = a;
17       if (a > 1) {
18           b = 1;
19           ...
20       }
21       ...
22       c = foo();
23       d = a + b + c;
24       memoryOperation(d);
25       ...
26   }
```

Fig. 5. Demonstration example of defect propagation.

The propagation process of the defect is calculated as follows. Line 15 is the defect source, so variable a will be assigned a default fatality score of 1. Base on the *instruction rule*, the fatality score of the global variable G will be updated to 1. According to the *assumption rule*, unpredictable value of a will affect whether the branch at line 17 will be executed. Thus, it affects the value of b and its fatality score is assigned a value of $1/2$. The assignment at line 16 will propagate the defect from a to global variable G. Then the defect will propagate to c through function `foo()`. As a result, c will obtain a fatality score of 1. Each operand in expression $a + b + c$ at line 23 is affected by the defect, which makes the assignment's left operand d being propagated by the defect. Since we only get the maximum fatality score of the three variables, the fatality score of variable d is assigned to 1. The defect will be propagated to function `memoryOperation` by function call at line 24. Since function `memoryOperation` is a critical function, the priority of the defect will be high enough in prioritization result. We do not enter the critical function body, so the defect propagation process ends.

4.3   Critical Function Set Calculation

Currently we have three strategies to calculate critical functions.

– *ALL_FUNCTION.* The first strategy naively takes all functions as critical functions. The defect prioritization results calculated by this strategy only show the scope of a defect's propagation.
– *TOP_K.* This strategy analyzes the call graph of the input program and extracts functions with a large number of callers.
– *USER_SPEC.* Users can manually specify critical functions with their knowledge of the subject program. For example, defects on memory operations are usually vulnerable to attackers, thus users can annotate all the functions that are relevant to memory operations as critical functions.

5   Implementation

As we described in Sect. 3, we need to calculate control dependency before analyzing defect. We have demonstrated detailedly how we use control dependency to propagate defects in Sect. 4.2. In this section, we will introduce the algorithm we used to calculate control dependency.

Cytron *et al.* [4] presented *reverse dominance frontier* algorithm to calculate dominance frontier and control dependency based on node dominance tree. We employ a simple and approximating algorithm rather than reverse dominance frontier in our approach to calculate control dependency.

Its procedure is shown in Algorithm 2 and generally it derives control dependency by calculating a least fixed point. Function exit note describes the function ends. $PN(X)$ denotes all nodes appears on the path from node X to Exit Node. $CD(X)$ denotes all nodes which have control dependency with node X. We first use function PATH-TO-EXITNODE to calculate $PN(X)$ for each node X in function. Then we calculate $CD(X)$ by comparing $PN(Y)$ for all node Y which is the successor of node X. In function PATH-TO-EXITNODE, we start at the function exit node and traverse backward to function entry node. Each time we put the current node into the path set S which records all node passed from current node to exit node. This function stops when the calculation of S saturates.

We optimize control dependency calculation in the following two aspects.

Algorithm 2. Control Dependency Calculation

Input: CFA of source files
Output: Control Dependency Map $M : \{Node : NodeSet\}$

CONTROL-DEPENDENCY-CALCULATION(CFA)

1 **for** $f \in CFA.functions$
2   PATH-TO-EXITNODE($\{\}, PM, f.exitNode$)
3   **for** $n \in f.nodes$
4          $PN = [PM.get(p)\ for\ p \in n.successors]$
5          $CD = symmetricDifference(PN)$
6          $M.put(n, CD)$
7 **return** M

PATH-TO-EXITNODE(S, PM, n)

1 **if** $PM.get(n).containsALL(S)$
2   **return**
3 **else**
4      $PM.get(n).addALL(S)$
5 $Sort(n.enteringNodes)$ in exploration priority
6 **for** $n' \in n.enteringNodes$
7      $S.add(n')$
8   PATH-TO-EXITNODE(S, PM, n')
9      $S.remove(n')$

- **Persistent structure.** We use persistent set to store the node set PN. Persistent set preserves the previous nodes when it is modified, thus better memory efficiency is achieved.
- **Exploration Priotity.** When we traverse backwards from current node to function entry, we traverse successors of the current node in exploration priority (line 5 of function PATH-TO-EXITNODE). Basically, exploration priority is determined by the distance between current node and function exit node. Exploration priority guarantees when there is a loop in successors, we will traverse the loop first. This helps to reduce useless traverse of other nodes when the loop exits.

6   Experimental Evaluation

In this section, we presented the evaluation results of our defect prioritization approach. We analyzed consecutive release versions of open source projects with clang's static analyzer *scan-build*. Then we located fixed defects of all defects by comparing the report of *scan-build*. At last, we prioritized those defects with our algorithm and present the effectiveness of it.

6.1   Experimental Data Preparation

Jureczko et al. [7] collected defect occurrence with a tool called BugInfo. BugInfo analyse the logs from source code repository (SVN or CVS) and decides whether a commit is a *bugfix* according to the log content. A commit is interpreted as a *bugfix* when it solves an issue reported in the bug tracking system.

Watanabe et al. [15] collected their experiment data following three steps. The first step is to identify the past release points for each project. Next, the log data is obtained from the past release points to the current commit. Finally, textual search is employed (using the keywords 'bug' and 'fixed') to count the frequency of bug fixes.

Similar to the existing work, our approach collects fixes for defects by digging version history of a certain software project. To evaluate the effectiveness of our defect prioritization approach, we examine whether the defect reports with high priority correspond to the real defects which are fixed in the later commits.

A defect reported by a static analysis tool is fixed if and only if the defect is no longer reported by the same static analysis tool in the subsequent versions. Based on the hypothesis, we can locate fixed defect by comparing the static analysis result of different release versions of a project. So we compute the fixed defect as follows: (1) We extract consecutive past release versions of a project. (2) We run static analysis on those release versions of the project base on the *scan-build* clang-analyzer. (3) We compare the bug reports of those release versions of the project and label all defects which disappear in latest release version's report as **fixed defect.** Other defects are labeled as unfixed defects.

We applied this approach to different releases of open-source projects from GitHub and got the defect numbers and fixed defect numbers shown in Table 2.

- Nuklear is a single-header ANSI C GUI library. It does not have any release currently. But it has 1,549 commits currently, so we use *scan-build* analyzed 5 former commits. We were able to found 3 fixed defects out of 8 defects in commit "1d7f024".
- MASSCAN is a TCP port scanner. It currently has 8 releases. We analyzed 3 of them and found 4 fixed defects out of 9 defects in version 1.0.1.
- GoAccess is a real-time web log analyzer and interactive viewer. It currently has 25 releases. We analyzed 3 of them and found 6 fixed defects out of 11 defects in version 0.7.
- Twemproxy is a fast, light-weight proxy for memcached and redis. It currently has 13 releases. We analyzed 5 of them and found 4 fixed defects out of 32 defects in version 0.1.16.

6.2   Evaluation Metrics

We evaluate the performance of our method with two experiments: accuracy experiment and prioritization improvement experiment.

We evaluate the accuracy of our method by checking if we set fixed defects' priority higher than all unfixed defects. Let function $N(x)$ denote the number

Table 2. Tested projects

Project name	Release	#Defects	#Fixed defects
Nuklear	*	8	3
	*	6	1
	*	10	0
	*	12	0
	*	12	0
MASSCAN	v1.0.1	9	4
	v1.0.3	9	3
	v1.0.5	8	0
GoAccess	v0.7	11	6
	v0.8	10	5
	v0.9	6	0
Twemproxy	v0.1.16	23	4
	v0.1.20	23	3
	v0.1.20	23	3
	v0.2.0	24	0
	v0.3.0	25	0

of fixed defects in top x of prioritized defects. Function $N\_E(x) = min(N_a, x)$ describes the ideal case when all fixed defects are in front of all unfixed defects, where N_a is the number of fixed defects in all defects. So to evaluate the accuracy of our method, we just need to calculate the correlation coefficient between $N(x)$ and $N\_E(x)$. The closer correlation coefficient to 1, the higher our accuracy.

To evaluate the prioritization improvement of our approach compared with the random approach, we check if the fixed defects ranked high enough in our prioritized defects than randomly ranked defects reported by the *scan-build* analyzer. Let function $P(x) = \frac{N(x)}{x}$ denote the rate of fixed defects in top x of prioritized defects. Function $P\_O(x) = \frac{N\_O(x)}{x}$ describes the rate of fixed defects in top x of randomly ranked defects, where $N\_O(x)$ is the number of fixed defects in top x of randomly ranked defects. So to evaluate the prioritization improvement of our method, we just compare the value of $P(x)$ and $P\_O(x)$

6.3   Experimental Result Evaluation

Currently, we implemented a version of our method which naively used *ALL_FUNCTION*. (Sect. 4.3) as our Critical Function Set. Then we applied our defect prioritization algorithm on 4 prepared open-source projects. Our experiment aims to find correlations between fixed defects and high-rank defects by our algorithm.

The results of accuracy experiment are shown in Fig. 6. The X-axis of the figure is top x defects. The Y-axis of the figure is fixed defects among those

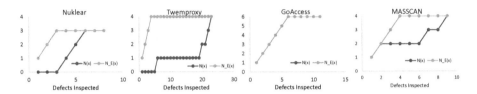

Fig. 6. Accuracy experiment.

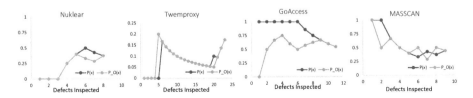

Fig. 7. Prioritization improvement experiment.

defects. The correlation coefficient between $N(x)$ and $N\_E(x)$ for 4 projects are $0.61, 0.42, 1$ and 0.65 respectively.

The results of prioritization improvement experiment are shown in Fig. 7. The X-axis of the figure is top x defects. The Y-axis of the figure is the rate of fixed defects among those defects. For most cases, $P(x)$ of in Fig. 7 are better than $P\_O(x)$. It means that our defect prioritization analysis can achieve better performance than the naively random approach. This leads to more serious defects assigned to the programmer to prioritize fixes.

Experiment results show that our method works well on some projects. But it also shows the limitation of *ALL_FUNCTION* strategy on some defects' analysis.

In the case of project *Nuklear*, the first fixed defect ranks at the 4th of all defects. All 3 fixed defects are ranked at 4th, 5th, and 6th. We looked into the source code and analyzed the propagation of those fixed defects. Unfortunately, all of them are *Dead Assignment*, which means value stored to variable is never read. So this kind of defect will not propagate. Since our defect prioritization algorithm is based on defect propagation, they could not have sufficient high rankings in defect reports.

In the case of project *MASSCAN*, 2 fixed defects are ranked at top-2 prioritized defects. However, the other 2 fixed defects rank at the end of prioritized defects. We dug into the source code and analyzed the propagation of those 2 defects. One of them is *Memory Leak*, a piece of memory which is no longer needed is incorrectly released. Such defects cannot be propagated by our data propagation analysis. The other fixed defect can be abstracted as the following code.

```
1   table = (transition_t*)malloc(sizeof(transition_t*) * row_count *
         column_count);
2   \\ code block
3   memset(table, 0, sizeof(transition_t*) * row_count * column_count);
```

Programmer allocated wrong size of memory for pointer `table` at line 1. Then they used `table` in function `memset`, which could lead to severe memory error. They fixed the bug at version 1.0.5 by change the `transition_t*` in `sizeof` to `transition_t`. While the variable `table` itself will not affect many functions, so the defect's ranking is low. This can be fixed by specifying memory related functions as critical functions. We will discuss this in Sect. 7.

In the case of project *GoAccess*, our algorithm works quite well. All the 6 fixed defects are before all unfixed defects.

In the case of project *Twemproxy*, our algorithm ranks the first fixed defect at the 6th of the results. The other 3 fixed defects are ranked at the end of the results. We dug into the source code and analyzed the propagation of those 4 fixed defects. We found 3 of them are *Dereference of null pointer*, the other is *Dead Assignments*. Although these defects did not affect a large amount of code, *Dereference of null pointer* clearly affected memory. With *ALL_FUNCTION* as critical functions, it is currently impossible to rank these fixed defects higher.

Based on the experiments, we found that our method with *ALL_FUNCTION* can get satisfying defect priority when there are no memory related defects in defects. But when there are memory related defects, like the *Memory Leak* in *MASSCAN* and *Dereference of null pointer* in *Twemproxy*, functions relevant to memory operations should be more critical than others.

7   Future Work

This section discusses the factors which may deter the effectiveness of our approach and give possible solutions to these problems in our future work.

Critical Function Set. In our experiment, we only implemented a version of our method which considered all functions as critical functions. But this implementation does not work well on memory related defects because memory related functions are more important than others in real-world projects.

Defect Location. Defect location is important to our approach. We used *scan-build* in our experiment to give method name and line number of defects, which helps to locate defects. For defect propagation analysis, we need to know which variable is first affected by a defect, then the defect can propagate through variables. Currently, all the variables at the line where a defect occurs are propagated as defects, which is an imprecise approximation.

Our method can be improved with the following approaches:

Combining with Categorical Attributes. Some defect analyzer may give defects some categorical attributes (such as the category of defect, defect severity, method, etc.) to help manage defects. Currently, most defect prioritization algorithms would combine those categorical attributes and try to classify or cluster the defects with machine learning algorithm. Those algorithms can achieve satisfying accuracy with enough labeled data, which substantiates the importance of attribute data to defect prioritization. We believe our defect prioritization algorithm will be more accurate if we combine defect propagation information with categorical attributes.

Mining Critical Functions. A proper set of critical functions may improve our method a lot. To handle memory related defects, memory related functions (*memset, memcpy, malloc, free, etc.*) can be specified as critical functions. Also, learning from CVE could be an effective way to acquire critical functions.

8 Conclusion

In this paper, we presented an approach to prioritize defects reported by static analysis tools. Given detailed information of defects (method, line number, etc.), we can trace the propagation of those defects with our static analysis algorithm. Then we can analyze the affection of defects with the defect propagation information. At last, we prioritize those defects by evaluating the fatality score of their propagation.

Currently, only the affection of defects is considered in our approach. Experiment results in Sect. 6.3 show that there is indeed a strong correlation between the affection domain of defects and the priority of defects. However, this is not enough to fully assess the priority of defects. In future work, we will take more defect attributes into consideration and try to build a stronger model for defect prioritization.

References

1. Abdelmoez, W., Kholief, M., Elsalmy, F.M.: Bug fix-time prediction model using naïve bayes classifier. In: 2012 22nd International Conference on Computer Theory and Applications (ICCTA), pp. 167–172. IEEE (2012)
2. Beyer, D., Henzinger, T.A., Théoduloz, G.: Configurable software verification: concretizing the convergence of model checking and program analysis. In: Damm, W., Hermanns, H. (eds.) CAV 2007. LNCS, vol. 4590, pp. 504–518. Springer, Heidelberg (2007). https://doi.org/10.1007/978-3-540-73368-3_51
3. Cheng, B.C., Hwu, W.M.W.: Modular interprocedural pointer analysis using access paths: design, implementation, and evaluation. ACM Sigplan Not. **35**(5), 57–69 (2000)
4. Cytron, R., Ferrante, J., Rosen, B.K., Wegman, M.N., Zadeck, F.K.: An efficient method of computing static single assignment form. In: Proceedings of the 16th ACM SIGPLAN-SIGACT Symposium on Principles of Programming Languages, pp. 25–35. ACM (1989)
5. Guo, P.J., Zimmermann, T., Nagappan, N., Murphy, B.: Characterizing and predicting which bugs get fixed: an empirical study of microsoft windows. In: 2010 ACM/IEEE 32nd International Conference on Software Engineering, vol. 1, pp. 495–504. IEEE (2010)
6. Jeong, G., Kim, S., Zimmermann, T.: Improving bug triage with bug tossing graphs. In: Proceedings of the 7th Joint Meeting of the European Software Engineering Conference and the ACM SIGSOFT Symposium on The Foundations of Software Engineering, pp. 111–120. ACM (2009)
7. Jureczko, M., Madeyski, L.: Towards identifying software project clusters with regard to defect prediction. In: Proceedings of the 6th International Conference on Predictive Models in Software Engineering, p. 9. ACM (2010)

8. Kanwal, J., Maqbool, O.: Managing open bug repositories through bug report prioritization using SVMs. In: Proceedings of the International Conference on Open-Source Systems and Technologies, Lahore, Pakistan (2010)
9. Kaushik, N., Amoui, M., Tahvildari, L., Liu, W., Li, S.: Defect prioritization in the software industry: challenges and opportunities. In: 2013 IEEE Sixth International Conference on Software Testing, Verification and Validation (ICST), pp. 70–73. IEEE (2013)
10. Kremenek, T., Engler, D.: Z-Ranking: using statistical analysis to counter the impact of static analysis approximations. In: Cousot, R. (ed.) SAS 2003. LNCS, vol. 2694, pp. 295–315. Springer, Heidelberg (2003). https://doi.org/10.1007/3-540-44898-5_16
11. Lamkanfi, A., Demeyer, S., Giger, E., Goethals, B.: Predicting the severity of a reported bug. In: 2010 7th IEEE Working Conference on Mining Software Repositories (MSR), pp. 1–10. IEEE (2010)
12. Liang, G., Wu, Q., Wang, Q., Mei, H.: An effective defect detection and warning prioritization approach for resource leaks. In: 2012 IEEE 36th Annual Computer Software and Applications Conference (COMPSAC), pp. 119–128. IEEE (2012)
13. Ruthruff, J.R., Penix, J., Morgenthaler, J.D., Elbaum, S., Rothermel, G.: Predicting accurate and actionable static analysis warnings: an experimental approach. In: Proceedings of the 30th International Conference on Software Engineering, pp. 341–350. ACM (2008)
14. Uddin, J., Ghazali, R., Deris, M.M., Naseem, R., Shah, H.: A survey on bug prioritization. Artif. Intell. Rev. **47**(2), 145–180 (2017)
15. Watanabe, S., Kaiya, H., Kaijiri, K.: Adapting a fault prediction model to allow inter languagereuse. In: Proceedings of the 4th International Workshop on Predictor Models in Software Engineering, pp. 19–24. ACM (2008)

Software Bug Localization Based on Key Range Invariants

Lin Ma[✉] and Zuohua Ding[✉]

School of Information Science and Technology, Zhejiang Sci-Tech University,
Hangzhou 310019, Zhejiang, China
624890917@qq.com, zouhuading@hotmail.com

Abstract. Bug localization is expensive and time-consuming during software debugging. The traditional software bug localization based on range invariants need to monitor all variables in the system, requires a large of runtime overhead. However, this overhead is not necessary. Because only a set of key variables can really affect the results of the system. Therefore, this paper proposes a software bug localization method based on key range invariants. First, add the key variables screening phase in the original method. By combining the dynamic filtering mechanism with the static reduction mechanism, the key variables set of the program are screened. Then, the values of the key variables in all successful test cases are counted to obtain the key range invariants. Finally, bug localization is performed by monitoring the values of the key variables in failure test cases. When we need to minimize the overhead of monitoring variables, we can use this method to ignore variables that are considered unimportant. The experimental results show that, the method can still maintain a good bug localization effect only monitoring the key variable set, which verifies the effectiveness of the method.

Keywords: Key variables · Range invariants · Bug localization
Suspicious statements

1 Introduction

Application's development is often limited by development budgets and time-to-market, which provide a trade-off for system reliability, leading to increased defects and disastrous consequences. Therefore, software bug localization techniques are critical to identifying and recovering faults as quickly as possible [1–3].

Software bug localization technology can be divided into lightweight software bug localization technology and heavyweight software bug localization technology according to different research methods [4]. The lightweight software bug localization technology analyzes the coverage information or execution trajectory of the program execution, uses statistical or data mining methods to process information, and finds a collection of suspicious bug codes for bug localization. It does not involve the dependency of the program, and the time overhead is

© Springer Nature Switzerland AG 2018
L. Bu and Y. Xiong (Eds.): SATE 2018, LNCS 11293, pp. 20–32, 2018.
https://doi.org/10.1007/978-3-030-04272-1_2

relatively small. The heavyweight software bug localization technology performs bug localization by analyzing the data dependence and control dependence of the program, which requires a large time overhead [5]. The invariants bug localization technique is a method of bug localization by analyzing the information of the variable value when the program executes, so it is a lightweight software bug localization technique. Compared with the heavyweight bug localization technology, the invariants bug localization technology has less time overhead and higher positioning accuracy [6].

The invariants are properties that remain constant in the program [7]. The invariants can be divided into the static invariants and the dynamic invariants according to whether or not the program under test is executed. The static invariants refers to the invariants obtained by static analysis of the program source code without executing the program under test, which are generally only used for small and medium programs. The dynamic invariants refers to the invariants obtained by analyzing the information of the program execution in the case of executing a successful test case, which are applicable to large programs [8]. The invariants can be automatically generated and trained during the test phase, and then detects learning behaviors that deviate from invariants during the detection phase [9]. The invariants have been studied for many years, producing a variety of types, such as range invariants, bitmask invariants, and Bloom invariants. They are mainly used for bug detection [10–13] and fault localization [14–17]. The invariants-based software bug localization is a proven method [14–17]. Compared with other invariants bug localization techniques, the range invariants bug localization technique is simpler and easier to implement. It reduces overhead, and makes it easier to detect variable-related bugs. Therefore, this paper studies the bug localization technology of range invariants. Although the bug localization technology based on range invariants has many advantages, in actual use of large software applications, it is hindered by the overhead required to monitor all variables in the system. However, we believe that monitoring each variable in each statement may not be necessary. Because only one subset of variables, called the collar variable [18], it can really affect the results of the system. In this paper, we call this a set of key variables. Therefore, we propose a software bug localization technique based on key range invariants.

Compared with the existing methods [6,12], the contributions of this paper are as follows. First, the key variables screening phase is added to the original range invariants bug localization method. Combing dynamic and static methods to screen the variables, and the key variables set of the program are obtained. Then, using the screened set of key variables for range invariants learning and bug localization. We establish discrete invariant intervals for variables when learning the range of variables. And the bug localization is carried out without knowing the correct program in this paper. Finally, the effectiveness of this method is verified in the open source test suite. And the experimental results still keeps a good bug location effect.

This paper is organized as the follows. Section 2 is an overview of our methods. Section 3 describes how to locate bugs based on key range invariants, including how to screen the key variables set and use the screened key variables set to locate bugs. Section 4 experimentally validates the effectiveness of this method through a classic open source test suite. Section 5 describes the work related to this paper. Section 6 concludes the paper.

2   Approach Overview

This section outlines our approach. Fig. 1 shows the basic framework of our method.

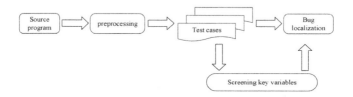

Fig. 1. The basic framework of our method.

Preprocessing. Since the range invariants bug localization method needs to analyze the value information of variables when the program executes, it is necessary to instrument the program source code before the program is executed. And then execute the instrumented program according to the given inputs to obtain a series of test cases that contain execution path information and variables value information.

Test Case Optimization. Our method is known the error program, inputs and expected output results. Distinguished successful test cases and failure test cases by checking whether the execution results are the same as the expected results. In general, there are accidental correct test cases (CC) in successful test cases. If the number of such accidental correct test cases is large, the scope of the range invariants is increased, and the possibility of violating the range invariants is reduced, so that there are many false negatives. Therefore, we reduce the scope of range invariants by deleting accidental correct test cases, thereby increasing the possibility of violating invariants during the bug localization phase, thereby reducing false negatives. In this paper, we use the algorithm proposed by Masri [19] to delete accidental correct test cases. And CCT is used to represent the set of successful test cases identified as CC.

Screening Key Variables. In this paper, we first optimize the two variable evolution pattern detectors proposed in reference [12], and obtain two dynamic filtering mechanisms. Then we combine two dynamic filtering mechanisms and a static reduction mechanism to filter the variables in the program and obtain the set of key variables in the program.

Bug Localization. First, we analyze the values of key variables in successful test cases, and obtain the range invariants of key variables statistically. Then, detect failure test cases. If the value of the key variable in failure test cases is not within the range of the corresponding invariant, the flag is violated. That is, the statement containing the variable is marked as a suspicious statement.

3   Bug Localization Using Key Range Invariants

This section introduces how to screen key variables set, and use the screened key variables set for bug localization. First, in the key variables screening phase, two dynamic filtering mechanisms and a static reduction mechanism are used to analyze the test cases, and the set of key variables in the program can be screened out. Then, the range invariants of key variables are statistically obtained by analyzing the values of key variables in successful test cases. Finally, it is determined whether the value of key variables in failure test cases is within the range of the corresponding invariants, thereby the suspicious statements set is obtained.

3.1   The Key Variables Screening Phase

In the key variables screening phase, we first use two simple dynamic filtering mechanisms to filter the variables when the program executes, and get a key variables set KEY. Then, we use a static reduction mechanism to reduce the KEY set, and get a reduced KEY set. It is important to note that, if a variable is only used for one execution of the program or is not executed in all successful executions, it is classified as a key variable.

Dynamic Filtering Mechanism I. The purpose of dynamic filtering mechanism I is to filter a class of non-key variables. This class of variables value increases or decreases in the same way during each execution of the program, regardless of the input. We regard such variables as non-key variables and do not need to be monitored. We use the delta (Δ) to implement an increase or decrease of the variable value. The delta is obtained by subtracting the recorded last observation value from the current observation value [9]. In the dynamic filtering mechanism I, only numerical variables (int, long, float, double) are trained.

Using the dynamic filtering mechanism I, we can filter a class of variables such as constants, counters, and loop variables. Because no matter what the input is, they are always increases or decreases in the same way. We believe that during the execution of the program, such variables have little effect on the output of the program and do not need to be monitored.

Dynamic Filtering Mechanism II. The purpose of dynamic filtering mechanism II is to filter a class of non-key variables. The range of this class of variables is always the same after each complete execution of the program, regardless of the input. We regard such variables as non-key variables and do not need to be monitored. In the dynamic filtering mechanism II, both numerical variables (int, long, float, double) and non-numerical variables (char, string) are trained. Integer variables (int, long) and non-numerical variables (char, string) establish discrete invariant intervals, and float variables (float, double) establish continuous invariant intervals.

Using the dynamic filtering mechanism II, we can filter a class of variables. Although they do not change in a linear manner during program execution, they subject to certain limitations in execution, which are the same in each execution, regardless of the input. We believe that during the execution of the program, such variables have little effect on the output of the program and do not need to be monitored.

Static Reduction Mechanism. After filtering the variables using two dynamic filtering mechanisms, we get a key variables set KEY. Then, we perform static analysis and reduction on the variables in the KEY set according to the function call relation.

The function call graph can describe the calling relationships between functions. It is divided into static function call graph and dynamic function call graph. The static function call graph is to record the function call case of the static program (that is, not running the program). The dynamic function call graph is to record the function call case when the program is actually running. In this paper, we use the tools Doxygen (http://www.doxygen.nl) and Graphviz (http://www.graphviz.org) to build static function call graphs of test sets [13, 20].

The variables in the KEY set are analyzed based on the function call graph. If a variable in the function has the same value before and after the function is called, the variable is regarded as a non-key variable and does not need to be monitored. And remove it from the KEY set. Using the static reduction mechanism to reduce the KEY set, we can filter a class of variables such as passing parameters. Although their range is different after each complete execution of the program, their values remain the same before and after the function is called. We believe that during the execution of the program, such variables have little effect on the output of the program and do not need to be monitored.

3.2   Bug Localization Phase

First, we analyze the values of the key variables in the successful test cases. The key range invariants corresponding to each key variable are obtained statistically. Thus, the set of key range invariant is obtained. It is important to note that integer variables (int, long) and non-numerical variables (char, string) establish discrete invariant intervals and float variables (float, double) establish continuous invariant intervals when learning variables. Algorithm 1 is the learning algorithm of key range invariants.

Then, we detect failure test cases. If the value of the key variable in failure test cases is not within the range of the corresponding invariant, the flag is violated. That is, the statement containing the variable is marked as a suspicious

Algorithm 1. Learning Algorithm of Key Range Invariants

Input: Successful Test Cases Set
Output: Key Range Invariants Set
 1: Key_Range_Invariable $= \varnothing$
 2: key_range_invariable $= \varnothing$
 3: **for all** Success_Execution $\notin$ CCT **do**
 4:    **for all** Statement **do**
 5:       **for all** Variable $\in$ KEY **do**
 6:          **for all** Observation **do**
 7:             Update key_range_invariable
 8:          **end for**
 9:          Key_Range_Invariable $\leftarrow$ key_range_invariable
10:          key_range_invariable $= \varnothing$
11:       **end for**
12:    **end for**
13: **end for**
14: **return** Key_Range_Invariable

statement. Thus, the set of suspicious statement is obtained. Algorithm 2 is the bug location algorithm based on key range invariants.

Algorithm 2. Bug Location Algorithm Based on Key Range Invariants

Input: Failure Test Cases Set
Output: Suspicious Statements Set
 1: Suspicious_Statement $= \varnothing$
 2: **for all** Failure_Execution **do**
 3:    **for all** Statement **do**
 4:       **for all** Variable $\in$ KEY **do**
 5:          **for all** Observation **do**
 6:             **if** the_Observation $\notin$ Range_Invariable **then**
 7:                Suspicious_Statement $\leftarrow$ the_Statement
 8:             **end if**
 9:          **end for**
10:       **end for**
11:    **end for**
12: **end for**
13: **return** Suspicious_Statement

4   Experiments

In this paper, we used a set of test programs called the Siemens set (http:// sir.unl.edu/content/sir.html) as experimental programs. It consists of seven programs, and each with a correct version and multiple error versions. And there is

Table 1. Details of the Siemens set.

Program	Faulty_Versions	LOC	Test_Cases	Description
print_tokens	7	564	4130	Lexical analyzer
print_tokens2	10	511	4115	Lexical analyzer
replace	32	564	5542	Pattern matching and substitution
schedule	9	413	2650	Priority scheduler
schedule2	10	308	2710	Priority scheduler
tcas	41	174	1608	Aircraft collision avoidance system
tot_info	23	407	1052	Computes statistics given input data

only one bug in each error version. Each program also has a set of inputs that ensure complete code coverage. Table 1 provides details of the test suite.

The Siemens set provides a total of 7 correct version programs and 132 error version programs. However, we have discarded some error versions that are not available for some reason: (a) the error is in the variable declaration of the header file; (b) a segment error occurred while the error version was running, resulting in incorrect recording of the program execution path; (c) no failure test cases; (d) error type is array declaration size error; (e) Error type is parameter declaration error. In addition, this article is based on the range invariants for bug location, so cannot locate for some errors: (a) an error occurred in the statement that not contain variables in the program; (b) an error occurred in the logic operator in the judgment statement in the program; (c) an error occurred in the pointer variable that not with "*". The program and the number of error versions used in this paper are shown in Table 2.

Table 2. Program and the number of versions.

Program	print_tokens	print_tokens2	replace	schedule	schedule2	tcas	tot_info
Faulty_Versions	2	4	16	4	2	15	17

In this paper, the range invariants bug localization is carried out by monitoring the key variables. Therefore, we compare the number of variables monitored, the number of suspicious statements checked and the number of versions located by the traditional method and our method, to verify the effectiveness of this method.

4.1 The Number of Variables Monitored

Compared with the traditional method, when the bug localization is performed on different error versions of seven test sets, the number of variables that need to monitor is shown in Fig. 2. In the figure, the horizontal axis is the different error version of the test set, and the vertical axis is the number of variables monitored.

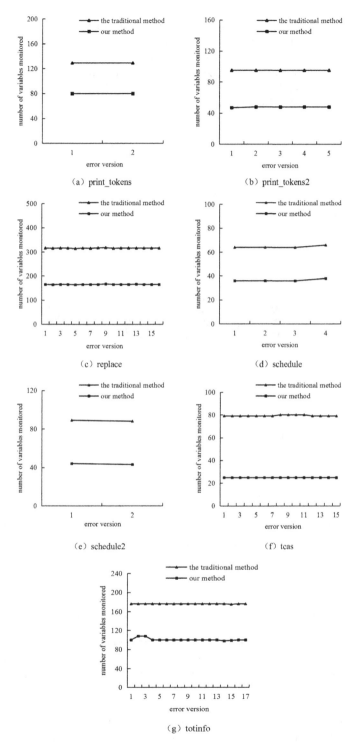

Fig. 2. Comparison of the number of variables monitored by the traditional method and our method.

In order to more clearly reflect that the number of variables monitored by our method is less than that of the traditional method, we give out the average number of variables monitored by the traditional method and our method, as shown in Fig. 3, when the bug localization is performed on different error versions of seven test sets. The horizontal axis in the figure is the test set and the vertical axis is the number of variables monitored.

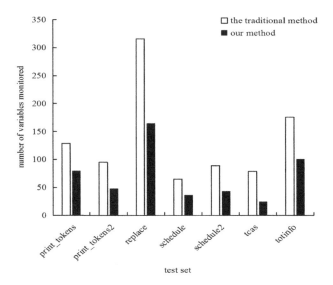

Fig. 3. Comparison of the average number of variables monitored by the traditional method and our method.

The experimental results show that the number of variables monitored for error versions of each test set is reduced after the key variables screening phase. The number of variables monitored for different error versions of the same test set is reduced by roughly the same percentage, but the number of variables monitored for different test sets is reduced by the different percentage. In general, the number of variables monitored after the key variables screening phase is reduced by an average of 48.77%.

4.2   The Number of Suspicious Statements Checked

Compared with the traditional method, the number of suspicious statements checked after the bug localization of different error version programs of the seven test sets is shown in Fig. 4. The horizontal axis in the figure is the different error version of the test set, and the vertical axis is the number of suspicious statements checked.

The experimental results show that the number of suspicious statements checked by our method is less than that of the traditional method after the

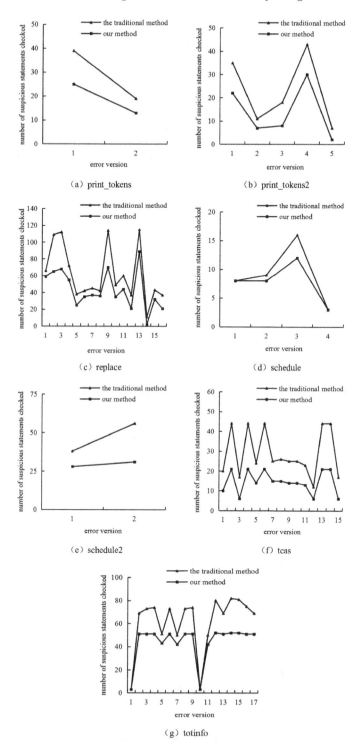

Fig. 4. Comparison of the number of suspicious statements checked by the traditional method and our method.

bug localization of different error versions of the test set. And the number of suspicious statements checked for different error versions of the same test set is reduced by the different percentage. But in general, after the bug localization of the test set, the number of suspicious statements checked by our method is reduced by an average of 32.92% compared with the traditional method.

4.3   The Number of Versions Located

After the bug localization, comparison of the number of versions located by the traditional method and our method is shown in Table 3. V_T is the number of versions located by the traditional method, and V_O is the number of versions located by our method.

Table 3. Comparison of the number of versions located by the traditional method and our method.

Program	print_tokens	print_tokens2	replace	schedule	schedule2	tcas	tot_info	total
V_T	2	4	16	4	2	15	17	60
V_O	2	2	16	4	1	15	14	54

In summary, except for some special cases. After the key variables screening phase, the reduction in the number of invariants used is quite significant when bug localization of the test set, and the reduction in the number of suspicious statements checked is also quite significant after bug localization of the test set. At the same time, good bug location effect is still maintained.

5   Related Work

Ernst et al. [7] proposed a method for dynamically generating likely program invariants. The method can generate invariants based on the size relation $(x \leq y)$, simple function relation $(x = fn(y))$, linear relation $(y = ax + b)$ and element inclusion relation $(x \in y)$ between variables according to the information of program execution. The Daikon tool is implemented to generate invariants. Pytlik et al. [16] used invariants generated by Daikon for software bug localization. First, he used the Daikon tool to dynamically extract the invariants in the program, and then detected the violation of the invariants in the failed test cases to locate bugs. The range invariants bug localization is located by analyzing the value range of variables. Compared with the Daikon invariants bug localization, the range invariants bug localization is easier to implement.

Range invariants and bitmask invariants are an easy implement lightweight dynamic invariants extraction method. Rui et al. [15] used range invariants and bitmask invariants to judge the successful or failure of test cases, and concluded that range invariants have smaller false positive and false negative relatives to bitmask invariants. Sahoo et al. [17] proposed an algorithm to automatically generate the correct input that is close to the fault-triggering input. That is, the successful test cases similar to the failure test cases is generated, thereby improved the accuracy of the range invariants bug localization. Compared with other invariants bug localization methods, the range invariants bug localization method is easier to implement, and it is easier to locate variable-related bugs, and it has higher positioning accuracy.

Liu [6] optimized some problems in the software bug localization method of range invariants. He proposed four optimization methods. The number of false negatives are reduced by optimization, and the localization efficiency is improved. But this method needed to learn and monitor all variables in the system, which will be a large and not necessary overhead.

Santos et al. [12] proposed two variable evolution pattern detectors to detect variables that do not need to monitor in the system. By this method, the number of variants monitored was reduced, while the quality of detection was maintained. However, the method trained variables on the condition that the correct program is known; the method only analyzed numerical variables and not considered the non-numerical variables; and the method was not applied to bug localization.

6   Conclusions and Future Work

This paper proposes a bug localization method based on key range invariants. A set of key variables can be obtained by screening the variables before the invariants learning. Then, only the key variables are monitored during the invariant learning and bug localization phases. This method can not only reduce the number of variables monitored, but also reduce the number of suspicious statements checked. At the same time, good bug localization effect is still maintained.

In spite of this, the method in this paper also has some shortcomings. First, this method has higher requirements for test cases. Second, this method has different results in different test sets, so this means that a system with completely different characteristics may produce different results. Finally, this paper only considers the cost of monitoring variables, not the cost of training variables. So in the future, it is necessary to experiment on more and larger test sets to verify the effectiveness of this method. Second, it is necessary to weigh consider the cost of monitoring variables and training variables. Finally, it is necessary to find more ideal methods to screen the variables, and further reduce the number of invariants used.

References

1. Yu, K., Lin, M.X.: Advances in automatic fault localization techniques. Chin. J. Comput. **34**(8), 1411–1422 (2011)
2. Patterson, D., et al.: Recovery oriented computing (ROC): motivation, definition, techniques, and case studies. Berkeley Computer Science, vol. 9, no. 2, pp. 14–16 (2002)

3. Xie, M., Yang, B.: A study of the effect of imperfect debugging on software development cost. IEEE Trans. Softw. Eng. TSE **29**(5), 471–473 (2003)
4. Santelices, R., Jones, J.A., Yu, Y., Harrold, M.J.: Lightweight fault-localization using multiple coverage types. In: International Conference on Software Engineering, ICSE 2009, pp. 56–66. IEEE, Vancouver (2009). https://doi.org/10.1109/ICSE.2009.5070508
5. Cao, H.L., Jiang, S.J., Ju, X.L.: Survey of software fault localization. Comput. Sci. **41**(2), 1–6 (2014)
6. Liu, X.: Research on optimization of fault localization with range invariant. Harbin Institute of Technology (2016)
7. Ernst, M.D., Notkin, D.: Dynamically discovering likely program invariants. IEEE Trans. Softw. Eng. **27**(2), 99–123 (2000)
8. Liu, S.K., Yang, X.H., Luo, J.Q., Liu, J.: Dynamically discovering likely program invariants based on the contract. Microcomput. Inf. **22**(30), 233–235 (2006)
9. Racunas, P., Constantinides, K., Manne, S., Mukherjee, S.S.: Perturbation-based fault screening. In: High Performance Computer Architecture, HPCA 2007, Scottsdale, AZ, USA, pp. 169–180. IEEE Computer Society (2007). https://doi.org/10.1109/HPCA.2007.346195
10. Hangal, S., Lam, M.S.: Tracking down software bugs using automatic anomaly detection. In: International Conference on Software Engineering, ICSE 2002, Orlando, FL, USA, pp. 291–301. IEEE (2002). https://doi.org/10.1145/581376.581377
11. Abreu, R., González, A., Zoeteweij, P., van Gemund, A.J.C.: Using fault screeners for software error detection. In: Maciaszek, L.A., González-Pérez, C., Jablonski, S. (eds.) ENASE 2008. CCIS, vol. 69, pp. 60–74. Springer, Heidelberg (2010). https://doi.org/10.1007/978-3-642-14819-4_5
12. Santos, J., Abreu, R.: Lightweight automatic error detection by monitoring collar variables. In: Nielsen, B., Weise, C. (eds.) ICTSS 2012. LNCS, vol. 7641, pp. 215–230. Springer, Heidelberg (2012). https://doi.org/10.1007/978-3-642-34691-0_16
13. Wang, R., Ding, Z., Gui, N., Liu, Y.: Detecting bugs of concurrent programs with program invariants. IEEE Trans. Reliab. **66**(2), 425–439 (2017)
14. Le, T.D.B., Lo, D., Goues, C.L., Grunske, L.: A learning-to-rank based fault localization approach using likely invariants. In: International Symposium on Software Testing and Analysis 2016, pp. 177–188. ACM, New York (2016). https://doi.org/10.1145/2931037.2931049
15. Rui, A., Zoeteweij, P., van Gemund, A.J.C.: Automatic software fault localization using generic program invariants. In: ACM Symposium on Applied Computing 2008, Fortaleza, Ceara, Brazil, pp. 712–717. ACM (2008). https://doi.org/10.1145/1363686.1363855
16. Pytlik, B., Renieris, M., Krishnamurthi, S., Reiss, S.P.: Automated fault localization using potential invariants. Computer Science, pp. 273–276 (2003)
17. Sahoo, S.K., Criswell, J., Geigle, C., Adve, V.: Using likely invariants for automated software fault localization. ACM SIGPLAN Not. **41**(1), 139–152 (2013)
18. Menzies, T., Owen, D., Richardson, J.: The strangest thing about software. Computer **40**(1), 54–60 (2007)
19. Masri, W., Assi, R.A.: Cleansing test suites from coincidental correctness to enhance fault-localization. In: Third International Conference on Software Testing, Verification and Validation 2010, Paris, France, pp. 165–174. IEEE (2010). https://doi.org/10.1109/ICST.2010.22
20. Zong, F.F., Huang, H.Y., Ding, Z.H.: Software fault location based on double-times-locating strategy. J. Softw. **27**(8), 1993–2007 (2016)

Evaluating the Strategies of Statement Selection in Automated Program Repair

Deheng Yang[1], Yuhua Qi[2($\boxtimes$)], and Xiaoguang Mao[1,3]

[1] National University of Defense Technology, Changsha 410073, China
{yangdeheng13, xgmao}@nudt.edu.cn
[2] Beijing Institute of Tracking and Communication Technology,
Beijing 100094, China
yuhua.qi@outlook.com
[3] Laboratory of Software Engineering for Complex Systems,
National University of Defense Technology, Changsha 410073, China

Abstract. Automated program repair has drawn significant attention in recent years for its potential to alleviate the heavy burden of debugging activities. Fault localization, which generally provides a rank list of suspicious statements, is necessary for automated repair tools to identify the fault. With such rank list, existing repair tools have two statement selecting strategies for statement modification: suspiciousness-first algorithm (SFA) based on the suspiciousness of statements and rank-first algorithm (RFA) relying on the rank of statements. However, despite the extensive application of SFA and RFA in repair tools and different selecting methods between both strategies, little is known about the performance of the two strategies in automated program repair.

In this paper we conduct an empirical study to compare the effectiveness of SFA and RFA in automated program repair. We implement SFA and RFA as well as 6 popular spectrum-based fault localization techniques into 4 automated program repair tools, and then use these tools to perform repair experiments on 44 real-world bugs from Defects4J to compare SFA against RFA in automated program repair. The results suggest that: (1) RFA performs statistically significantly better than SFA in 64.76% cases according to the number of candidate patches generated before a valid patch is found (NCP), (2) SFA achieves better performance in parallel repair and patch diversity, (3) The performance of SFA can be improved by increasing the suspiciousness accuracy of fault localization techniques. These observations provide directions for future research on the usage of statement selecting strategies and a new avenue for improving the effectiveness of fault localization techniques in automated program repair.

Keywords: Automated program repair · Fault localization · Empirical study

1 Introduction

With massive scale and growing complexity of modern software programs, manual debugging is commonly regarded to be extremely tedious and time consuming as well as expensive. As a result, automated program repair, which aims to reduce the debugging effort by automatically generating a fix for the faulty program [1, 5, 35, 36, 40], has been

© Springer Nature Switzerland AG 2018
L. Bu and Y. Xiong (Eds.): SATE 2018, LNCS 11293, pp. 33–48, 2018.
https://doi.org/10.1007/978-3-030-04272-1_3

an active research subject in the software community. Automated program repair typically consists of three stages [2]: fault localization that identifies the suspicious statements potentially containing faults, patch generation that generates candidate patches by modifying the suspicious statements, and patch validation that verifies the validity of candidate patches. For the first stage of automated program repair, spectrum-based fault localization (SFL for short) techniques are extensively used due to its practicality and feasibility [1, 3, 4]. Accordingly, various automated program repair tools implementing SFL techniques have been continuously proposed in recent years [6–12].

Taking a faulty program and a test suite containing both failing and passing test cases as input, SFL techniques output a rank list of suspicious program elements (e.g., statements, declarations, and branches) [13]. Note that we focus on studying the SFL techniques at the statement level, as most existing automated repair tools work at the level of program statement [1]. With the rank list of statements, existing repair tools have two strategies to select statements for patch generation [14]: (1) Suspiciousness-first algorithm (SFA): a stochastic algorithm, for which the probability of each statement being selected for modification depends on its suspiciousness value [2, 15–18], and (2) Rank-first algorithm (RFA): a deterministic algorithm, which always selects the top (or next top if it fails to generate a valid patch by modifying current top ranked statement) ranked statement as target statement [6, 7, 9, 11, 12].

SFA and RFA have different strategies on the usage of fault localization information. For instance, given a rank list produced by an SFL technique: {(Statement$_3$, 0.9), (Statement$_9$, 0.7), (Statement$_5$, 0.3), ...}, where the former element in the ordered pair indicates the location ID of the suspicious statement, and the latter is the corresponding suspiciousness value. During the repair process, RFA-based repair tools directly select Statement$_3$ as the first target statement and produce candidate patches by modifying Statement$_3$. If these patches are invalid, they then select next top ranked statement (i.e., Statement$_9$) as target statement. In contrast, for SFA-based repair tools, the probability of each statement being selected relies on its suspiciousness. That is, every suspicious statement has the chance to be selected first, but Statement$_3$ has the largest chance to be selected as the first target statement.

With the different strategies in using the fault localization information, SFA and RFA directly impact the number of statements modified before a valid patch is found, thus further influencing the number of candidate patches generated before a valid fix is reached (NCP) [2, 17, 24], which is used to evaluate the effectiveness of program repair tools. Unfortunately, despite the wide application and potentially differing performance of RFA and SFA in automated program repair, little is known about the relative performance of both strategies in the context of automated program repair.

To fill this gap, we compare the effectiveness of SFA and RFA by conducting an empirical evaluation considering the NCP metric [2] and patch diversity metric. In the evaluation experiment, we select Nopol [12], jKali [10], jMutRepair [10] and SimFix [40], all of which are targeted at repairing Java programs, as our experimental tools, and perform repairing experiments on 44 buggy programs from Defects4J [19], which provides a set of real-world bugs for evaluating Java program repair systems.

The main contributions of this paper include:

- We are the first to conduct the empirical study on the two statement selecting strategies in automated program repair. In addition, to facilitate the comparison between SFA and RFA, we implement 6 well-studied SFL techniques and the 2 statement selection strategies into the 4 selected repair tools to get 48 versions of repair tools in the experiment (see Sect. 4). We make the revised tools and experimental data publicly available at [41].
- Our study highlights the different performance achieved by both strategies in automated program repair. RFA outperforms SFA under the measurement of NCP, while SFA achieves better performance in parallel repair and patch diversity.
- Our experiment finds that the performance of SFA can be improved by increasing the suspiciousness accuracy of SFL techniques, which sheds light on the direction of improving SFL techniques by focusing on increasing the suspiciousness value of the faulty statement rather than the absolute rank.

This paper builds on our prior work [14], studying more repair tools with different repair approaches and conducting further statistical analyses. The new findings facilitate future usage of statement selecting strategies as well as open a new avenue for improving fault localization in automated program repair, especially for the SFA-based tools (see Sect. 2.2). The rest of the paper is organized as follows. Section 2 first presents the background and related work. Section 3 introduces the three research questions, and Sect. 4 describes the design of our experiment. Section 5 presents the evaluation of the result data. Section 6 presents further discussions on SFA and RFA. Conclusions and future work are described in Sect. 7.

2 Background and Related Work

2.1 Spectrum-Based Fault Localization Techniques

Spectrum-based fault localization (SFL) techniques, which are recognized as the most studied and evaluated fault localization techniques [13], are originally proposed for assisting developers in localizing faults, and also extensively used in automated program repair [1, 21]. To localize a fault, SFL techniques utilize a program spectrum to assign each program entity a suspiciousness score. The program spectrum is a collection of program entities, which are statements in general [20], and exploits information of executing failing and passing test cases on the buggy program. Specifically, SFL techniques first execute the test suite to obtain the program spectrum. Then, SFL techniques use risk evaluation formulas to calculate the suspiciousness score of each statement according to the program spectrum [21]. As an output, a sorted list of suspicious statements in descending order of their suspiciousness is provided for automated program repair to select statements for modification.

2.2 Automated Program Repair

The enormous number of program bugs in our world have posed huge threats to the human society and consumed a large amount of time of developers in debugging [5, 23]. To reduce the heavy workload of developers, automated program repair has attracted much attention of researchers and has been extensively studied in recent literature [1, 5], in which promising results of repairing large real-world bugs have been achieved [6–12, 25, 36]. Existing program repair tools often use the rank list of suspicious statements deriving from fault localization techniques, particularly the SFL techniques, to generate patches [1].

There exist two statement selecting strategies for automated program repair tools to use the fault localization information [14]: RFA and SFA. Both strategies are conducted on the rank list of statements produced by SFL techniques, but SFA does not rely on the absolute rank but the concrete suspiciousness values. As shown in Fig. 1, given the sorted list, SFA first converts the suspiciousness score of each statement into probability to be selected. Based on the calculated probabilities, SFA then takes a statement randomly with probability proportional to its suspiciousness from the rank list to generate patch candidates for validation. Unlike SFA, RFA selects statements in a simpler way (see Fig. 2), that is, it always chooses the highest ranked statement, which is then removed from the list, for patch generation and validation. If the patch candidates are invalid, the next top ranked statement will be selected for generation. The selection process does not end until a valid patch is generated, or the list is empty, or the time limit expires.

Input: rankList {(stmt$_1$, sp$_1$), (stmt$_2$, sp$_2$) ... (stmt$_n$, sp$_n$)}
Output: A valid patch
1: **repeat**
2:    **for** i = 1 to |rankList| **do**
3:        probList[i] ← sp$_i$/SumOfSusp(rankList)
4:    **end for**
5:    **let** randNum = rand(0,1)
6:    **let** sumProb = 0
7:    **for** i = 1 to |probList| **do**
8:        sumProb ←sumProb + prob$_i$
9:        **if** sumProb ≥ randNum **then**
10:            stmt ← stmt$_i$
11:            rankList ← rankList − stmt$_i$
12:            candidatePatches ← modify(stmt)
13:            validate(candidatePatches)
14:            **break**
15:        **end if**
16:    **end for**
17: **until** a valid patch is found ∪ list is empty ∪ timeout

---

Fig. 1. Suspiciousness-first algorithm (SFA) is a weighted randomly strategy. The probability of being selected for each statement is proportional to its suspiciousness value. stmt$_i$ represents the statement ranking number i in the list, and sp$_i$ is the corresponding suspiciousness value.

Statement selection strategies are commonly used in automated program repair but are seldom investigated or studied. For C program repair tools, Genprog [16] employs

---

Input: rankList {(stmt$_1$, sp$_1$), (stmt$_2$, sp$_2$) ... (stmt$_n$, sp$_n$)}
Output: A valid patch
1: **repeat**
2:   stmt ← TopRankedStm(rankList)
3:   rankList ← rankList − stmt
4:   candidatePatches ← modify(stmt)
5:   validate(candidatePatches)
6: **until** a valid patch is found ∪ list is empty ∪ timeout

---

Fig. 2. Rank-first algorithm (RFA) is a deterministic algorithm relying on the rank of suspicious statements.

SFA in the mutation operation, selecting statements randomly according to their suspiciousness scores for mutation. PAR [15] also adopts SFA as an approach to operate on the rank list of suspicious statements. In automated repair tools for Java programs, both jGenprog [10] and HDRepair [18] implement SFA when performing the mutation procedure. On the other hand, Jaid [6], the Java repair tool capable of constructing detailed state abstractions, uses RFA for statement selection. Also, ACS [11], Nopol [12], and ELIXIR [7] choose RFA as their statement selecting strategy.

We further study SFA and RFA in the context of automated program repair based on our prior work [14], studying more experimental tools (i.e., jKali [10], jMutRepair [10] and SimFix [40]) with different repair approaches and conducting further statistical analyses to evaluate the experimental results qualitatively and quantitatively. Based on the experiments, we have more concrete findings compared to previous conclusions [14]: (1) RFA outperforms SFA in most cases under the measurement of NCP, while our prior work only observes the inequivalence of the two statement selection strategies, (2) we explore the reasons behind the better performance of RFA as well as propose a new approach to improve suspiciousness accuracy, which has not been done in previous work. These conclusions facilitate future usage of statement selecting strategies in automated program repair. In addition, the new observations in Sect. 5.3 open a new avenue for improving fault localization techniques in automated program repair, especially for the SFA-based repair tools.

3 Research Questions

This research aims to explore the differences of RFA and SFA and compare their effectiveness in automated program repair, and thus leads to three research questions for measurement and analysis as follows:

RQ 1: Does there exist a statement selecting strategy achieving statistically significantly better performance than the other under the measurement of NCP metric?

Considering that the difference of RFA and SFA may result in different NCP, empirical experiments and statistical analyses are necessary. Thus, **RQ 1** concerns whether RFA or SFA has statistically significantly different performance in automated program repair when evaluated by NCP.

RQ 2: If so, why does this strategy achieve better performance than the other?

The lower NCP score obtained in the independent repair trials, the better effectiveness can be reached by the statement selecting strategy in automated repair (see Sect. 4.4). If RFA or SFA performs statistically significantly better in NCP, **RQ 2** then concerns the reasons behind the better performance.

RQ 3: Does SFA outperform RFA in patch diversity?

As discussed in Sect. 4.4, SFA may outperform RFA in patch diversity when the buggy program has more than one suspicious statement that can be modified to generate a fix. However, this still remains an issue that needs to be empirically verified. **RQ 3** plans to use patch diversity to evaluate the effectiveness of SFA and RFA.

4   Experimental Design

4.1   Overview

As presented in Fig. 3, our experimental design consists of four procedures: repair tools implementation, benchmark selection, data collection and statistical analysis. First, we obtain the RFA-based and SFA-based tools by modifying the selected repair tools. To evaluate the performance of SFA and RFA under different SFL, we further implement 6 popular SFL techniques into the repair tools. Then, we select a set of benchmark programs, which are used in repair experiments to evaluate these versions of repair tools. During the repair experiments, the data of evaluation metrics (i.e., NCP and patch diversity) are collected. Based on the result data, the statistical analysis is performed to qualitatively and quantitatively compare SFA and RFA. In the rest of this section, we give detailed descriptions for the four procedures respectively.

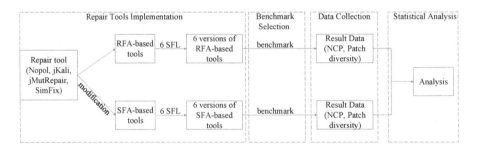

Fig. 3. Overview of the experimental design

4.2   Repair Tools Implementation

The objective of this paper is to compare the effectiveness of SFA and RFA on the usage of fault localization information (i.e., the rank list of statements) in automated program repair. As a result, we select repair tools that are publicly available as well as implement SFL techniques to produce a rank list of suspicious statements. Accordingly, we choose Nopol [12], jKali [10], jMutRepair [10] and SimFix [40] as our experimental tools. Note that the ACS [11] is not selected as it uses an extra technique called predicate switching to combine with SFL techniques during the fault localization stage, and S3 [42], Angelix [8], JFix [9] are not chosen because they do not share the same benchmark (i.e., Defects4J) as our selected tools. For the selected tools, Nopol, jKali and jMutRepair are well-developed with an active GitHub community and extensively used in previous studies [25–29], while SimFix implements the state-of-art repair approach to successfully fix the largest number of bugs in Defects4J compared to other automated program repair technologies [40].

All the tools we select are RFA-based tools that go through the suspicious rank list from the most suspicious statement to the least suspicious statement. The reason why we do not select SFA-based tools is that SFA-based tools cannot be transformed into RFA-based tools (see Sect. 6). For example, jGenprog, which can also be obtained from Astor [10], is an SFA-based tool that relies on SFA to perform the mutation operator in automated program repair due to the genetic programming algorithm [16], and thus cannot be converted into RFA-based tools.

To perform the comparison between SFA and RFA, we obtain SFA-based tools by modifying the source code of the four tools according to the pseudocode of SFA and RFA as illustrated in Fig. 1 and Fig. 2. Specifically, when all suspicious statements are collected in a sorted list, we perform following steps to modify RFA-based tools into SFA-based tools: (1) Suspiciousness conversion: we convert the suspiciousness scores of these statements into probabilities to be selected, by calculating the percentage of suspiciousness of each statement in the list, (2) Random Selection: we implement the random selection, in which a statement is randomly selected with its calculated probability, (3) Statement Removal: the selected statement will be removed from the list and modified to generate candidate patches. Then step (1), (2) and (3) will be iterated until the rank list is empty, or a valid patch is found, or the time limit expires.

In automated program repair, both RFA and SFA operate on the rank list of statements produced by SFL techniques. To evaluate the performance of two statement selecting strategies under different rank lists, we introduce 6 SFL techniques with different risk evaluation formulas including Barinel [13], Ochiai [13], Op2 [13], Tarantula [13], DStar [13] and Jaccard [3], as they are widely studied in recent researches [2, 3, 13, 39]. Note that for DStar (abbreviated as D*), we set the * as 2, which is the most thoroughly-explored value [13]. As Nopol, jKali, jMutRepair, and SimFix provide extension points for adding new risk evaluation formulas, we directly replace the default risk evaluation formula (i.e., Ochiai) with the 6 formulas to obtain versions of repair tools with different SFL techniques.

4.3   Benchmark Selection

We choose Defects4J, a Java bug database provided by Just et al. [14], as our experimental benchmark. In recent years, Defects4J is extensively used in automatic repair to test the effectiveness of repair tools and compare the performance of various SFL techniques [13, 25, 27, 28, 38]. Note that the result data of NCP (see Sect. 4.4) can only be generated when there is a valid fix produced in the repair process. Therefore, the benchmark programs in our experiment need to be successfully repaired by the four experimental repair tools. According to the prior experiments of using Nopol, jKali and jMutRepair to repair bugs in Defects4J [10, 31], Nopol successfully repairs 103 bugs in Defecst4J, while jKali and jMutRepair generate valid patches for 27 and 17 bugs respectively. We randomly select 44, 9 and 9 bugs for Nopol, jKali and jMutRepair respectively from Defects4J bugs that can be repaired successfully without any bias. For SimFix that generates correct patches for 34 bugs and test-suite adequate patches for 22 bugs [40], we select 7 bugs from the 56 bugs for our experiment.

Note that collecting the result data of NCP metric requires 100 independent repair trials for each bug, which often leads to high time cost [2, 14]. Although we do not perform the empirical study on the whole benchmark programs, the time consumed for running experiments with all versions of repair tools and selected bugs has reached up to two and a half months on the Ubuntu 14.04 machine.

4.4   Data Collection

To compare the effectiveness of two statement selecting strategies, we consider two evaluation metrics to capture the features and differences of RFA and SFA in automated program repair:

(1) NCP: The number of candidate patches generated before a valid patch is found. This metric has been used in previous experiments to study the effectiveness of automated program repair tools and SFL techniques [2, 17, 24]. In our experiment, for the same rank list of suspicious statements, RFA and SFA have completely different operations on choosing candidate statements to generate possible patches, which directly cause the differences of NCP. Therefore, we choose NCP as our main evaluation metric in the experiment. In addition, the lower NCP score obtained, the better effectiveness of the repair tool, which indicates the better performance of corresponding statement selecting strategy implemented into the repair tool. Note that measuring NCP requires at least 100 independent repair trials for each faulty program [2].

(2) Patch Diversity: The number of inequivalent validated patches found in a certain number of independent repair trials. In theory, if the rank list produced by SFL contains more than one statement that can be modified to generate valid patches, SFA may obtain different patch diversity compared to RFA due to the random selection strategy of SFA in repeated repair trials. That is, SFA may have the potential to find more inequivalent fixes passing all test cases than RFA in repeated trials. Also, we believe that more inequivalent fixes can provide more clue information to assist developers in eliminating bugs. Therefore, we propose this metric to explore the potential benefits of statement selecting strategies in finding more useful patches.

Note that we discard the repair time metric which was introduced in our prior work [14], because the repair time does not only depend on the statement selecting strategies but also the time of executing test cases and repairing statements.

We obtain 48 versions of repair tools totally in Sect. 4.2 by implementing 6 SFL techniques into 4 SFA-based and 4 RFA-based repair tools. For collecting the result data of NCP, we performed 100 independent repeated trials on both SFA-based and RFA-based repair tools for each bug from the benchmark programs. For the patch diversity metric that also requires an enough number of repeated runs, we extract and count the inequivalent valid patches from the patch information of 100 independent trials for each benchmark program.

5 Evaluation

5.1 Statistical Analysis

Since SFA is a randomized algorithm that may generate different results (e.g., NCP) on each repair, we use statistical tests to compare the result data of NCP obtained by RFA-based and SFA-based repair tools.

To qualitatively measure the difference between NCP results of SFA and RFA, we first perform qualitatively Mann-Whitney-Wilcoxon test [2, 32] to verify whether there exists significant difference between SFA and RFA in each case. As a non-parametric statistical test, the Mann-Whitney-Wilcoxon method tests the null hypothesis that the NCP scores of SFA and RFA in each case have the same distributions, against the alternative that they do not. In each group of data compared, if the test rejects the null hypothesis, the difference between SFA and RFA is considered statistically significant at the 5% significance level.

If the difference is statistically significant with Mann-Whitney-Wilcoxon test, to further assess the improvement quantitatively (i.e., effect size), we use Vargha-Delaney A-test [2, 32] to evaluate the magnitude of the improvement by calculating effect sizes. The A-statistic with value greater than 0.71 or less than 0.29 indicates a "large" effect size, while the A-statistic of greater than 0.64 or less than 0.36 means "medium" effect size. For the A-statistic value greater than 0.36 or less than 0.64, a "small" effect size for the differences between RFA and SFA is indicated.

5.2 Result of RQ 1

The Better Performance of RFA Under the Measurement of NCP. We focus on displaying the NCP results obtained from SimFix. The results of NCP from jKali, jMutRepair and Nopol are used for facilitating the comparison between SFA and RFA. All the NCP result data and figures are available at [41].

Figure 4 presents 42 grouped boxplots of NCP data for SFA and RFA (i.e., 7 bugs and 6 SFL techniques correspond to 42 cases in the figure). As shown in the figure, RFA-based SimFix achieves a fixed NCP score in 100 repeated repair runs for each case. That is, when the repair tool uses RFA to fix the same bug in repeated trials, the repair tool always selects the same suspicious statement to generate a valid patch. On the other hand, the NCP scores obtained by SFA-based SimFix vary in each boxplot, which reflects the more flexible selecting strategy of SFA compared to RFA. However, judged by the 42 cases in Fig. 4, RFA achieves lower NCP scores, which means the better effectiveness, than SFA in most cases.

Table 1 lists the statistical comparison results of SFA and RFA from four experimental tools when evaluated by NCP metric. Note that we finally obtain 403 cases by discarding 11 cases that contain "infinite" suspiciousness values from DStar. These

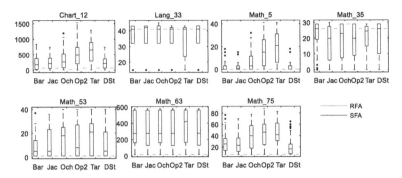

Fig. 4. The grouped boxplots of NCP obtained by SFA-based and RFA-based SimFix for each bug and SFL technique. In each grouped boxplot, the NCP of SFA-based SimFix is displayed on the left side, marked with black, while the NCP of RFA-based SimFix is shown in red on the right side. The performance of RFA and SFA varies with different bugs and SFL techniques. (Color figure online)

"infinite" values cannot be transformed into probabilities for SFA, thus being discarded in the evaluation. In Table 1, 64.76% (=261/403) cases indicate the statistical significance that RFA outperforms SFA in NCP. Only 12.41% (=50/403) cases show that SFA achieves better performance than RFA. For the rest 43 cases, they show no significant difference between RFA and SFA. Therefore, *RFA performs statistically significantly better than SFA in 64.76% cases when evaluated by NCP*.

Table 1. The statistical comparison of SFA and RFA using Mann-Whitney-Wilcoxon test and Vargha-Delaney A-test under the measurement of NCP. We first used Wilcoxon test to compare SFA and RFA in all cases. For these cases having statistically significant differences, we then performed A-test to measure the effect sizes. Note that RFA > SFA means RFA outperforms SFA, and vice versa.

Tools	A-test (effect size)	Number of cases (significant) (RFA > SFA)	Number of cases (significant) (SFA > RFA)	Number of cases (insignificant)
Nopol	Large	124	41	27
	Medium	21	19	
	Small	17	8	
jKali	Large	22	3	10
	Medium	11	1	
	Small	2	2	
jMutRepair	Large	34	4	9
	Medium	0	2	
	Small	0	4	
SimFix	Large	29	1	4
	Medium	1	1	
	Small	0	6	
Total		**261**	**92**	**50**

The Higher Efficiency of SFA in Parallel Repair. With the NCP results, we also compare the minimum NCP of SFA and RFA. We observe that the minimum NCP of SFA for each bug in 100 repeated trials reaches as small as 0 or 1, while that of RFA in independent trials ranges from 0 to approximately 2000. The lower minimum NCP obtained by SFA in 100 repair trials suggests that *SFA finds the valid patch more efficiently with lower NCP score when parallel repair is allowed.*

Given that huge computing resources can be obtained by reusing and paralleling computers, the parallel advantage of SFA can make it produce valid patches faster than RFA. In fact, GenProg adopted parallel repair strategy in its repair process on C program benchmark and achieved satisfactory results [16].

5.3   Result of RQ 2

To explore the reasons why RFA outperforms SFA in most cases in Sect. 5.2, we studied the rank lists for each bug and SFL technique. We found that the 6 experimental SFL techniques have high rank accuracy but low suspiciousness accuracy for most benchmark programs. That is, for most experimental programs, SFL techniques always rank the faulty statement high in the rank list. Therefore, RFA, which is a deterministic algorithm relying on the absolute rank, can reach relatively low NCP scores. On the other hand, although these SFL techniques do rank faulty statements high, they also produce not too low suspiciousness of many normal statements (i.e., flatter score), thus leading to low suspiciousness accuracy and resulting in low performance of SFA that selects statements randomly with different probabilities.

To further verify the finding that low suspiciousness accuracy of existing SFL techniques results in poor performance of SFA, we conducted a new experiment to improve the suspiciousness accuracy of SFL without changing the rank. In fact, Parnin and Orso [22] manually increased the rank accuracy of Tarantula formula in their experiment to observe the debugging aids of SFL techniques. Unlike that work focusing on the rank, we propose a useful approach to increase the suspiciousness accuracy of SFL techniques without changing the rank accuracy. As described in Fig. 5, the approach increases the probability of being selected of the faulty statement by decreasing the suspiciousness values of correct statements that do not rank in the top 40% to zero. We set the cut-off point as 40% because in our experiment the faulty statement in most cases ranks in the top 40%. In the experiment, we select Ochiai and 6 bugs (see Fig. 6), and then implement this approach into Ochiai to obtain "Och-New", which is then employed in SFA-based Nopol to perform 100 independent repair trials for NCP collection.

As shown in Fig. 6, compared to the NCP of SFA using Ochiai, the NCP scores of SFA using "Och-New" are obviously improved. We further conduct Wilcoxon test and A-test to evaluate the improvements of "Och-New" over Ochiai. According to the results [41], all 6 benchmark programs indicate that the improvement is statistically significant, with 3 of them presenting promising "large" effect sizes and 2 of them displaying "medium" effect sizes. Based on the results, we can conclude that *the low performance of SFL is caused by the suspiciousness inaccuracy of SFL and can be improved through increasing the accuracy of the suspiciousness of the faulty statement.*

Input: RankList A = {$(stm_1, susp_1)$, $(stm_2, susp_2)$ ... $(stm_n, susp_n)$}
Output: Rank list A
1: **let** cutoff = ceil(length(A)*40%)
2: **for** i = cutoff to length(A) **do**
3:    **let** $A(i).susp$ = 0
4: **end for**
5: **return** rank list A

Fig. 5. The approach to improve the suspiciousness accuracy of SFL techniques

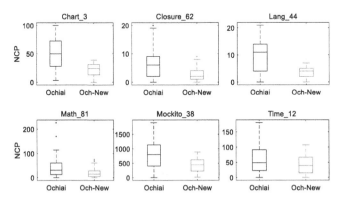

Fig. 6. The NCP of SFA from Ochiai and "Och-New".

This finding indicates a new direction for improving the fault localization techniques in automated program repair. More details can be found in Sect. 6.

5.4 Result of RQ 3

In automated program repair, most patches generated by automated repair tools are plausible patches rather than correct patches [30, 33]. Therefore, when a faulty program has more than one statement that can be modified to generate a plausible patch, the patch diversity of RFA and SFA may differ. To investigate the performance of RFA and SFA in patch diversity, we compare the patch information of all the benchmark programs repaired by four experimental tools. As indicated in Table 2, RFA-based tools reach the same results in patch diversity, that it, they get only 1 plausible patch in repeated trials. On the contrary, SFA-based Nopol, jKali and jMutRepair obtain more inequivalent valid patches than the corresponding RFA-based tools in 75% (=33/44), 55.56% (=5/9) and 33.33% (=3/9) buggy programs respectively. For the rest of benchmark programs, the three SFA-based tools achieve the same performance as their corresponding RFA-based tools, as these bugs only have one statement that can be repaired by experimental repair tools. Interestingly, both SFA-based and RFA-based SimFix generate only one patch for each bug, which results from the narrowed search space of these bugs obtained by SimFix [40].

Table 2. The number of inequivalent patches obtained by SFA and RFA in 100 independent repeated trials for each program

Tool	Strategy	Number of inequivalent patches	Number of buggy programs
Nopol	SFA	1	11
		>1	33
	RFA	1	44
jKali	SFA	1	4
		>1	5
	RFA	1	9
jMutRepair	SFA	1	6
		>1	3
	RFA	1	9
SimFix	SFA	1	7
	RFA	1	7

Overall, *SFA outperforms RFA in patch diversity* by stimulating the repair tools to repair statements randomly rather than depending on the absolute rank. The better performance achieved by SFA in patch diversity produces more inequivalent patches in repeated repair or parallel repair, thus providing more clue information to help developers find the correct patch [34].

5.5 Threats to Validity

Internal validity threats are concerned with the errors in our implementation and experiments. In our experiment, Op2 produced negative suspiciousness scores for many statements in buggy programs according to its risk evaluation formula [13]. Such statements, if considered by SFA, may be transformed into negative probabilities, thus deviating the definition of SFA. To mitigate this threat, we discarded the statements with negative suspiciousness scores in the rank list.

Threats to external validity relate to the generalizability of our experimental results. In our experiment, we obtained 48 versions of automated program repair tools. Although we did our best to make the study generalizable through studying more repair tools and bugs, these experiments may not be representative of all buggy programs and repair tools. As future work, we plan to extend our experiment by studying more repair tools and benchmark programs, such as Jaid [6] and QuixBugs [26].

Construct validity threats concern the suitability of our evaluation metrics. We introduce NCP and propose patch diversity as evaluation metrics in our work. For the two metrics, we performed the same number of independent repeated trials for each bug as the study [2, 17] did to avoid occasionality and inaccuracy. In addition, we conducted statistical analyses to measure the NCP for comparing SFA and RFA.

6 Discussion

Though RFA obtains lower NCP that represents better effectiveness in the experiment compared to SFA, RFA has two limitations in automated program repair: (1) RFA-based repair tools can be easily converted into SFA-based tools, but not vice versa. That is, SFA cannot be replaced by RFA in the automated program repair tools, especially for tools that use many modification operators or heuristic approaches when repairing the suspicious statements. These tools, such as Genprog [16] and PAR [15] always explore prohibitively large search space, in which SFA is indispensable as an effective strategy. On the other hand, RFA-based tools can be easily transformed into SFA-based tools by suspiciousness conversion and random selection (See Sect. 4.2), (2) As a deterministic algorithm, RFA is less flexible than SFA in selecting statements, thus achieving comparatively poor performance in the patch diversity and low efficiency in parallel repair.

Many recently proposed automated program repair tools [6, 7, 9, 11, 12], however, directly employ RFA as their statement selecting strategy, regardless of SFA that has great potential to assist automated program repair. This is mainly because: (1) existing repair tools still select fault localization techniques from the viewpoint of developers which prefer localization techniques that rank the faulty statement higher [2], despite the fact that higher suspiciousness accuracy can improve the effectiveness of fault localization techniques in automated program repair. That is, the usage of fault localization information (i.e., SFA and RFA), which has the potential to move the automated repair towards industrial applications, are neglected in current automated program repair. (2) existing studies [13, 37] focus too much on improving the rank accuracy with rank-based metrics (e.g., EXAM [37] and Top-10 [13]) while ignoring the suspiciousness accuracy that impacts the effectiveness of automated program repair, especially for the SFA-based tools. Although the LIL metric [24] focusing on suspiciousness accuracy is proposed, there are still no studies improving the effectiveness of SFA in automated program repair to our knowledge. To fill such gaps, in this paper we empirically evaluate the performance of SFA and RFA. Furthermore, our study yields insights into the construction of more effective fault localization techniques in automated program repair through improving the suspiciousness accuracy.

7 Conclusion

In this paper, we have performed an empirical study on the two statement selecting strategies (i.e., SFA and RFA) based on our prior work [14]. We introduce more repair tools and benchmark programs as well as statistical analyses to further evaluate the performance of SFA and RFA in automated program repair. As our evaluation shows, RFA outperforms SFA in 64.76% cases when evaluated by NCP, while SFA performs better in parallel repair and patch diversity. The two findings provide directions for future research on the usage of fault localization information. In addition, we explore the reasons behind the lower performance of SFA under the measurement of NCP by increasing the suspiciousness accuracy of the faulty statement. The results suggest that improving the suspiciousness accuracy can be a promising way to propose more effective fault localization techniques in automated program repair.

As future work, we plan to evaluate the correctness of patches obtained by SFA and RFA to further compare their abilities in finding correct patches. Also, we plan to construct a fault localization technique with higher suspiciousness accuracy that can benefit automated program repair, especially the SFA-based repair tools.

Acknowledgements. This research was partially supported by National Natural Science Foundation of China (61502015, 61672529, 61379054, 61602504).

References

1. Gazzola, L., Micucci, D., Mariani, L.: Automatic software repair: a survey. In: ICSE (2018)
2. Qi, Y., et al.: Using automated program repair for evaluating the effectiveness of fault localization techniques. In: ISSTA (2013)
3. Wong, W.E., et al.: A survey on software fault localization. IEEE Trans. Softw. Eng. (TSE) **42**(8), 707–740 (2016)
4. Assiri, F.Y., Bieman, J.M.: Fault localization for automated program repair: effectiveness, performance, repair correctness. Softw. Qual. J. (SQJ) **25**(1), 171–199 (2017)
5. Monperrus, M.: Automatic software repair: a bibliography. ACM Comput. Surv. (CSUR) **51**(1), 17 (2018)
6. Chen, L., Pei, Y., Furia, C.A.: Contract-based program repair without the contracts. In: ASE (2017)
7. Saha, R.K., et al.: ELIXIR: effective object oriented program repair. In: ASE (2017)
8. Mechtaev, S., Yi, J., Roychoudhury, A.: Angelix: scalable multiline program patch synthesis via symbolic analysis. In: ICSE (2016)
9. Le, X.-B.D., et al.: JFIX: semantics-based repair of Java programs via symbolic PathFinder. In: ISSTA (2017)
10. Martinez, M., Monperrus, M.: Astor: a program repair library for Java. In: ISSTA (2016)
11. Xiong, Y., et al.: Precise condition synthesis for program repair. In: ICSE (2017)
12. Xuan, J., et al.: Nopol: automatic repair of conditional statement bugs in Java programs. IEEE Trans. Softw. Eng. (TSE) **43**(1), 34–55 (2017)
13. Pearson, S., et al.: Evaluating and improving fault localization. In: ICSE (2017)
14. Yang, D., Qi, Y., Mao, X.: An empirical study on the usage of fault localization in automated program repair. In: 2017 IEEE International Conference on Software Maintenance and Evolution (ICSME NIER Track). IEEE (2017)
15. Kim, D., et al.: Automatic patch generation learned from human-written patches. In: ICSE (2013)
16. Le Goues, C., et al.: Genprog: a generic method for automatic software repair. TSE **38**(1), 54–72 (2012)
17. Qi, Y., et al.: The strength of random search on automated program repair. In: ICSE (2014)
18. Le, X.B.D., Lo, D., Le Goues, C.: History driven program repair. In: SANER (2016)
19. Just, R., Jalali, D., Ernst, M.D.: Defects4J: a database of existing faults to enable controlled testing studies for Java programs. In: ISSTA (2014)
20. Keller, F., et al.: A critical evaluation of spectrum-based fault localization techniques on a large-scale software system. In: 2017 IEEE International Conference on Software Quality, Reliability and Security (QRS). IEEE (2017)

21. Xie, X., et al.: A theoretical analysis of the risk evaluation formulas for spectrum-based fault localization. TOSEM **22**(4), 31 (2013)
22. Parnin, C., Orso, A.: Are automated debugging techniques actually helping programmers? In: ISSTA (2011)
23. Kochhar, P.S., et al.: Practitioners' expectations on automated fault localization. In: ISSTA (2016)
24. Moon, S., et al.: Ask the mutants: mutating faulty programs for fault localization. In: ICST (2014)
25. Xiong, Y., et al.: Identifying patch correctness in test-based program repair. In: ICSE (2018)
26. Ye, H., Martinez, M., Monperrus, M.: A comprehensive study of automatic program repair on the QuixBugs benchmark. arXiv preprint arXiv:1805.03454 (2018)
27. Martinez, M., et al.: Automatic repair of real bugs in Java: a large-scale experiment on the Defects4J dataset. Empir. Softw. Eng. **22**(4), 1936–1964 (2017)
28. Tanikado, A., et al.: New strategies for selecting reuse candidates on automated program repair. In: COMPSAC (2017)
29. Xin, Q., Reiss, S.P.: Leveraging syntax-related code for automated program repair. In: ASE (2017)
30. Qi, Z., et al.: An analysis of patch plausibility and correctness for generate-and-validate patch generation systems. In: ISSTA (2015)
31. Durieux, T., et al.: The patches of the Nopol automatic repair system on the bugs of Defects4J version 1.1. 0. Dissertation, Université Lille 1-Sciences et Technologies (2017)
32. Arcuri, A., Briand, L.: A practical guide for using statistical tests to assess randomized algorithms in software engineering. In: ICSE (2011)
33. Xin, Q., Reiss, S.P.: Identifying test-suite-overfitted patches through test case generation. In: ISSTA (2017)
34. Tao, Y., et al.: Automatically generated patches as debugging aids: a human study. In: FSE (2014)
35. Mechtaev, S., et al.: Semantic program repair using a reference implementation. In: ICSE (2018)
36. Jia Y., et al.: Finding and fixing software bugs automatically with SapFix and Sapienz. https://code.fb.com/developer-tools/finding-and-fixing-software-bugs-automatically-with-sapfix-and-sapienz/ (2018)
37. Wong, W.E., et al.: The DStar method for effective software fault localization. IEEE Trans. Reliab. **63**, 290–308 (2014)
38. Wen, M., et al.: Context-aware patch generation for better automated program repair. In: ICSE (2018)
39. Just, R., et al.: Comparing developer-provided to user-provided tests for fault localization and automated program repair. In: ISSTA (2018)
40. Jiang, J., et al.: Shaping program repair space with existing patches and similar code. In: ISSTA (2018)
41. Yang, D.: SFA-RFA. https://github.com/DehengYang/sfa-rfa (2018)
42. Le, X.-B.D., et al.: S3: syntax-and semantic-guided repair synthesis via programming by examples. In: FSE (2017)

Program Analysis

Evaluating and Integrating Diverse Bug Finders for Effective Program Analysis

Bailin Lu[1], Wei Dong[1(✉)], Liangze Yin[1], and Li Zhang[2]

[1] National University of Defense Technology, Changsha, China
lubailin12@163.com, wdong@nudt.edu.cn, yinliangze@163.com
[2] Meituan Corporation, Beijing, China
zhangli31@meituan.com

Abstract. Many static analysis methods and tools have been developed for program bug detection. They are based on diverse theoretical principles, such as pattern matching, abstract interpretation, model checking and symbolic execution. Unfortunately, none of them can meet most requirements for bug finding. Individual tool always faces high false negatives and/or false positives, which is the main obstacle for using them in practice. A direct and promising way to improve the capability of static analysis is to integrate diverse bug finders. In this paper, we first selected five state-of-the-art C/C++ static analysis tools implemented with different theories. We then evaluated them over different defect types and code structures in detail. To increase the precision and recall for tool integration, we studied how to properly employ machine learning algorithms based on features of programs and tools. Evaluation results show that: (1) the abilities of diverse tools are quite different for defect types and code structures, and their overlaps are quite small; (2) the integration based on machine learning can obviously improve the overall performance of static analysis. Finally, we investigated the defect types and code structures which are still challenging for existing tools. They should be addressed in future research on static analysis.

Keywords: Static analysis · Tool integration · Machine learning

1 Introduction

Static analysis (SA) is the method of analyzing program without executing it [10], which has been widely used for program bug detection. A large number of SA methods (such as flow-based pattern matching [5], abstract interpretation [11], symbolic execution [16] and program model checking [12]) have been studied, and corresponding tools have been implemented. However, current SA research still faces the following challenges.

First, the capabilities of different SA methods and tools over different defect types and program features are still unclear [13]. For example, we know that program model checking can detect and locate defects with complex semantics,

© Springer Nature Switzerland AG 2018
L. Bu and Y. Xiong (Eds.): SATE 2018, LNCS 11293, pp. 51–67, 2018.
https://doi.org/10.1007/978-3-030-04272-1_4

while abstract interpretation can reduce the complexity of numerical computation [11,12]. However, given a real program that contains some unknown defects, which technique and tool should we select? It is usually difficult to make decision.

Second, how to appropriately integrate existing tools together to improve the capability of SA is still an open problem. Large number of false positives and false negatives is the main obstacles for applying SA in practice [13]. Integrating existing SA tools might decrease the number of false negatives. However, simply merging the results of various tools may greatly increase the number of false positives. Therefore, we need a better method to give full play to the specialty of each tool, and effectively reduce both the false positives and false negatives.

Third, the defect types and program features that are not well-supported by current SA techniques and tools have not been clarified yet. There are still some kinds of defects that frustrate all current SA tools. These defects have been rarely detected by existing SA tools. More studies should be carried out to improve the methods of detecting these kinds of defects. For this, one should first make certain which kinds of defects and code structures frustrate current SA methods and tools, then corresponding academic and implementation work could be carried out in future.

To investigate the above problems, we considered five state-of-the-art SA tools for C/C++ programs, including Cppcheck [3], CBMC [1], Frama-C [4], Clang Static Analyzer [2] and a commercial tool. These tools implement different SA techniques, including data and control flow analysis using bug patterns, abstract interpretation, symbolic execution and model checking. The first four tools are open source, reflecting the up-to-date research improvement. The last one is well known, and we chose it as the representative of commercial tools. We used Juliet Test Suite [8] as our benchmark. It contains 61387 test cases, covers more than one hundred Common Weakness Enumeration (CWE) types and tens of different code structures. The main contributions of this paper include:

(1) We evaluated the capability of each tool on 91 CWE types and 48 kinds of code structures. Experiment results show that the abilities of these tools are quite different from each other, and they have quite small overlaps in defects types. These evaluations can also support tool selection for special analysis purposes.

(2) To improve both the precision and recall, we proposed a method using machine learning to merge the results of diverse tools with consideration of specialties of different tools and program features. We evaluated six ML algorithms, and the experiment results show that our method performs much better than any individual tool and simple integration.

(3) We analyzed the defect types and code structures that are still not well-supported by these five tools. These results are valuable for determining the future research directions of program analysis methods and tools.

Section 2 reviews the related work. Section 3 introduces the research questions and the design of our study. Section 4 evaluates five SA tools in detail. Section 5 presents the ML-based tool integration method. Section 6 studies the defect types and code structures that are still challenging. Finally, Sects. 7 and 8 discuss the threats to validity and concludes this paper respectively.

2   Related Work

2.1   Static Analysis Tools

SA methods have been deeply studied in recent years, such as abstract interpretation, program model checking and symbolic execution. There is also some work on combining these methods [25]. Accordingly, many good tools have been developed for each technique, such as Frama-C [4] for abstract interpretation, CBMC [1] for model checking, KLEE [6] for symbolic execution, Cppcheck [3] for pattern and flow analysis. Compared with dynamic analysis, SA does not actually execute programs and usually scan the programs quickly [14]. However, it may produce a large number of false positives and false negatives [25].

2.2   Evaluation of Static Analysis Tools

Thung et al. evaluated the performance of various bug finders in terms of false negative rates [24]. McLean et al. compared Flawfinder and RATS on some open source software by the number of detected defects [19]. Wagner et al. compared the defects found by bug finders with dynamic tests and reviews, and analyzed their false positives [27]. They also evaluated practical effectiveness and efficiency of two bug pattern tools in industrial projects [26]. Rutar et al. compared the number of warning generated by various bug finders and analyzed the overlapped bugs of them [23]. In 2012, NSA CAS employed four evaluation indexes, including precision, recall, F-Score and discrimination rate, to evaluate several SA tools. Their experiments were done on 15 defect types of Juliet Test Suite. Their results showed that these tools performed differently over different defect types [7].

In our work, we tried to evaluate the capabilities of tools with different theoretic background in detail. Particularly, we evaluated diverse tools on both defect types and code structures, and tried to identify which ones each tool is good at.

2.3   Integration of Static Analysis Tools

Rutar et al. proposed a meta-tool that combines outputs of bug finders together, and studied two metrics for ranking the bug reported [23]. Deguang Kong et al. developed an integrating system based on data fusion, making different tools complement each other [9]. Meng et al. merged the defect reports of several SA tools based on the consideration that defect reported by multiple tools would be more likely to be a true positive [20]. TOIF (the Blade Tool Output Integration Framework) [15] works by merging the defect results of different tools with a unified format and removing those duplicated warnings.

However, all of them didn't take full advantage of the specialties of different SA tools. For example, a SA tool might be adept at detecting some kinds of defects and be weak at detecting others. It usually gives accurate reports on the former while produces a mass of false positives on the latter. In our work, to obtain better precision and recall, we tried to employ features like this and also features in program with machine learning to identify whether a detected defect is true or false.

3   Methodology Design

3.1   Research Questions

When people use SA in software development, they always confuse which SA method and tool will be more suitable for them, and how to evaluate the results after usage. They also didn't know how to choose and use different tools together. More tools will introduce more reduplicate results, and even much more false positives. These factors have seriously impeded the utilization of SA tools in practice. Therefore, we would like to answer the following five research questions.

Research Question 1: For diverse SA methods and respective tools, what's the effects when these tools are applied in programs contain all kinds of defects, and which defect types is each tool most adept at respectively?

Different SA methods normally target on different defects. Even the tools using same technique have different ability because of the implementation details [25]. To clarify the specific ability of each tool, we need a detailed evaluation of these tools over different defect types such as ones included in CWE.

Research Question 2: Program structure and complexity have large influence on SA, what are the impacts of different code structures (data and control flow types) on detection ability of diverse methods and tools?

The more complex the structure of a program is, the harder the program is analyzed. Many work in program analysis focused on finding tricky errors in complex codes. Evaluating SA tools over different code structures can help us further understand the capabilities of SA methods and tools.

Research Question 3: If the abilities of diverse tools are quite different, to what extents the overlaps of these tools will be?

Overlap rate is the ratio of the number of defects detected commonly by multiple tools to that of all detected defects. It can be used to represent the similarity of different SA tools. Evaluating the overlap rates of different tools is of great significance to tool integration.

Research Question 4: When we have large amount of data on usage of different SA tools, how to utilize related machine learning algorithms to obtain a better integration result?

Integrating multiple tools together can usually find more defects. However, simple integration might also produce plenty of false positives. If we have enough data such as evaluation results and corresponding program features, machine learning may be useful in tool integration.

Research Question 5: To promote future SA research, which defect types and code structures are still challenging for state-of-the-art methods and tools?

It is obvious that some defect types are still challenging for almost all tools. For these types, tool integration can hardly enhance the detection capability. The only way to improve the results of detecting such defects is to improve SA technique itself. It is the same for code structures. To improve existing SA methods and tools, we need to investigate these defect types and code structures.

3.2   Design of the Experimental Study

(1) Choice of SA Tools. To evaluate and compare the SA tools with most diversity, we determined several rules for tools selection. The rules include:

– These tools are implemented with different mainstream SA technologies.
– Each tool is the representative for the technology it uses.
– Selected tools have relatively better usability and have been widely accepted by developers.
– Excellent open source tools are preferred to, but we also select one well-known commercial tool for comparison.

Since C/C++ programs have more subtle defects and are usually more difficult to analyze, and many critical software still use them, here we focus on C/C++ SA tools. With above rules, we chose five state-of-the-art SA tools for study, including Cppcheck, CBMC, Clang Static Analyzer, Frama-C and a commercial tool A (its name will not appear here because of the business reason).

Cppcheck [3] conducts a generic context-sensitive value flow analysis before any checker is executed. It primarily focuses on undefined behaviour and dangerous coding constructs. It has been widely used by developers, although there are still many bugs cannot be detected [28].

CBMC [1] is a bounded model checker for C/C++ programs. It verifies properties like array bounds, pointer safety, and user-specified assertions. The verification is performed by unwinding the loops and encoding the program behavior into logical formula, which is then solved by constraint solver [18].

Clang Static Analyzer [2] employs symbolic execution to find bugs of C, C++ and Objective-C programs. The default set of checkers covers a variety of aims target at finding security and API usage bugs, dead code, and other logic errors (It is referred as Clang for short in the following).

Frama-C [4] is an extensible and collaborative platform dedicates to source-code analysis of C programs. It is based on abstract interpretation and gathers several SA techniques in a single collaborative framework. Frama-C allows its users to manipulate functional specifications, and proves the source code satisfies these specifications [17].

Commercial tool A is famous in industry for finding software defects and security vulnerabilities. It wants to provide full path coverage, ensuring that every line of code and every potential execution path are analyzed. We chose it since we want to compare the capabilities between commercial and open source tools, and check the effect of their integration.

(2) Benchmark Used. We selected Juliet Test Suite v1.2 for C/C++ [8] as our benchmark. Juliet Test Suite is provided by NSA Center for Assured Software. It has been widely accepted for SA tool evaluation [7]. The reasons we choose Juliet Test Suite include:

- It contains a total of 61387 test cases and is large enough to yield statistical significance.
- All defects in this suite are already known, which makes it feasible to calculate accurate values of evaluation indexes.
- It covers many well-known defect types and common code structures. Actually, 118 CWE types and 48 data and control flow variants are covered in this test suite.
- For each defect in the suite, both buggy and correct versions are provided. It can better support the evaluation of false positives.

In this suite, each test case can be uniquely identified by the combination of CWE ID, data or control flow variant and functional variant. With these characteristics, experiments can give a comprehensive evaluation on the defect detection capability of a SA tool. Our experiments were performed on Ubuntu 14.04. We chose 51399 test cases that could run on Linux as our benchmark (the others focus on defects only exist in Windows platform), which cover 91 CWE types and 48 data/control flow variants.

(3) Evaluation Indexes. We used six indexes to evaluate the capability of SA tool. The calculation of these indexes involves several conventional statistical values including True positive (TP), False positive (FP), True negative (TN), and False negative (FN). It can be concluded that $TP+FP$ represents the number of reported defects, while $TP+FN$ represents the number of actual defects. Besides these values, we also use some other statistical values to compute following six evaluation indexes.

(i) *Precision* represents the reliability of a defect report to be a real bug. The higher the precision is, the higher probability the detected defects to be real bugs. We have $precision = \frac{TP}{TP+FP}$.

(ii) *Recall* describes the capability of a tool to detect potential defects. The higher the recall is, the less the number of undetected true defects will be. We have $recall = \frac{TP}{TP+FN}$.

(iii) *F-score* is used to evaluate the comprehensive capability of a tool over precision and recall, since a trade-off between precision and recall should usually be considered when implementing real tools. The higher the *F-score* is, the better a tool performs. It is defined as $F\text{-}score = \frac{2}{1/precision+1/recall}$.

(iv) *Discrimination rate* is the ratio of the number of discriminated cases to that of all cases, where a discriminated case is the one that only positive defects are detected. The higher the discrimination rate is, the higher precision might be obtained. There is $Disc.\ rate = \frac{number\ of\ discrimination\ cases}{number\ of\ all\ cases}$.

(v) *CWE coverage* is the ratio of the number of detected CWE types to that of all CWE types in Juliet. It is used to evaluate the capability of a tool to detect more kinds of defects. We have $CWE\ coverage = \frac{number\ of\ detected\ CWE\ types}{number\ of\ all\ CWE\ types}$.

(vi) *Overlap rate* is the ratio of the number of defects that are commonly detected by multiple tools to that of all detected defects. It reflects the similarity of different tools. It is defined as $Overlap\ rate = \frac{number\ of\ commonly\ detected\ defects}{number\ of\ all\ detected\ defects}$.

(4) Process of Our Experiment. The procedures of our experiment were devised as follows.

(a) We identified those cases that can be compiled on Linux platform, and 51399 test cases were selected.
(b) We extracted information such as CWE ID, flow variant of code, file path, error type and error line, of these cases, and stored them into the database.
(c) We ran five SA tools separately over these 51399 test cases, and received a result report for each tool.
(d) A unified report format based on XML was devised, and the reports of all tools were converted into that format.
(e) The evaluation indexes were computed to evaluate each tool over CWE types and flow variants. Research questions 1 to 3 were then answered.
(f) We studied how to employ ML algorithms on results of five tools to obtain better performance. Research question 4 was then answered.
(g) We analyzed the defect types and flow variants that were still not well-supported by existing SA techniques and tools. Research question 5 was then answered.

Table 1. Commands used for five tools

Tool	Command
CBMC	cbmc file_name -I include_path -D INCLUDEMAIN −−bounds-check −−pointer-check −−div-by-zero-check −−signed-overflow-check −−unsigned-overflow-check −−nan-check −−unwind 6 −−no-unwinding-assertions −−xml-ui
Clang	scan-build -o . make
Cppcheck	cppcheck −−quiet −−enable=style −−xml
Frama-C	frama-c -val file_name -cpp-extra-args='-D INCLUDEMAIN -I include_path'
Commercial tool A	−− (*The command is not listed since business reason.*)

The execution commands and options of five tools are shown in Table 1. Since there may be many special options for each tool, in our experiments, we executed the typical commands and options. For Clang and tool A, their normal commands were used; For Frama-C, *-val* was used to perform value analysis; For CBMC, *–unwind 6* is used to set the loop unwinding bound to 6; For Cppcheck, *enable=style* is used to enable all coding style check.

4 Tool Evaluation

4.1 Evaluation on Ability of Finding Bugs

Figure 1 summaries the bug finding results of five tools. The capability of each tool is evaluated by the precision, recall, F-score, discrimination rate, and CWE coverage. According to the results, we can observe that:

(1) The highest recall of these tools is 36.7%, which means that none of tools can find most defects in the benchmark. Furthermore, none precision are higher than 50% (Cppcheck with 49.1%), which means more than half warnings are false positives for each tool.

(2) Cppcheck has the best F-score (34.1%), and the F-scores of four tools except CBMC are similar. But no tool has good precision and recall at the same time. Cppcheck has the best precision, its recall is only the third. Frama-C has the best recall, but the worst precision.

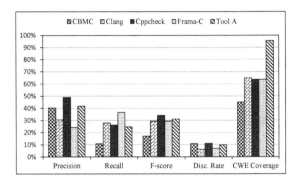

Fig. 1. Evaluate the bug finding ability of five tools.

(3) The numbers of CWE types detected by these tools vary greatly. CBMC, Clang, Cppcheck, Frama-C and tool A can detect 41, 59, 58, 58 and 87 CWEs respectively. The disc. rates of them are not quite different.

(4) The defects found by tool A covers 95% of the CWE types, which seems very good. However, its recall is only the forth in all tools, and its precision, F-score and disc. rate are also not highlighted. It might be concluded that commercial tools often try to find more types of defects which will be beneficial to their market, but for each defect type, commercial tools are not as good as open source tools. They can find more defects types, but cannot find more defects.

Obviously no individual tool can satisfy the requirements in SA. Each tool can only find small part of defects, and most of their results are false positives. Therefore, next we want to know is which defect types will each tool be good at.

4.2   Evaluation over CWE Types

To show the capabilities of tools over different defect types, for each tool we select its top 15 CWE types with the largest F-score, i.e., the 15 kinds of defects that this tool is more skilled. The evaluation results are shown in Fig. 2. The horizontal axis represents the CWE IDs sorted by F-score in descending order.

We can observe that: (i) The adept CWE types of different tools are quite different. For each pair of tools, the overlap of top 15 adept defect types is only four on average. (ii) There are some special defect types for each tool that can obtain a high precision. For example, the precision of CWE197, 23, 36 and 590 for CBMC are 100%. It means that all detected defects of CBMC over these defect types are true positives. (iii) High recall is very difficult, there is no CWE type can obtain 100% recall for any tool. For each tool, these observed results can then be used to estimate the reliability of its reports in the integration.

ANSWER of RQ1: For SA tools implementing different techniques, their abilities of bug finding and their adept defect types are quite different. Moreover, each tool may be especially adept at detecting some special defect types.

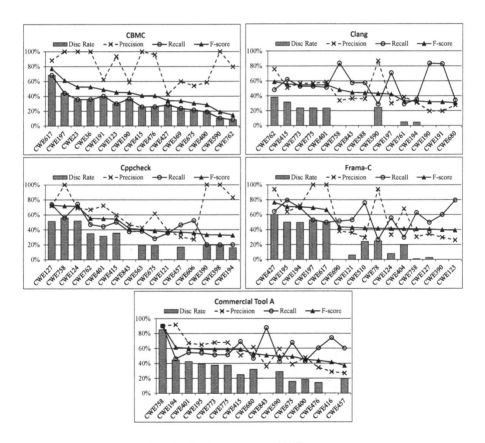

Fig. 2. Evaluation over CWE types.

4.3 Evaluation over Flow Variants

Since code structures heavily affect the results of SA, we then evaluated five tools over different data and control flow variants. In Juliet, test cases are also classified by their typical flow which is numbered [8]. Number 01 represents the simplest variant of flow, Number 02–22 represent control flows, and Number 31–84 represent data flows. Now there are 48 flow variants, since some numbers are reserved. For data or control flows separately, the larger the number is, the more complex the code will be. For example, variant 31 represents *"data flow using a copy of data within the same function"*, while variant 45 is *"data passed as a static global variable from one function to another in the same source file"*.

In Fig. 3, horizontal axis represents the flow variant numbers. There is no successive decreases when the flow number increases, but there are some cliff decreases when flow reach some complexity. Generally speaking, the more complex the flow is, the more difficult it will be to find the bugs. In the figure, CBMC seems working with stable performance before variant 68, but all its indexes immediately reach bottom after that. Frama-C has the similar results.

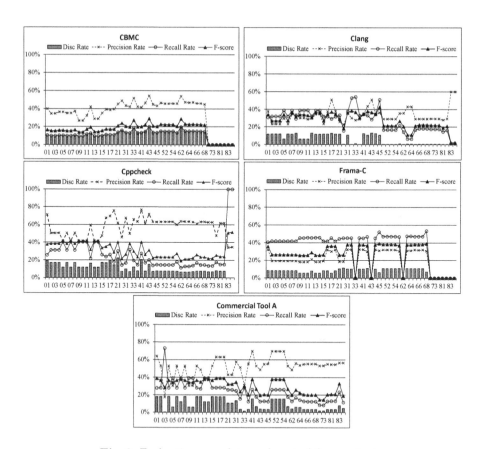

Fig. 3. Evaluation over data and control flow variants.

It may be that model checking and abstraction interpretation are both more sensitive to complex data flow. For Clang, Cppcheck and tool A, the recall and F-score decrease obviously for higher variant numbers. We can conclude that complex data flow has more negative influences than complex control flow.

ANSWER of RQ2: For SA tools implementing different techniques, their bug detection abilities over different data and control flows are obviously different. Taking flow variants into consideration for tool integration is important.

4.4   Overlaps of Different SA Tools

Here we know diverse tools have quite different capabilities, then we wonder what the actual overlaps of these tools are for effectively integrating them.

Figure 4 shows the percents of defects that can be detected by multiple tools. 28.00% of all defects cannot be detected by any tool, and 34.50% of them can be found by only one tool. Only one third of the defects can be commonly detected by more than one tool. What's more, the number of defects that can be detected by several tools decreases drastically as the number of tools increases. The defects that can be detected by two tools account for 23.36%. This rate decreases to 11.54% for three tools, and 2.25% for four tools. The percent for all five tools even can be neglected. Then, we have more proofs to conclude that capabilities of different tools are usually diverse from each other.

Table 2 lists the overlap rates for each pair of tools. In the best case, the overlap rate is 31.2% (Clang and Tool A); while in the worst case, this rate is just 2.79% (CBMC and Cppcheck). Particularly, CBMC and Frama-C have relatively lower overlap rates with the other four tools. They have average overlap rates of 8.35% and 16.1% with the other four tools, respectively. The reason may be that CBMC and Frama-C employ bounded model checking and abstract interpretation for program analysis respectively, which are special theories for semantic reasoning.

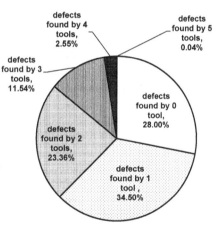

Fig. 4. Overlaps of the five tools.

ANSWER of RQ3: The overlaps of SA tools implementing different methods are usually quite small. Integrating these tools together may obtain promising results.

5   Machine Learning Based Tool Integration

5.1   Integration Method Overview

According to the experiment results shown in Sect. 4, tools implementing different techniques complement each other. An intuitive idea to reduce the false negatives of using one tool is to merge the results of multiple tools together. However, it will also bring all false positives together, which frustrate SA in practice. Many factors can affect the detection results of a tool, including the SA methods used, defect types and code structures, implementation techniques and the ability of tool developers. Thus, it is very difficult to automatically decide which warnings are real defects.

Machine learning (ML) gives computer the ability to learn without being explicitly programmed. It includes the algorithms that build analytical model automatically and use it to predict future data [21]. When we have enough experimental data for SA tools, ML algorithms can be used to predict the correctness of warnings, which can be regarded as a classification problem. To obtain better effect of tool integration, we studied how to employ ML to exploit the specialty of each tool over features such as defect types and code structures.

Table 2. Overlap rates of each pair of tools

	Clang	Cppcheck	Tool A	Frama-C
CBMC	15.88%	2.79%	4.94%	9.80%
Clang	-	19.78%	31.20%	24.16%
Cppcheck	-	-	28.06%	13.04%
Tool A	-	-	-	17.46%

Here we first considered six popular classification algorithms, including Multinomial Naive Bayes (M_NB), Gaussian Naive Bayes (G_NB), Bernoulli Naive Bayes (B_NB), SVM, Decision Tree (DT) and Logistic Regression (LR). Implementations of all these algorithms are from scikit-learn library [22]. The features we select follow two principles: (1) they could be extracted from Juliet Test Suite and

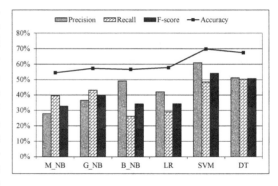

Fig. 5. Comparison of the six ML algorithms.

detection results of the five tools, (2) they could apparently affect the predict result of ML. Therefore, the features we finally chose to learn are: CWE ID, flow variant of code that contain the warning, defect type, tool name, and whether the result is a true positive. We use k-fold cross validation method to divide data set into five parts randomly, and take any four parts as the training set and the remaining part as the test set. Our study contains following steps:

Step 1. We first simply merge the results of five tools without using any ML algorithms, and evaluate the results. It is called *Simple* integration.
Step 2. We then employ six ML algorithms to learn prediction models from training set, which are then used to filter results of the test set. The prediction results are evaluated to distinguish which algorithms are better.

Step 3. Finally we compare the results of using individual SA tools, simple integration and individual ML algorithms.

For ML algorithms, it is important to evaluate if the good and bad cases in the test data are correctly predicted as good and bad respectively. Therefore, another index $accuracy = \frac{TP+TN}{TP+FP+TN+FN}$ is added for evaluating ML algorithms.

5.2   Experimental Results

Figure 5 shows the evaluation results of six ML algorithms. We can see that SVM achieves the best result. Actually, almost all the four evaluation indexes of SVM are higher than those of other five algorithms, except that recall of DT is a few higher. Therefore, we select SVM as the best one of six ML algorithms for SA tool integration. SVM is selected to join the next round of experiments.

After that, we evaluate the effect of simple integration, which is only merging the results of each SA tool. As shown in Fig. 6, we finally compared the precision, recall and F-score of applying individual tool, simple integration and SVM algorithm. From the figure, we will see that:

(1) Compared with individual tool, simple integration improves the recall greatly. It can find 72% defects, while the best recall of five tools is only 37% (Frama-C). Unfortunately, it also merges all false negatives. Since the redundant true positives are removed in simple integration, its precision (22%) is lower than any individual tool.

(2) ML-based method (SVM) has lower recall (48.5%) compared with simple integration, but it greatly improves the precision (61%). At the same time, recall of SVM is still much higher than any individual tool, and precision is also higher than other tools. Therefore, the F-score of SVM

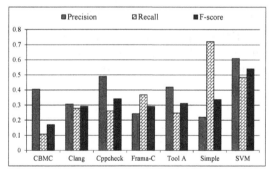

Fig. 6. Comparison of ML based integration, individual tools and simple integration.

(54%) is much higher than any tool and simple integration. ML removes a large number of false positives at the expense of missing a small number of true positives.

Based on above observation, we can conclude that ML-based methods will bring a balance which makes the integration more practical, and has much higher F-score than simple integration.

ANSWER of RQ4: ML is an appropriate method for tool integration that balance the false negatives and false positives. It is much better than any individual tool and simple integration.

6 Challenges for Existing Methods and Tools

We first gather those test cases whose defects cannot be detected by any tool (we call them missed cases in the following). Then 28% of the whole test suite are obtained. We analyzed their distribution on CWE types and flow variants. To ensure the reliability of our conclusion, only those CWE types with more than 50 test cases are considered. The missed test cases distribute on 66 CWE types. The top 15 CWE types with the highest missed ratio are shown in Table 3. For the extreme cases, 94% of the defects are missed (for CWE396 and CWE546). The missed ratios of the top six entries are all higher than 75%. Their corresponding descriptions are also shown in Table 3.

Figure 7 demonstrates the distribution of these missed test cases over flow variants. We can see that the missed ratios of flow variants 01–22 are still manageable, which are mostly around 20%. However, as the number goes on, i.e. the flow becomes more complex, the false negatives increase more and more. For those most complex structures, nearly 70% of the defects are missed by all tools.

It indicates that these complex code structures are still challenging for existing SA techniques, such as number 81 *"Data passed in an argument to a virtual function called via a reference"*. We can observe that the flow variants 43, 62 and 72–82 are especially difficult for these tools, and complex data flows are more difficult to cope with than control flows.

ANSWER of RQ5: There are indeed some defect types and code structures have not been well-supported by state-of-the-art tools. To improve the abilities of SA methods and tools, we should pay more attention to them in future research.

Table 3. The top 15 CWE types with the highest missed ratios.

No.	CWE ID	CWE description	Missed num	Total num	Missed ratio
1	CWE396	Declaration of catch for generic exception	51	54	0.94
2	CWE546	Suspicious comment	85	90	0.94
3	CWE426	Untrusted search path	174	192	0.91
4	CWE252	Unchecked return value	516	630	0.82
5	CWE506	Embedded malicious code	124	158	0.78
6	CWE665	Improper initialization	146	192	0.76
7	CWE511	Logic/time bomb	48	72	0.67
8	CWE78	OS command injection	1534	2304	0.67
9	CWE398	Indicator of poor code quality	119	181	0.66
10	CWE404	Memory leak	248	384	0.65
11	CWE23	Relative path traversal	704	1152	0.61
12	CWE36	Absolute path traversal	704	1152	0.61
13	CWE377	Insecure temporary file	87	144	0.60
14	CWE253	Incorrect check of function return value	389	684	0.57
15	CWE563	Unused variable	286	510	0.56

7   Threats to Validity

We will discuss the threats come from three dimensions: benchmark used, selected tools, and experiment method.

Juliet Test Suite we used is an artificial test set. The codes in Juliet are simpler than real codes. Furthermore, the number of test cases for certain defect might not reflect its actual distribution in real programs, so that two tools that have similar evaluation results on this suit may perform differently on real programs. However, since Juliet covers most common

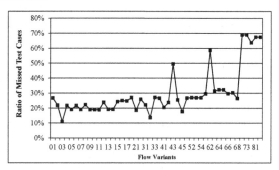

Fig. 7. Ratios of missed test cases over flow variants.

defect types, and they are real defects even are not from real programs, selecting this suite can give a comprehensive evaluation of SA tools.

We selected five SA tools, which are only a small portion of hundreds academic and commercial tools. Some of them are also famous and may have many different specialties, some others may not be famous but are very good at certain kinds of subtle defects by devising special strategies. Thus, if we select more tools or different tool combination, better result on Juliet might be obtained. However, peoples in practice also cannot select too many tools. The five tools implementing diverse SA technologies are representative enough to properly reflect the intent of our study.

In our ML-based integration method, only some traditional classification algorithms were used. Other algorithms and some up-to-date methods of ML such as deep learning might obtain different results. We used data and control flow variants as one of the features for learning. These variants may not be complete, and there might be many other features which seriously affect ability of bug finding. But current algorithms and features can already obtain the expected effects. More ML methods and features are also part of our future work.

8   Conclusion

In this paper, we evaluated five representative tools implementing different SA methods. Their abilities of detecting defects for different CWE types and flow variants, together with their overlaps are investigated in detail. Then the method of properly using ML algorithms to integrate these tools to improve the SA effects is proposed. Finally, we analyzed the CWE types and flow variants that are still challenging for current SA methods and tools.

The results of the paper are valuable for software developers to find more bugs with an accurate manner in practice, since many open source tools are available now. They can use similar method to improve their SA work based on their customized tool set. This work also provides the directions for SA researchers by presenting challenging problems.

Acknowledgments. This work was funded by the National Nature Science Foundation of China (No.61690203, No.61802415, No.61532007).

References

1. CBMC. http://www.cprover.org/cbmc/
2. Clang Static Analyzer. http://clang-analyzer.llvm.org/
3. Cppcheck. http://cppcheck.sourceforge.net/
4. Frama-C. http://frama-c.com/
5. Ayewah, N., Penix, J., Morgenthaler, J.D., Pugh, W., Hovemeyer, D.: Using static analysis to find bugs. IEEE Softw. **25**, 22–29 (2008). https://doi.org/10.1109/MS.2008.130
6. Cadar, C., Dunbar, D., Engler, D.: KLEE: unassisted and automatic generation of high-coverage tests for complex systems programs. In: Usenix Conference on Operating Systems Design and Implementation, pp. 209–224 (2009)
7. CAS: CAS static analysis tool study methodology. NSA (2012)
8. CAS: Juliet test suite v1.2 for C/verb/C++ user guide. NSA (2012)
9. Chen, C., Li, J., Kong, D.: Source code static analysis based on data fusion. Comput. Eng. **34**(20), 66–68 (2008)
10. Chess, B., West, J.: Secure Programming with Static Analysis. Addison-Wesley Professional, Boston (2007)
11. Cousot, P., Cousot, R.: Abstract interpretation frameworks. J. Log. Comput. **2**(4), 511–547 (1992)
12. Clarke, E.M., Emerson, E.A., Sifakis, J.: Model checking: algorithmic verification and debugging. Commun. ACM **52**(11), 74–84 (2009)
13. Heckman, S.S., Williams, L.A.: A systematic literature review of actionable alert identification techniques for automated static code analysis. Inf. Softw. Technol. **53**(4), 363–387 (2011)
14. Johnson, B., Song, Y., Murphy-Hill, E.R., Bowdidge, R.W.: Why don't software developers use static analysis tools to find bugs? In: Notkin, D., Cheng, B.H.C., Pohl, K. (eds.) 35th International Conference on Software Engineering, ICSE 2013, San Francisco, CA, USA, 18–26 May 2013, pp. 672–681. IEEE Computer Society (2013)
15. kgirard: The tool output integration framework (TOIF) is a powerful composite vulnerability detection platform (2016). https://github.com/KdmAnalytics/toif
16. King, J.C.: Symbolic execution and program testing. Commun. ACM **19**(7), 385–394 (1976)
17. Kirchner, F., Kosmatov, N., Prevosto, V., Signoles, J., Yakobowski, B.: Frama-C: a software analysis perspective. Formal Aspects Comput. **27**(3), 573–609 (2015)
18. Kroening, D., Tautschnig, M.: CBMC – C bounded model checker. In: Ábrahám, E., Havelund, K. (eds.) TACAS 2014. LNCS, vol. 8413, pp. 389–391. Springer, Heidelberg (2014). https://doi.org/10.1007/978-3-642-54862-8_26
19. McLean, R.K.: Comparing static security analysis tools using open source software. In: IEEE Sixth International Conference on Software Security and Reliability Companion, pp. 68–74. IEEE (2012)

20. Meng, N., Wang, Q., Wu, Q., Mei, H.: An approach to merge results of multiple static analysis tools (short paper). In: Zhu, H. (ed.) Proceedings of the Eighth International Conference on Quality Software, pp. 169–174. IEEE Computer Society (2008)
21. Omidiora, E.O., Adeyanju, I.A., Fenwa, O.D.: Comparison of machine learning classifiers for recognition of online and offline handwritten digits. Comput. Eng. Intell. Syst. **4**(13), 39–47 (2013)
22. Pedregosa, F., et al.: Scikit-learn: machine learning in python. J. Mach. Learn. Res. **12**(10), 2825–2830 (2012)
23. Rutar, N., Almazan, C.B., Foster, J.S.: A comparison of bug finding tools for java. In: International Symposium on Software Reliability Engineering, pp. 245–256 (2004)
24. Thung, F.: To what extent could we detect field defects? An empirical study of false negatives in static bug finding tools. In: Proceedings of the IEEE/ACM International Conference on Automated Software Engineering, pp. 50–59 (2012)
25. Thung, F., Lucia, Lo, D., Jiang, L., Devanbu, P.T.: To what extent could we detect field defects? An empirical study of false negatives in static bug finding tools. In: Proceedings of the IEEE/ACM International Conference on Automated Software Engineering, pp. 50–59. SelectedWorks (2013)
26. Wagner, S., Deissenboeck, F., Aichner, M., Wimmer, J., Schwalb, M.: An evaluation of two bug pattern tools for java. In: International Conference on Software Testing, Verification, and Validation, pp. 248–257 (2008)
27. Wagner, S., Jürjens, J., Koller, C., Trischberger, P.: Comparing bug finding tools with reviews and tests. In: Khendek, F., Dssouli, R. (eds.) TestCom 2005. LNCS, vol. 3502, pp. 40–55. Springer, Heidelberg (2005). https://doi.org/10.1007/11430230_4
28. Zhang, S., Shang, Z.: Software defect pattern analysis and location based on Cppcheck. Comput. Eng. Appl. **51**(3), 69–73 (2015)

Recognizing Potential Runtime Types
from Python Docstrings

Yang Luo, Wanwangying Ma, Yanhui Li, Zhifei Chen, and Lin Chen[✉]

State Key Laboratory for Novel Software Technology, Nanjing University,
Nanjing, China
{yluo,wwyma,chenzhifei}@smail.nju.edu.cn, {yanhuili,lchen}@nju.edu.cn

Abstract. Docstring plays an important role in software development
and maintanance as it is used in source code to document a specific segment of code. In dynamic language programming, docstring is usually
used to annotate types of parameters and return values.

Docstrings can help developers remind the expected types of a parameter, without process of comprehending the context which is time-
consuming. In this study, we propose an automatic approach to recognize
potential types of a parameter from its description.

In our approach, we utilize feature selection to select useful features
for classifier training. Then we adopt four different kinds of classifiers
to recognize potential types and evaluate their performances using seven
metrics.

We collect a dataset of 314 type descriptions from ten prevalent
Python projects. Our experimental results show that, Decision Tree classifier has the best performances among four studied classifiers, whose precision, recall, F1-score, jaccard index, hamming loss, accuracy and MRR
achieve 0.681, 0.548, 0.582, 0.542, 1.234, 0.432 and 0.778 respectively.
Multi-layer perceptron has the weakest performances. Futher more, we
discover that the performances of four classifiers achieve their best performances when select top 20% or 40% features with the highest χ^2
statistic.

This study archive a dataset of type descriptions and propose a framework of automatically recognizing potential types of a parameter from
its description.

Keywords: Python · Docstring · Random forest · Decision tree

1 Introduction

In programming, a docstring is a string literal specified in source code that
is used to document a segment of code. Unlike conventional source code comments, docstrings are not stripped from the source tree when it is parsed, but are
retained throughout the runtime of the program. Due to this feature, docstring
is supported by many dynamic programming languages, such as Python [1].

© Springer Nature Switzerland AG 2018
L. Bu and Y. Xiong (Eds.): SATE 2018, LNCS 11293, pp. 68–84, 2018.
https://doi.org/10.1007/978-3-030-04272-1_5

As a dynamic programming language, Python does not support static type declaration. How to describe type information to facilitate program comprehension is an important issue in Python development community. Docstring is supported by Python PEP 257 since 2001 [7]. PEP, short for Python Enhancement Proposals, is a serial of proposals raised to improve source code quality of Python projects. A docstring is a string literal that occurs as the first statement in a module, function, class, or method definition. Docstrings are not recognized by the Python bytecode compiler and are not accessible as runtime object attributes. One of the key role of docstring is to describe type information in Python programs.

A simple docstring example adopted form *hbmqtt* is shown as Fig. 1. The method *bytes_to_int* accepts an input parameter *data* and returns a integer value. Line 4 is the description of parameter *data :param data: byte sequence*. We observe that the parameter *data* receives data with the type *byte sequence*, while there doesn't exist a type named *byte sequence* in Python or in the program. In Python, there is a built-in basic type *bytes* which has the meaning of *byte sequence*. After running the test cases provided by developers, we found that the parameter *data* exactly receives objects of *bytes* type at runtime.

```
1  def bytes_to_int(data):
2      """
3      convert a sequence of bytes to an integer using big endian
        ↪ byte ordering
4          :param data: byte sequence
5          :return: integer value
6      """
7      try:
8          return int.from_bytes(data,byteorder='big')
9      except:
10         return data
```

Fig. 1. Code segment with docstring

High quality docstrings help developers remind the function of methods. Understanding and writing high quality type descriptions in docstrings is essential for dynamic programming languages. However, little work has been done to address this problem. Therefore, in this paper, we propose a framework to automatically recognize potential types of parameters in their descriptions. We build our classification model using parameter descriptions collected from ten open source Python projects as training data to classify the potential types which corresponding parameter receives. In our approach, we first preprocess the parameter descriptions and apply feature selection, namely χ^2 to select the top 20% of features with highest statistic value. Then we use the selected features to train a classifier to predict the potential types of a new input parameter description.

To summarize, we mainly make the following contributions in this paper:

- We archive a dataset of parameter descriptions on ten prevalent open source Python projects. Futher research can base on the dataset without collecting projects data from a fresh start.
- To the best of our knowledge, this is the first study of recognizing type descriptions in Python docstrings. In this study, we propose a framework to recognize potential types from type descriptions.

Paper Organization. The rest of this paper is structured as follows. Section 2 describes the overall framework and technical details of our approach. Sections 3 and 4 present our experimental setup and results. Section 5 discuss the implications of our study and threats to validity. Section 6 introduces related work. Section 7 concludes the paper and outlines directions for future research.

2   Approach

2.1   Overall Framework

Figure 2 presents the overall framework of our approach. It contains two phases: a model building phase and a recognition phase. In the model building phase, our approach builds classifiers for each individual project, usings corpus from the other projects. In the recognition phase, the trained classifier receives new parameter descriptions, and label the potential types of these parameters. To evaluate the performance of our approach, we perform leave-one-out cross-project validation: first, we choose one project as "target project", then the rest projects are called as "source projects" and train our multilabel classification model using the docstrings from these source projects.

Our framework takes as input training docstrings with known actual types from different source projects. It first collects all docstrings from source codes of studied projects (Step 1). Next, we extract parameter descriptions from these docstrings (Step 2). Then, we preprocess these descriptions and extract features (i.e., terms) to represent these descriptions (Step 3) and apply feature selection to select features that are useful for classification (Step 4). At the end of the model building phase, we train a decision tree classifier with the filtered features (Step 5). In the recognition phase, for each new parameter description, we first preprocess the description to extract features (Step 6) and classifier receive it as input (Step 7). Finally, the classifier output labels corresponding to the potential types of the input parameter (Step 8).

2.2   Text Preprocessing

We extract features (i.e. terms) in two steps: tokenization, stop-word removal.

Tokenization. Tokenization is the process that separates a stream of text into tokens. We first convert all terms to lowercase. Then, we split sentences with

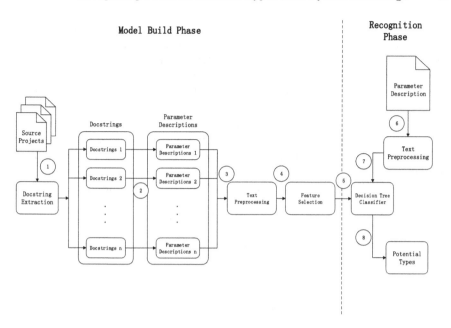

Fig. 2. Framework

blank and punctuation other than periods. We employ a popular Python natural language toolkit library *nltk* for this process. Finally, we filter the tokens that do not contain English letters.

Stop-Word Removal. Stop words are terms that are used frequently and carry little information to recognize types of parameters. Examples of stop words include "I", "me", "you" and so on. There are many text mining toolkits providing standard stop-words. In our experience, we use the stop-words supplied in *nltk* library.

Stemming. Stemming is also an import process in preprocessing. This process reduces inflected terms to their word stem. For example, the terms "stems", "stemmer" and "stemmed" would all be reduced to "stem". However, in our scenario, inflected words may hint different types. For example, a parameter named *value* may receive *int* type while the parameter *values* is more likely to accept *list* type. So we leave all terms unchanged.

2.3 Feature Selection

After preprocessing and tokenizing the descriptions, we use the Vector Space Model (VSM) [23] to represent each description with a term vector. In this model, a feature can be viewed as a dimension, and a parameter description can then be viewed as data point in a high-dimensional space. In total, we have a large number of features for each project. An overly high number of dimensions can cause the curse-of-dimensionality problem [19].

χ^2 **Test.** To handle with these problems, we apply feature selection to identify a subset of features that are most useful in recognizing different types. In this paper, we employ the widely used feature selection technique, namely χ^2 test [15] to select useful features.

The χ^2 statistic measures the lack of independence between the text feature term t and the its class c. Assume that we have a dataset of descriptions $Corpus = \{(D_1, L_1), \ldots, (D_N, L_N)\}$, where D_i represents the ith description, L_i is the label of the description (i.e., types that the parameter of this description can receive) and N denote the size of $Corpus$. For each type t, t represent the parameter can accept type t as its input and the meaning of $\bar{t}$ is opposite. The term vector of $D_i = \{w_1, \ldots, w_n\}$, where n represents the number of different terms appeared in C_i and w_i represents the ith term. For a feature w and a description D_i, there would be four possible relationships:

1. (w, t): description D_i contains the feature w, and the corresponding parameter can receive type t as its type.
2. $(w, \bar{t})$: description D_i contains the feature w, and the corresponding parameter cannot receive type t as its type.
3. $(\bar{w}, t)$: description D_i does not contains the feature w, and the corresponding parameter can receive type t as its type.
4. $(\bar{w}, \bar{t})$: description D_i does not contains the feature w, and the corresponding parameter cannot receive type t as its type.

Then the χ^2 statistic is defined as follows:

$$A = \#(w, t), B = \#(w, \bar{t}) \tag{1}$$

$$C = \#(\bar{w}, t), D = \#(\bar{w}, \bar{t}) \tag{2}$$

$$\chi^2(t, c) = \frac{N \times (AD - BC)^2}{(A + C) \times (B + D) \times (A + B) \times (C + D)} \tag{3}$$

χ^2 statistic measures the independence of two events. In the scenario of feature selection, the two events are occurrence of a term and occurrence of the types. After calculating the scores for each feature, we rank these scores in descending order. The higher the score is, the more important the feature is to distinguish types. We select the top k% features whose feature selection scores are in the top k% of the ranked list, and remove the other features. In this way, we reduce the number of features not only in the model building phase, but also in the recognition phase. By default, we empirically choose the top 20% of the total number of features. We examine the impact of different percentages of features in our classifiers in Sect. 4.

2.4   Training Multi-label Classifiers

Multi-label classification is a generalization of multiclass classification, which assigns to each sample a set of target labels. In our experiment, given the description of a parameter, we attempt to label the parameter with all potential types.

So the problem can be regarded as a multi-label classification problem. We select decision tree classifier as our classifer, and then compare the performance with three other classifiers namely, random forest, k-nearest neighbors and multi-layer perceptron. All classifiers selected support multi-labeling natively.

Decision Tree [9]. Decision tree is a potentially powerful predictor and provides an explicit concept description for a dataset. Decision tree learners are popular due to the reason that they are fast and produce models that perform well on variety of features. Decision tree learning uses a decision tree (as a predictive model) to go from observations about an item (represented in the branches) to conclusions about the item's target value (represented in the leaves).

Random Forest [14]. Random forest is an ensemble learning method for classification, regression and other tasks, that operate by constructing a multitude of decision trees at training time and outputting the class that is the mode of the classes (classification) or mean prediction (regression) of the individual trees. Random decision forests correct for decision trees' habit of overfitting to their training set.

K-Nearest Neighbors [13]. K-nearest neighbors algorithm (KNN) is a non-parametric method used for classification and regression. The basic idea is to determine the category of a given description based not only on the description that is nearest to it in the document space, but on the categories of the k documents that are nearest to it.

Multi-layer Perceptron [2]. A multi-layer perceptron (MLP) is a class of feed-forward artificial neural network. A MLP consists of at least three layers of nodes. MLP utilizes a supervised learning technique called back-propagation for training. Its multiple layers and non-linear activation distinguish MLP from a linear perceptron. It can distinguish data that is not linearly separable.

3 Experiment Setup

In this section, we describe the experiment setup that we follow to evaluate the performance of our approach. The experimental environment is a computer equipped with Intel(R) Core(TM) i7-6700 CPU and 16 GB RAM, running Windows 10 (64-bit). We first present our data collection and then present our evaluation metrics. The experiment result and research questions are presented in the next section.

3.1 Projects Selection

To make our methodology more convincing, the selected projects follow these criteria: (i) the project is mainly developed in Python; (ii) the project is active and has a life cycle with at least one year; (iii) the project still receives both commits and pull requests; (iv) the project gains at least 150 stars on Github; (v) the application area of chosen repositories cover wide domains.

According the above criteria, we select ten repositories from Github and 1 widely-used Python library, i.e., asphalt, faker, hbmqtt, httpie, oauthlib, pycookiecheat, pydantic, requests, shand BeautifulSoup4.

Table 1 summarizes the basic information of the ten projects. We cloned these repositories on April 30th, 2018.

Table 1. Summary of studied repositories

Repository	Owner	Stars	Description
asphalt	asphalt-framework	186	An asyncio based microframework
bs4	\	\	Pulling data out of HTML and XML files
faker	joke2k	6k	Generates fake data
hbmqtt	beerfactory	360	MQTT client and broker implementation
httpie	jakubroztocil	35.2k	Modern command line HTTP client
oauthlib	oauthlib	1.6k	OAuth request-signing logic
pycookiecheat	n8henrie	276	Borrow cookies from user's session
pydantic	samuelcolvin	433	Data validation and settings management
requests	requests	32.1k	Non-GMO HTTP library for Python
sh	amoffat	4.4k	A full-fledged subprocess replacement

3.2   Extracting Project Data

Extracting Runtime Types. A test case is a specification of the inputs, execution conditions, testing procedure, and expected results that define a single test to be executed to achieve a particular software testing objective. That is to say, test cases provided in projects usually represent the expected inputs of methods designed by developers and they will test most of expected inputs to verify the methods performing correctly.

Based on this assumption, we run test cases provided by developers to collect runtime types. *Monkeytype* is a system that generates static type annotations by collecting runtime types[1]. It record the types of arguments/return values/yield values. As a result, we extract a set of two-tuple $<varname, types>$, of which each item record a parameter name and its actual types observed at runtime.

Extracting Parameter Descriptions. To extract parameter descriptions more precisely, first we manually review the docstrings to find patterns. We find that although type descriptions of docstrings are various from projects to projects, there are some patterns.

Structured Docstring. One common pattern of docstrings is shown in Fig. 1. In this pattern the first line describe the function of the method. The following lines started with :*param* and the name of parameter are descriptions of the

---

[1] https://github.com/Instagram/MonkeyType.

corresponding parameter. The descriptions range from empty or one sentence about the utility of the parameter to a detailed specification of the parameter, often including acceptable input types, format of expected input and so on. Finally, the docstring ends with a line which describes the specification of return value. We call docstring of this pattern as **structured docstring**.

In structured docstrings, we can extract two-tuple $<varname, description>$ by separating docstring lines using the pattern like *:param varname: description*.

Unstructured Docstring. In the meanwhile, most of other docstrings have various patterns written in natural language. These docstrings are hard to extract tiny type descriptions. We called them **unstructured docstring**. After manually reviewing all the unstructured docstring, we discover that the first sentence of the docstring often describes the function of the method and gives specification of the parameter when the method has only one parameter. We can also extract a two-tuple in a similar way as extracting descriptions from structured docstrings.

3.3   Generating Dataset

After the previous two steps, we obtain a set of two-tuple $<varname, types>$ and a set of $<varname, description>$. Then we inner join these two set of two-tuple by *varname* and generate the dataset containing three-tuple $<varname, types, description>$.

Basic Types. However, the use frequency of types used in different projects vary a lot. Some types may occur frequently in some projects while rarely occur in other projects as they are domain-related. In this paper, we only consider nine built-in types in Python, namely, *int*, *str*, *Dict*, *bool*, *List*, *Type*, *Callable*, *bytes* and *Tuple* respectively, we call the nine types as **basic types**.

Our dataset will only reserve three-tuples whose *types* at least contain one basic types. As a result, we totally collect 314 instances of such three-tuple, 280 from structured docstrings and 34 from unstructured docstrings. Finally, we use one-hot encoding [10] to encode the runtime types of each parameter as its label.

3.4   Evaluation Metrics

Based on the dataset, our approach will recognize potential types of each parameter description in the testing corpus. We record the labels classified by our approach as PL, and AL denotes the actual types of the parameter. Using these two statistics, we compute precision, recall, f1-score, jaccard index, hamming loss, accuracy, that are usually used to evaluate the performance of multi-label classifiers, and a symthesis metric MRR to give a summary evaluation of our approach. They are defined as follows:

Precision. The proportion of the types that are correctly recognized as actual types among those recognized as potential types.

Recall. The proportion of the types that are correctly recognized among those actual types.

F1-Score. A summary measure that combines both precision and recall. It evaluates if an increase in precision (recall) outweighs a reduction in recall (precision):

$$P = \frac{|PL \cap AL|}{|PL|} \tag{4}$$

$$R = \frac{|PL \cap AL|}{|AL|} \tag{5}$$

$$F1 = \frac{2 \times P \times R}{P + R} \tag{6}$$

Jaccard Index. Also called intersection over union in the multi-label setting. Jaccard index is defined as the number of correctly predicted labels divided by the union of predicted and true labels:

$$J = \frac{|PL \cap AL|}{|PL \cup AL|} \tag{7}$$

Hamming Loss. The fraction of the wrong labels to the total number of labels, The lower hamming loss, the better a classifier performs:

$$H = \sum_i^{|L|} xor(PL_i, AL_i) \tag{8}$$

Accuracy. Indicating whether PL and AL are exactly same, it is also the most strict metric among these fix metrics:

$$A = \begin{cases} 1 & PL = AL \\ 0 & PL \neq AL \end{cases} \tag{9}$$

MRR. The performance over above six metrics of different classifiers have their own merits. To give a summary which classifier has the best performance in terms of these metrics, we introduce MRR. MRR, short for mean reciprocal rank, is a statistic measure for evaluating relevance of document retrieved. Concerned on our studied problem, the reciprocal rank of the terms is the multiplicative inverse of the rank of the first correct answer. Let $Metrics$ denotes the collection of above six metrics, m denotes a kind of metric. $rank_c(m)$ is the rank of c in term of m in descent order. MRR of classifier c is defined as below:

$$MRR_c = \frac{1}{|Metrics|} \sum_{m \in Metrics} \frac{1}{rank_c(m)} \tag{10}$$

MRR is a synthesis metric over the above six metrics in our experiment setup. The higher the MRR is, the better the classifier performs.

All of above metrics are often used to evaluate the multi-label classification performance and majority of them have been used in past studies [6,8,20]. We believe these metrics can help us distinguish the classifier with better performance.

4 Experiment Results

In this section, we present our experiment results which answer two research questions. We present these questions and their answers in the following sections. We implement four classifiers provided by a prevalent Python machine learning library *scikit-learn* and set all hyber-parameters with default values in the implementation. Our approach simulates a realistic scenario that each time we choose one project as "test project" (i.e., for prediction), whose parameter descriptions are to be recognized by the classifiers. Then we denote the rest projects as "train projects" and train our classifiers using the parameter descriptions from these projects. Futher more, To eliminate the influence of random state of classifiers, we run the experiment for 100 times and calculate the average of each metric.

4.1 RQ1: Can We Automatically Recognizing Expected Types from Parameter Descriptions?

Motivation. Our goal is to provide an approach that can automatically recognize expected types. However, to verify our approach is feasible, the first question is to see how effective it is in performing its recognization. This research question would answer whether our approach is feasible to recognize potential types from descriptions.

Approach. Based on the framework proposed in previous section, we choose four multi-label classifiers to recognize types from descriptions and compare their performance. In this research question, we select top 20% features with the highest χ^2 statistic in feature selection process.

Results. Table 2 presents experiment results. The best results of each metric are highlighted in bold.

Among four studied classifiers, decision tree has best performance with MRR of 0.778. And its precision, recall, F1-score and hamming loss have best performance among the four studied classifiers, achieve 0.681, 0.548, 0.582 and 1.234 respectively on average across the ten projects.

Random forest and k-nearest neighbors have similar effect with decision tree, whose MRR achieve 0.500 and 0.556 respectively. Random forest have the best performance in term of jaccard index, achieving 0.581. K-nearest neighbors outperform other three classifiers in term of accuracy, which reaches 0.468.

Multi-layer perceptron, with the MRR of 0.250, has the weakest performance among these four classifiers, all metrics are far worse than the other three classifiers.

Table 2. Experiment results of four classifiers

Classifier	P.	R.	F1.	J.	H.	A.	MRR
RF	0.643	0.530	0.561	**0.581**	1.235	0.442	0.500
KNN	0.656	0.546	0.575	0.546	1.274	**0.468**	0.556
MLP	0.222	0.167	0.180	0.167	1.598	0.134	0.250
DT	**0.681**	**0.548**	**0.582**	0.542	**1.234**	0.432	**0.778**

In the studied classifiers, decision tree has the best performance, whose MRR achieve 0.778. Its precision, recall, f1-score and hamming loss rank 1st among these classifiers. Random forest and k-nearest neighbors have similar performance with MRR of 0.500 and 0.556 respectively. Multi-layer perceptron has weakest performance with the MRR of 0.250.

4.2 RQ2: How Feature Selection Influence the Performance of Classifiers?

Motivation. In our approach, for each source project, we apply feature selection to preprocess the input of classifiers before training them. By default, we only keep the top 20% features with the highest χ^2 statistic. But the performance of our approach may vary between different percentage of features are selected. Besides, since a large of feature are removed during feature selection phase, it is possible that some features with important semantic information are also removed, which may impact the performance of our approach. Therefore, we investigate how feature selection influence the performance of classifiers.

Approach. To answer this research question, we vary the percentage of selected features from 20% to 100% (with a step of 20%) of the total number of features and compute the corresponding precision, recall, F1-score, jaccard index, hamming loss and accuracy of our approach. To futher investigate the impact of feature selection, we also compare the performance of our approach with and without feature selection.

Results. Table 3 present the seven metrics of the four classifiers when selecting different percentage of features. The best results of each metric in each classifier are highlighted in bold. Figure 3 shows the MRR of four classifiers with the change of the feature selected.

The results illustrate that decision tree, random forest and k-nearest neighbors have the best performance when select top 20% features in term of MRR. As a special case, achieving its best performance needs to select top 40% features for multi-layer perceptron. And from the change trend of MRR, we discover that the

Table 3. Results of four classifiers with change amount of features selected

Classifier	Feature(%)	P.	R.	F1.	J.	H.	A.	MRR
RF	20	**0.643**	**0.530**	**0.561**	**0.581**	**1.235**	**0.442**	**1.000**
	40	0.596	0.493	0.521	0.493	1.284	0.417	0.500
	60	0.571	0.471	0.498	0.471	1.301	0.398	0.333
	80	0.561	0.464	0.490	0.463	1.302	0.391	0.250
	100	0.539	0.445	0.470	0.445	1.324	0.376	0.200
KNN	20	**0.656**	**0.546**	**0.575**	**0.546**	**1.274**	**0.468**	**1.000**
	40	**0.656**	**0.546**	**0.575**	**0.546**	**1.274**	**0.468**	**1.000**
	60	0.592	0.507	0.527	0.498	1.293	0.420	0.333
	80	0.589	0.504	0.524	0.495	1.296	0.417	0.250
	100	0.589	0.504	0.524	0.495	1.296	0.417	0.250
MLP	20	0.222	0.167	0.180	0.167	1.598	0.134	0.208
	40	0.222	**0.524**	**0.440**	**0.464**	**1.286**	**0.373**	**0.875**
	60	0.450	0.382	0.401	0.381	1.307	0.329	0.444
	80	**0.451**	0.382	0.401	0.382	1.305	0.329	0.583
	100	0.449	0.381	0.399	0.380	1.307	0.328	0.278
DT	20	**0.681**	**0.548**	**0.582**	**0.542**	**1.234**	**0.432**	**1.000**
	40	0.675	0.540	0.575	0.535	1.247	0.427	0.375
	60	0.676	0.542	0.576	0.536	1.247	0.426	0.472
	80	0.675	0.541	0.575	0.535	1.250	0.425	0.306
	100	0.671	0.538	0.572	0.532	1.255	0.424	0.200

MRR keep descending with the increasing percentage of selected features, which represent most features contain little semantic information and it is worthy to adopt process of feature selection.

Concerned on the other six metrics, for almost all of these classifiers, our approach achieves the best performance in seven metrics when selecting the top 20% or 40% features. The only exception is that the precision of multi-layer perceptron achieves best performance when selecting the top 80% feature.

> As to the four studied classifiers, they achieve best performance when selecting top 20% or 40% features with the highest χ^2 statistic. And the performance of classifiers become worse with the increase of selected features.

5   Discussion

In this section, we first discuss the implications of our study. Then we discuss threats to validity.

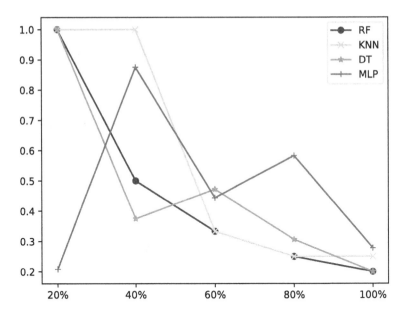

Fig. 3. MRR with change amount of features selected

5.1 Implications for Practitioners

For project managers, our approach may help them find the inconsistences between docstrings and method implements, and discover potential defects. If there is nothing wrong with method implements, they should take time to write docstrings more readable and understandable, otherwise, they are expected to improve the source code or add some test cases for better project evolution. For developers, our approach can help them remind the expected types of parameters without reviewing the context which is time-consuming.

5.2 Implications for Researchers

Our study provide a new sight into type inference. Existing studies on type inference mainly use hints of parameter types from data flow, patterns of parameter names, and context of points where parameters are used. No previous study consider the type descriptions in docstrings. Abundant type information of parameters hide in the parameter descriptions and making full use of these descriptions can improve the performance of type inference.

5.3 Threats to Validity

Threats to internal validity relate to the process of extracting runtime types. For a small fraction of parameters, their actual types extracted at runtime may not be correct. During manual inspection, we find some instances that our heuristic successfully comprehend and recognized expected types of a parameter, while types list which collected at runtime has some more types. We do further inspections and find that in some test cases input, an exception raise is required to ensure that the guard statement can detect invalid input. This introduce some false positive instances when measure classifiers.

Threats to external validity relate to the quantity and quality of our dataset. In the experiment, we studied 10 open source projects and totally extract 314 instances of parameter description, the size of dataset is insufficient. We will extend our dataset in future work.

Threats to construct validity relate to the suitability of our evaluation. In our experiment, we use seven metrics to evaluation the performance of classifiers, i.e., precision, recall, f1-score, jaccard index, hamming loss, accuracy and MRR respectively. All of these metrics are often used to evaluate the multi-label classification performance and majority of them have been used in past studies [6,8]. Thus, we believe we have little threats to construct validity.

6   Related Work

To the best of our knowledge, this study is the first about comprehending and recognizing types from descriptions of docstrings in dynamic language. The closest related work consists of docstring automatic generation and study of type hint.

6.1   Docstring Automatic Generation

McBurney et al. presented a novel approach that includes context by analyzing how the Java methods are invoked for automatically generating summaries of Java methods. In a user study, they found that programmers benefit from generated documentation because it includes context information [18].

Barone et al. introduce a large and diverse parallel corpus of a hundred thousands Python functions with their docstrings and describe baseline results for the code documentation generation tasks obtained by neural machine translation [1].

Iyer et al. generate summaries of source code using LSTM network by a completely data-driven approach for generating high level [12]. Loper implemented *Epydoc*, a tool for generating API documentation for Python modules, based on their docstrings [17]. However, studies that focus on docstrings are limited.

6.2   Type Hints

Milojkovic et al. analysis a corpus of more than 1,000 open source software systems developed in Smalltalk and found that nearly all projects define and use duck-typed methods [4]. Based on above study, they propose a lightweight heuristic algorithm *CPA** that utilizes the hints from method parameters' names. This heuristic algorithm outperforms the basic algorithm and correctly infers types for 81% more method parameters [5]. And there also exist lots of study focus on type inference with high precision in recent years [16, 21, 24].

Gao et al. quantify how much static type systems improve software quality by comparing JavaScript with Flow and TypeScript. The result shows that using Flow or TypeScript could have prevented 15% of the public bugs [3].

Type hints often serve as a kind of documentation. On the one hand, typed codes allow the compiler to find type errors earlier and potentially improve the readability of code, on the other hand, untyped code may be easier to change and require less work from developers. Developers should understand the tradeoffs between using or not type hints in their projects [11, 22].

7   Conclusion and Future Work

Type descriptions are useful for developers to understand the data types passed to a method. In this paper, we proposed an automated framework to recognize expected types in parameter descriptions, and compared four classifiers in this framework. The experimental results show that, decision tree achieves best performance among the four studied classifiers, whose MRR reaches 0.778. K-nearest neighbors and random forest has similar effect. And multi-layer perceptron has the worse performance on our dataset. Finally, we study the effect of selection percentage in feature selection. The results illustrate random forest, k-nearest neighbors and decision tree reach best performance when selecting top 20% features with the highest feature selection scores, while multi-layer perceptron needs top 40% feature to achieve its best performance.

Our future work will focus on extending the studied projects and build up a corpus of parameter descriptions. We also attempt to propose better approach to comprehend type hints from docstrings to improve the performance.

Acknowledgments. The work is supported by National Key R&D Program of China (2018YFB1003900), the Natural Science Foundation of Jiangsu Province of China (BK20140611), the National Natural Science Foundation of China (61872177, 61772263, 61432001), and the program B for Outstanding PhD candidate of Nanjing University.

References

1. Barone, A.V.M., Sennrich, R.: A parallel corpus of python functions and documentation strings for automated code documentation and code generation. arXiv preprint arXiv:1707.02275 (2017)
2. Belue, L.M., Bauer Jr., K.W.: Determining input features for multilayer perceptrons. Neurocomputing **7**(2), 111–121 (1995)
3. Gao, Z., Bird, C., Barr, E.T.: To type or not to type: quantifying detectable bugs in JavaScript. In: Proceedings of the 39th International Conference on Software Engineering, (ICSE) 2017, Buenos Aires, Argentina, 20–28 May 2017, pp. 758–769 (2017). https://doi.org/10.1109/ICSE.2017.75

4. Milojkovic, N., Ghafari, M., Nierstrasz, O.: It's duck (typing) season! In: Proceedings of the 25th International Conference on Program Comprehension, ICPC 2017, Buenos Aires, Argentina, 22–23 May 2017, pp. 312–315 (2017). https://doi.org/10.1109/ICPC.2017.10

5. Milojkovic, N., Ghafari, M., Nierstrasz, O.: Exploiting type hints in method argument names to improve lightweight type inference. In: Proceedings of the 25th International Conference on Program Comprehension, ICPC 2017, Buenos Aires, Argentina, 22–23 May 2017. pp. 77–87 (2017). https://doi.org/10.1109/ICPC.2017.33

6. Ghamrawi, N., McCallum, A.: Collective multi-label classification. In: Proceedings of the 14th ACM international conference on Information and knowledge management, pp. 195–200. ACM (2005)

7. Goodger, D.: Docstring Conventions (2001). https://www.python.org/dev/peps/pep-0257/

8. Herrera, F., Charte, F., Rivera, A.J., del Jesus, M.J.: Multilabel classification. In: Herrera, F., Charte, F., Rivera, A.J., del Jesus, M. (eds.) Multilabel Classification, pp. 17–31. Springer, Cham (2016). https://doi.org/10.1007/978-3-319-41111-8_2

9. Sikandar, A., et al.: Decision tree based approaches for detecting protein complex in protein protein interaction network (PPI) via link and sequence analysis. IEEE Access **6**, 22108–22120 (2018)

10. Johnson, R., Zhang, T.: Supervised and semi-supervised text categorization using LSTM for region embeddings. arXiv preprint arXiv:1602.02373 (2016)

11. Vitousek, M.M., Kent, A.M., Siek, J.G., Baker, J.: Design and evaluation of gradual typing for Python. In: ACM SIGPLAN Notices, vol. 50, pp. 45–56. ACM (2014)

12. Iyer, S., Konstas, I., Cheung, A.: Summarizing source code using a neural attention model. In: Proceedings of the 54th Annual Meeting of the Association for Computational Linguistics Volume 1: Long Papers, vol. 1, pp. 2073–2083 (2016)

13. Bijalwan, V., Kumar, V., Kumari, P., Pascual, J.: KNN based machine learning approach for text and document mining. Int. J. Database Theory Appl. **7**(1), 61–70 (2014)

14. Taherzadeh, G., Zhou, Y., Liew, A.W.C., Yang, Y.: Structure-based prediction of protein-peptide binding regions using random forest. Bioinformatics **34**(3), 477–484 (2017)

15. Liu, H., Setiono, R.: Chi2: feature selection and discretization of numeric attributes. In: Proceedings Seventh International Conference on Tools with Artificial Intelligence, pp. 388–391. IEEE (1995)

16. Xu, Z., Liu, P., Zhang, X., Xu, B.: Python predictive analysis for bug detection. In: Proceedings of the 2016 24th ACM SIGSOFT International Symposium on Foundations of Software Engineering, pp. 121–132. ACM (2016)

17. Loper, E.: Epydoc: API documentation extraction in Python. http://epydoc.sourceforge.net/pycon-epydoc.ps. Accessed 13 2008

18. McBurney, P.W., McMillan, C.: Automatic documentation generation via source code summarization of method context. In: Proceedings of the 22nd International Conference on Program Comprehension. ICPC 2014, pp. 279–290. ACM, New York, NY, USA (2014). http://doi.acm.org/10.1145/2597008.2597149

19. Mining, W.I.D.: Data Mining: Concepts And Techniques. Morgan Kaufmann, Burlington (2006)

20. Papanikolaou, Y., Dimitriadis, D., Tsoumakas, G., Laliotis, M., Markantonatos, N., Vlahavas, I.P.: Ensemble approaches for large-scale multi-label classification and question answering in biomedicine. In: CLEF (Working Notes), pp. 1348–1360 (2014)

21. Xu, Z., Zhang, X., Chen, L., Pei, K., Xu, B.: Python probabilistic type inference with natural language support. In: Proceedings of the 2016 24th ACM SIGSOFT International Symposium on Foundations of Software Engineering, pp. 607–618. ACM (2016)

22. Souza, C., Figueiredo, E.: How do programmers use optional typing?: an empirical study. In: Proceedings of the 13th International Conference on Modularity, pp. 109–120. ACM (2014)

23. Salton, G., Wong, A., Yang, C.S.: A vector space model for automatic indexing. Commun. ACM **18**(11), 613–620 (1975)

24. Chen, L., Xu, B., Zhou, T., Zhou, X.: A constraint based bug checking approach for Python. In: 33rd Annual IEEE International Computer Software and Applications Conference, 2009. COMPSAC 2009, vol. 2, pp. 306–311. IEEE (2009)

An Empirical Study of Dynamic Types for Python Projects

Xinmeng Xia[1,2], Xincheng He[1,2], Yanyan Yan[3], Lei Xu[1,2(✉)],
and Baowen Xu[1,2(✉)]

[1] State Key Laboratory for Novel Software Technology, Nanjing, China
[2] Department of Computer Science, Nanjing University, Nanjing, China
`{xlei,bwxu}@nju.edu.cn`
[3] School of Software, Nanjing University, Nanjing, China

Abstract. Python is a well-known dynamically-typed programming
language. Due to its dynamic type, Python is flexible to solve complex situations. However, the use of dynamic type may cause many problems on
correctness, security and performance. In this paper, we make an empirical study on the dynamic type of Python. First, we collect a dataset
with 81 categories from the project list of *Awesome Python*. Then all
Python files in this dataset are analyzed by Pysonar2. Type information
is collected and saved for each identifier. Next, we proposed to recognize the dynamic type by comparing the analysis results from Pysonar2.
After that, two research questions are put up to investigate the popularity of Python dynamic type in actual programming and the patterns of
dynamic type for Python variables. The results show that 6.9% of identifiers in this dataset involve dynamic type and 79.7% of identifiers do
not involve dynamic type. Besides, the patterns of dynamic type mainly
appear among Transfer assignment methods. Finally, our results give
implications such as optimization of naming space to improve the design
of Python type system.

Keywords: Dynamic type · Python program · Dynamic patterns

1 Introduction

Python is becoming more and more popular. In the latest 2017 IEEE Spectrum
rankings [1], the popularity of Python ranked first. As a dynamic programming
language, the dynamic type is the soul for Python. A good design of Python's
dynamic type can lead to higher development efficiency and higher software
quality. However, the type in Python is allowed to change from one to another
dynamically, which may lead to unexpected bugs. These bugs are different from
the traditional ones and probably fatal to the programs. They are caused by the
dynamic features of Python.

Richards et al. [17] made an empirical study of the dynamic behavior of
JavaScript programs in order to improve the correctness, security and performance of JavaScript applications. They analyzes how and why the dynamic

© Springer Nature Switzerland AG 2018
L. Bu and Y. Xiong (Eds.): SATE 2018, LNCS 11293, pp. 85–100, 2018.
https://doi.org/10.1007/978-3-030-04272-1_6

features are used in JavaScript Programs. However, for Python programs, it is also important to know how often these dynamic features of Python are used by software developers, whether these dynamic features are necessary when it comes to Python type system design, what pattern it is when the dynamic type shows up and so forth.

In this paper, we make an empirical study of Python's dynamic type. We try to figure out how often dynamic types appear and what patterns they are when dynamic changes appear. First, we collect a big dataset and then we analyze the dataset with Pysonar2 [3]. Next we propose an approach to detect the dynamic type of Python by comparing the difference of Pysonar2's analysis results and research the frequency of the dynamic type for all kinds of identifiers in Python. Finally, we analyze the patterns of dynamic type to see how the types change dynamically and give our implications on how to design Python type system and Python analysis tool.

In order to complete this work, the following challenges can not be ignored.

- **Dataset:** The selection of dataset is important. The dataset needs to be huge and balanced enough to support the reliability of our conclusions.
- **Analysis Tool:** There is no mature static analysis tool that can return precise type of identifier in Python. Note that we can not run this experiment dynamically by dynamic analysis tool since our conclusion is based on big data and it will be huge time cost to run all Python code.
- **Pattern Analysis:** As far as we know, there is no existing work researching the changing patterns of dynamic type. So there is no off-the-shelf tool to analyze this dynamic change.

The work of Holkner and Harland [14] is similar to ours. They evaluate the dynamic behavior of Python applications. However, they only measure the dynamic behavior on 24 production-stage open source Python programs by analyzing them dynamically. Their work focus on the problem when there exists a dynamic activity for the running of a program. For our work, we focus on the analysis of the dynamic type of Python. We try to conclude the statistical law from big data. So it is difficult to analyze our research by dynamic analysis tool since it will cost too much time and resources. We propose an approach to detect dynamic type statically so that we can analyze plenty of data with little cost. We make, therefore, the following contributions:

- A dataset *Awesome Python* [2] is chosen, collected, preprocessed after we inspect the dataset and compare it with 500 Python projects of "most stars" on Github.
- An approach is proposed to recognize dynamic type in Python by comparing the difference of results given by a static analysis tool Pysonar2.
- The patterns of dynamic type are mined by analyzing the assignment methods of variables in Python.

The rest of this paper is structured as follows. We discuss our related work in Sect. 2. In Sect. 3, we give details on our data collection and preprocess. Then we address our research questions. We next discuss the results of experiments, give implications and present the threats to validity in Sect. 4. Finally, we conclude this work in Sect. 5.

2 Related Work

Since Python is a dynamic programming language, the lack of type information has been a huge challenge for developers. Recently, there have been many researches that pay attention to dynamic behaviors and type inference of different languages. In this section, we will introduce recent works related to dynamic evaluation and type inference of dynamic languages.

2.1 Dynamic Evaluation

Many researchers pay their attention to dynamic evaluation. Dynamic evaluation is to evaluate the dynamic features for dynamic programming languages such as Python, JavaScript. Program analysis tools are developed and many empirical studies are conducted for this target.

First, Chen et al. [10] make a study on the changes of dynamic feature of code when fixing bugs. They focus on the benefits and costs. Kneuss et al. [16] describe a combination of runtime information and static analysis for checking properties of complex and configurable systems. Sapra et al. [19] find errors in Python programs using dynamic symbolic execution and Chen et al. [8] propose a dynamic slicing approach for Python programs at the bytecode level. Beatrice et al. [20] describe early results from trace-based collection of run-time data about the use of built-in language features which are inherently hard to type, such as dynamic code generation.

Besides, Chen et al. [9] conduct a comprehensive study of a large Python codebase to investigate the changes of dynamic feature code against software evolution. Alex et al. [14] have tested 24 production open source Python programs to measure the extent to which they are amenable to static analysis. Vitousek et al. [22] provide dynamic typing in situations that require rapid prototyping, heterogeneous data structures, and reflection, while supporting static typing when safety, modularity, and efficiency are primary concerns. Apart from that, Wang et al. [23] make an empirical study on the impact of Python dynamic features on change-proneness and find that (1) files with dynamic features are more change-prone, (2) files with a higher number of dynamic features are more change-prone, and (3) Introspection is shown to be more correlated to change-proneness than the other three categories in most systems.

In above work, they analyze and evaluate dynamic features of Python by dynamic methods. However, the size of experiment is limited due to the nature of dynamic methods. For our work, we evaluate the dynamic type by static methods so that we can run big data to come to a more convincing results. Besides, our work only focus on dynamic type of Python so that we can conduct more in-depth research on this point.

2.2 Type Inference

Apart from dynamic features and behaviors of Python languages, researchers also pay attention to type inference of Python. The type plays an important role in dynamic programming. However, we can not know the exact types due to its dynamic nature. Researchers have proposed various solutions for type inference [3,6,7,24], many of which have been worked by leveraging data flow between untyped variables and variables with known types.

PySonar2 [3] has been one of the most popular tool for Python type inference and can type 49.47% of variables in programs. Xu et al. [24] proposed a method to solve the problem of Python type inference by probability. They synthesized four information so as to improve the precisions of type inference apparently by probability graph model. Aycock [6] describes an application for type inference unrelated to optimization, and presents a new method for divining type information - aggressive type inference which determines the types of variables in the absence of explicit cues. Gorbovitski et al. [13] describe the development and experimental evaluation of a may-alias analysis for a full dynamic object-oriented language, for program optimization by incrementalization and specialization, which shows that this is necessary for effective optimization of dynamic languages. Salib [18] proposes a tool called Starkiller that analyzes Python source programs and converts them into equivalent C++ programs. Starkiller's type inference algorithm is based on the Cartesian Product Algorithm but has been significantly modified to support a radically different language.

Apart from researches above, there are many other methods which pay attention to type inference for other dynamic languages. Jensen et al. [15] present a static program analysis infrastructure that can infer detailed and sound type information for JavaScript programs using abstract interpretation. Anderson et al. [5] define a type inference algorithm for JavaScript that is sound with respect to the type system. Thiemann [21] presents a first attempt at defining a type system for analyzing a weakly typescripting language, JavaScript. It does so by defining a type system that tracks the possible traits of an object and flags suspicious type conversions. Furr [11] presents PRuby, a profile-guided type inference system for Ruby. Furr et al. [12] and An et al. [4] present static methods for type inference for Ruby.

In their work, type inference tools or type inference systems are designed. However, few of them are used in actual program analysis due to the limit of precision. In this paper, we proposed a method to use a type inference tool to research the dynamic type in Python. And we also give implications to help improve type inference tools based on the findings of our research in the end.

3 Empirical Analysis

In order to clarify the use of dynamic type in actual Python programming, we conducted an empirical analysis. The specific process is shown in Fig. 1. This empirical analysis starts from collection of dataset. We collect a dataset according to the project list of *Awesome Python*. Then a static code analysis tool called Pysonar2 is introduced to analyze the type of identifiers in Python programs. After analyzing these Python programs statically, Pysonar2 shows its analysis results in HTML form. We next parse these HTML files that contain raw information, extract useful information including identifier names, the result of type inference and so on. And then an information set is generated for later experiments. After that, we analyze the distribution of identifiers with dynamic type and the pattern of dynamic changes. Finally, implications are given based on our results.

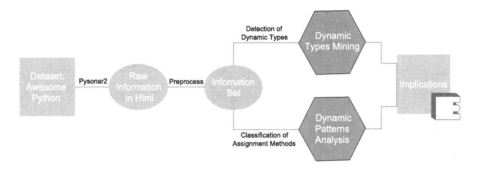

Fig. 1. Overview of this work.

3.1   Data Collection

The first challenge of our research is to collect a balanced dataset which can make our conclusions more reliable. A balanced dataset should contain all kinds of projects. Actually if all projects in a dataset is topic-related, the use of the type is probably limited. For example, if all projects come from a men in a company, the naming style, programming style of all projects may be similar. This will lead to inaccurate results. It is not easy to find such a dataset. We manually inspect 500 Python projects with "most stars" on Github. However, for these projects, we can not assure their balance. Some of them are topic-related. It is difficult to classify them. However, during our inspection on Github, we find a dataset that is possible to be balanced. It is a well-known dataset called *Awesome Python*, which contains awesome frameworks, libraries, software and resources of Python. It is a large but balanced dataset since it contains all kinds of categories of frequently used Python projects. There is a list of projects categories of *Awesome Python* on GitHub, which owns more than 52k stars. Some of these projects lie in GitHub. For this part, we cloned the code directly to the local. For other projects with code on their own websites, we manually downloaded the code to the local. The original dataset contains around 90 categories such as Natural Language Process category, Machine Learning category and so forth. Each category contains lots of related projects. However, some categories can not be found because of protection of privacy, commercial restriction and so on. We exclude these categories and finally, we get a dataset containing 81 categories.

Figure 2 describes this dataset. Figure 2(a) and (b) describe the number of Python files and the number of code lines for each category respectively. Every point in Fig. 2 represents a category. The X axis represents the serial number of the category. The Y axis represents the number of Python files and the number of code lines, respectively. In this 81 categories, 77,522 Python files and 1,615,120 lines of code, according to the statistics, are included. On average, there are 957 files and 208,828 lines of code per category. For these 81 categories, the median value of the number of Python files is 517 and the median value of the number of lines of code is 112,975.

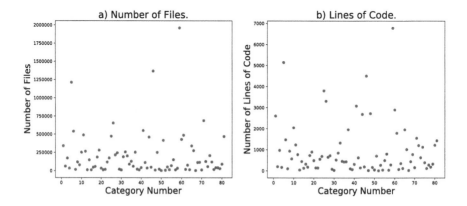

Fig. 2. Description of dataset.

3.2 Data Extraction and Preprocess

After getting our dataset of *Awesome Python*, we start our step of data extraction and preprocess.

As mentioned above, the second challenge of our work is the selection of analysis tool. In general, dynamic features can only be analyzed by dynamic analysis tools. However, there is no dynamic analysis tool that can analyze our dataset since it is too huge. Conducting a dynamic analysis for our dataset will consume lots of time and resources. So we figure out a walk around solution. We use a static analysis tool to replace the dynamic analysis tool to deal with our dataset. Pysonar2 is a tool chosen for this research. We infer the type of Python identifiers by Pysonar2 and then compare the inferred result to analyze dynamic changes of identifiers' type.

Pysonar is a static analysis tool developed by Google which can be used to infer types for Python programs. Pysonar2 is the upgraded version by the same developer of Pysonar. Pysonar2 is the most accurate static type inference tool

Fig. 3. An example of HTML forms. (Color figure online)

so far. Pysonar2 provides a command to analyze all Python files in a directory and to return the inferred results in HTML form. However, the HTML form is a web-based graphic user interface for demo but not for research. As we can see in Fig. 3, this is a HTML page that contains the type inference results given by Pysonar2 after we run the command. We move our mouse to the identifiers with color green, then the inferred result will show up. In this example, we move our mouse to the identifier *wrapper*, and the inferred result is $()->None$.

So in our work, first, we use this command to analyze all Python source code files and get the corresponding HTML files. Next, we parse the source code of these HTMLs in order to get the necessary information. Note that we do not need all the information of Pysonar2 and only the information of inference of identifiers' type initialization is needed. For the parsing part, regular expressions are used to recognize and extract the necessary information including line numbers, classes of identifiers, identifier scopes. Then we parse the scopes to obtain identifier names and file paths. Next, according to the line number and the file path, we locate and extract the source code of the line where the identifier is assigned to a certain type.

Finally, we set up a seven-tuple for each identifier in these Python programs. We call this seven-tuple **"identifier tuple"**. The identifier tuple contains all information we obtain above and it can be formally defined as follows.

Definition 1. *An identifier tuple is a seven-tuple* (c, n, l, p, s, ct, t) *containing elementary information of this identifier.*

where c represents the category of the identifier including class, function, variable and parameter of function. n represents the name of the identifier while l

represents the line number of the identifier in the Python file. p is the absolute path of the file that contains the identifier while s is the absolute scope of the identifier. ct represents the content of the line where the identifier is assigned to a type. t represents the result of type inference. The reason we pick these elements as our identifier tuples is that all of these elements contain necessary information and will be applied in the following analysis.

Then we get a list of identifier tuples for all identifiers in our dataset and we store them in a csv table. In this csv table, we calculate the distributions of all kinds of identifiers. In total, 4,155,657 identifiers are included in this dataset. Among them, variable names are the majority accounting for 46.96%. 31.72% of these identifiers are parameter names, 18.06% of them are function names and 3.26% of them are class names. All of these identifiers will be analyzed in the following section.

3.3   Analysis and Results of RQs

RQ1. How often is the dynamic type applied in actual programming tasks of Python?

As we all know, Python is a dynamically typed language. In the actual Python project, to what extent does the developer use the dynamic typing mechanism? Is it normal or occasional? In this RQ, we try to figure out the using frequency of dynamic type of identifiers so that it can help us evaluate whether the dynamic nature is necessary. That means if few even no people use a dynamic nature in Python, we can assume that either the dynamic nature is complex to be applied during programming or it is not suitable for actual programming. On the contrary, if a dynamic feature is used frequently, we can assume this feature is indispensable during the actual programming.

The first thing we need to know is when the dynamic type appears in Python. Actually, we can not know the precise type of an identifier without running the code by the dynamic analysis tool since the type information is not given when the program is initially written. The time cost and resource cost, however, are huge to run the whole Awesome Dataset by dynamic analysis tools in our experiment since our conclusion is based on big data. However, we can obtain all possible types by static analysis tool. That means we can infer the changes of type by comparing all these types. We propose an approach to compare and recognize dynamic type of identifiers in our dataset. We play, actually, a little trick on this research target. Pysonar2, a static analysis tool, is used to replace the dynamic analysis tool for this research. We run Pysonar2 to infer all types of identifiers in our dataset and then we analyze the inferred result of Pysonar2. In our approach, we assume that if the inferred results of Pysonar2 are the same for two identical identifiers with identical scopes, their types are probably not changed. Identical scopes, here, mean the absolute scopes in the program, for example, an identical function or an identical while-loop. If the inferred results are different for two identical identifiers with same scopes, their types are probably changed. It can be formally expressed as follows.

Definition 2. *Two identifiers with identifier tuple* $(c1, n1, l1, p1, s1, ct1, t1)$ *and identifier tuple* $(c2, n2, l2, p2, s2, ct2, t2)$ *own the attribute of dynamic type if and only if* $n1 = n2$, $s1 = s2$ *and* $t1! = t2$.

After defining the approach to find out whether the types of two identifiers are dynamic, we write a program to scan the csv by our approach and find out all identifiers with dynamic type according to the definition above. Note that, in actually experiment, there are few identifiers that can not be inferred by Pysonar2 and that the inferred results returning by Pysonar2 are "?". For these identifiers with inferred results "?", we calculate their numbers as our potential deviation analysis and we ignore them when calculating identifiers with dynamic type. Figure 4 shows the results. Y-axis represents the times that the type of 2 identifiers are dynamic. X-axis represent the category of identifiers. v means the variable name, f means the function name, p means the parameter name and c means the class name.

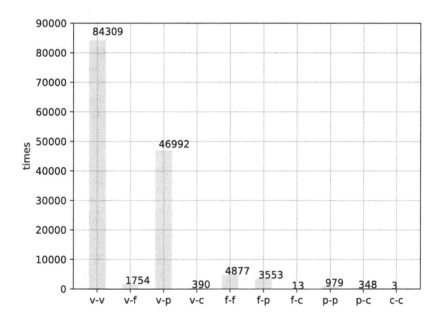

Fig. 4. Identifiers with dynamic type.

Finding1: Most dynamic type (58.9%) for identifiers in Python programs appears between variable names and variable names.

As we can see from Fig. 4, column v-f, column v-c, column f-f, column f-p, column f-c, column p-p, column p-c, column c-c are near but low. All of them are less than 5,000 times. However, the column of v-v and v-p are far higher than other column and the times of v-v pairs are almost two times $(84309/46992 = 1.794)$ of v-p pairs.

Therefore, for a variable identifier, the type is more likely to be dynamic. (58.9% = 84,309/(84,309 + 1,754 + 46,992 + 390 + 4,877 + 3,553 + 13 + 979 + 348 + 3) * 100%).

Finding2: 6.9% of identifiers involve dynamic type and 13.4% of identifiers are not sure whether they involve dynamic type. Most identifiers (79.7%) do not involve dynamic type.

In Fig. 4, 143,218 times (84,309 + 1,754 + 46,992 + 390 + 4,877 + 3,553 + 13 + 979 + 348 + 3) in total are observed. That means in all 4,155,657 identifiers (calculated during data extraction and preprocess in Sect. 3.2), at most 286,436 (143,218 × 2) identifiers are involved in dynamic type accounting for 6.9% (286,436/4,155,657 * 100%) of total identifiers.

For our potential deviation analysis, we count the times of the identifiers with the inferred type of "?". 279,146 pair identifiers with same names and scopes have at least one identifier with type of "?". That means 558,292 (279,146 × 2) identifiers are not sure whether they involve dynamic type accounting for 13.4% (558,292/4,155,657 * 100%) of total identifiers. 79.7% of identifiers (100% − 6.9% − 13.4%) do not involve dynamic type.

RQ2. What pattern is it when the type of a variable changes?

As we know in Sect. 3.2, most of the identifiers are variable names. In Finding 1, we know that variable names are the majority (58.9%) of total identifiers that can possibly own dynamic type. So in this research question, we try to concentrate more on the detail patterns of dynamic type for variable names.

Table 1. Assignment model.

Class	Method	Example
Simple	1: A string with single quote	x = 'apple'
	2: A string with double quotes	x = "apple"
	3: Real number	x = 1
	4: Boolean	x = True
	5: Complex number	x = 1 + 2j
	6: Dictionary	x = {}
	7: List	x = [ ]
	8: Tuple	x = ()
Transfer	9: Attribute	x = tree.apple
	10: Function	x = apple()
	11: Variable	x = apple
	12: Index	x = apple[1]
	13: Expressions or combinations etc.	x = apple + 1

The research method of this RQ is a little different from RQ 1. First, we classify several common assignment methods in Python as our assignment model.

The reason we focus on the assignment methods is that the corresponding type will be assigned to the variable when a value is assigned to a variable. We can, therefore, come to the source of dynamic type and research how identifiers are actually dynamic by researching the changes of assignment methods. Every initialization assignment method is related to one or more kind of types. If initialization assignment methods for two identifiers are different, the values of the variables are probably different. Therefore, the corresponding types are probably different. For example, if a variable is assigned by method 7, the type of this variable is probably *List*. If another variable with an identical name is assigned by method 8, the type of this variable is probably *Tuple*. Therefore even though these two variables share identical names, they probably own different types. We make a research how the types change by study the changes of assignment method between two identifiers with same names and scopes.

Table 1 shows our classification of assignment methods. Here we have 13 assignment methods. *"Simple"* means simple and direct assignment methods including assignments of strings, numbers, boolean values, dictionary, list and tuple. Examples are given in the third column of the table. *"Transfer"* means indirect assignment methods including assignments by transfer of attributes, functions, variables and indexes, expressions or some other combinations of method 1–12.

After defining our assignment model, we classify all variable identifiers by our assignment model. In our step of preprocess, the content that an identifier assigned to a value is taken out according to its line number and absolute path and stored in the csv table. So here, we first find out all identifiers with same names and scopes and then we analyze the assignment method for every identifier tuple. If the assignment method changes, the identifier that shares the same name and scope probably involves dynamic type. The judgement approach can be formally expressed as follows.

Definition 3. *For two identifiers i1, i2 with identifier tuple (c1, n1, l1, p1, s1, ct1, t1) and identifier tuple (c2, n2, l2, p2, s2, ct2, t2), the assignment methods change (new pattern) if and only if n1 = n2, s1 = s2 and assignment method of ct1 != assignment method of ct2.*

The result shows in Fig. 5. Figure 5 is a heatmap. Y-axis represents the assignment methods of original identifiers in Table 1. X-axis represents the assignment methods of identifiers after changes. For example, in a Python file, variable1 *"apple = 1"* is defined in line 17. The assignment method of this variable belongs to method 3. variable2 *"apple = tree.child()"* is defined in line 20. The assignment method of this variable belongs to method 10. The assignment method changes from method 3 to method 1o. In this heatmap, the times of the coordinate that x-height is method 3 and y-height is method 10 will plus 1. The color in this figure represents the total times of these transition. The deeper the color is, the larger the number is.

Finding 3: Function assignments and expression assignments are probably the major ways to lead to dynamic type.

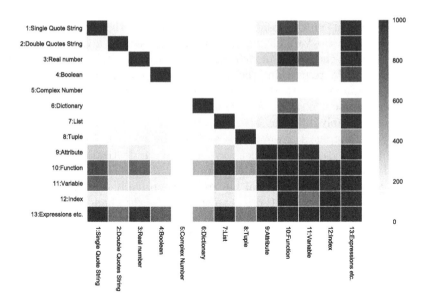

Fig. 5. Dynamic changes of assignment methods. (Color figure online)

As we can see in Fig. 5, the distribution of data is roughly symmetrical. We do not concern coordinates on the diagonal since they are ones whose assignment methods remain unchanged. For other coordinates in this heatmap, almost all coordinates related to method 10 and method 13 have deep colors. That means function assignments and expression assignments are probably the major ways to lead to dynamic type.

Finding 4: Dynamic type appears mainly inside "Transfer" methods.

In Fig. 5, deep colors are concentrated in "Transfer" methods area. That means this area may involve more dynamic type. However, the coordinate (12:Index, 11:Variable) is lighter than other coordinates around it. That means the pattern that variable assignments are changed to index assignments is less involved in dynamic type. For other coordinate in this area, almost all of them are deep blue. So dynamic type appears mainly inside "Transfer" methods.

4   Implications and Discussions

In last Section, we analyze two research questions and give four findings of our experiment. In this section, we will give our implications according to our findings and experiment results. And then we will discuss the threats to validity of our researches.

4.1   Implications

Implication 1: Dynamic type should be restricted regarding to the frequency of use.

According to Finding 2, the frequency of dynamic type is not high. Only 6.9% of identifiers involve dynamic type and 13.4% of identifiers are not sure whether involves in dynamic type. That means at least 79.7% (100% − 6.9% − 13.4%) of identifiers do not involve in dynamic type. So most identifiers do not involve in dynamic type. We can come to a conclusion that this dynamic feature exists but is not so popular as our expected in actually programming. As we mentioned in the beginning, the use of dynamic type may cause some problems of software quality in programming and provide some trouble for program analysis such as type inference. So it is reasonable to restrict the use of dynamic type or add some type annotations to Python grammar.

Implication 2: Naming space of Python can probably be optimized.

Every name contains specific meaning. In Python, due to its dynamic, names of identifiers are allowed to be identical even between different kinds of identifiers such as between variables and functions. However, this may cause some problems in program comprehension. If two different kinds of identifiers share an identical name, a programmer, especially in a big program, might be confused when comprehending the code. Finding 1 describes that most dynamic type appears between variable names and variable names. That means for other kinds of identifiers, little dynamic type is used. We propose, therefore, to optimize the design of naming space of Python to avoid the identical name. In this way, we can probably help improve the quality of program comprehension.

Implication 3: For the type inference tools of Python, combining assignment methods information into the tools may help improve its accuracy.

The mainstream design of type inference tool is based on traditional program analysis such data flow analysis, control flow analysis and so forth. However, the information of the code itself is also important. As we know from Finding 4, dynamic type appears mainly inside "Transfer" methods. That means for "Simple" methods little dynamic type is involved. On the other hand, the types with "Simple" method assignment are easy to be inferred since the type informations are given directly. For "Transfer" methods, we can probably research the relationship between assignment patterns and dynamic type to get some type hints. Combining these hints into the tools may help improve the accuracy of existing Python type inference tools.

4.2   Threats to Validity

Although we try our best to make the experiments fair and reasonable, there are still several concerns to the validity of this work.

First, few projects that can not be analyzed by Pysonar2 are excluded from our dataset. We assume that these projects have little impact on balance of dataset and have no influence on our results since our conclusions are based on big data. However, in actual case, it is not sure whether they will have impact on our results.

Second, the precision of Pysonar2 may affect our conclusions. The first part of our research relies on Pysonar2's results. Although we analyzed the situation that the inferred results are "?", there still exist some inaccurate inferred results and our precision may be influenced. For example, for an identifier in line 17, its inferred result is "$\{float \mid int\ \}$" (The type is "$float$" or "int") and its real type is "int". For another identifier with same name and scope in line 20, its inferred result is also "$\{float \mid int\ \}$" and its real type is "$float$". In our approach, we judge that the inferred results of these two identifiers are consistent and we assume that the types remain unchanged. Actually, they are changed.

Third, for research question 2, we analyze the assignment methods to research the patterns of type changes. For general, it is effective. However, for some special cases, it does not work well. For example, identifier i is in line 1 and line 4. "$i = 1$" is for line 1 and "$i = app$" is for line 4. If app is a int number 2, the type is not changed for this case.

5   Conclusion and Future Work

Python is well-known for its dynamic. Dynamic type of Python may cause many problems on correctness, security and performance. In this paper, we make an empirical study of dynamic types of Python. We try to figure out the popularity of Python dynamic type in actual programming and the patterns of dynamic type for Python variables.

A well-known dataset is collected for our experiment from a project list called *Awesome Python*. Then we extract necessary information with Pysonar2, a well-known static analysis tool, initially developed by Google.

First, in our work, we propose an approach to detect dynamic type between two identifiers by comparing the results of Pysonar2. We calculate the number of dynamic type in dataset and find that most identifiers do not involve in dynamic type and most dynamic type appears between variable names and variable names. Then we analyze the assignment methods and their transformations in order to analyze type change patterns and we find that function assignments and expression assignments are probably the major ways to lead to dynamic type. Finally, we give some implications based on our findings and discuss the threats to validity of our experiments. Our implications mainly focus on improvement of Python type system design and optimization of existing analysis tools.

In future, we will put up new Python grammars to improve the design of Python type system. We plan to add static types and annotations to Python so that we can control the use of dynamic type in Python and reduce related concerning issues.

References

1. 2017 IEEE spectrum rankings. https://spectrum.ieee.org/computing/software/the-2017-top-programming-languages
2. Awesome Python. https://github.com/vinta/awesome-python
3. Pysonar2. https://github.com/yinwang0/pysonar2
4. An, J.h., Chaudhuri, A., Foster, J.S.: Static typing for ruby on rails. In: 24th IEEE/ACM International Conference on Automated Software Engineering, ASE 2009, pp. 590–594. IEEE (2009)
5. Anderson, C., Giannini, P., Drossopoulou, S.: Towards type inference for JavaScript. In: Black, A.P. (ed.) ECOOP 2005. LNCS, vol. 3586, pp. 428–452. Springer, Heidelberg (2005). https://doi.org/10.1007/11531142_19
6. Aycock, J.: Aggressive type inference. Language **1050**, 18 (2000)
7. Cannon, B.: Localized type inference of atomic types in Python. Ph.D. thesis. Citeseer (2005)
8. Chen, Z., Chen, L., Zhou, Y., Xu, Z., Chu, W.C., Xu, B.: Dynamic slicing of Python programs. In: IEEE Computer Software and Applications Conference, pp. 219–228 (2014)
9. Chen, Z., Ma, W., Lin, W., Chen, L., Xu, B.: Tracking down dynamic feature code changes against Python software evolution. In: Third International Conference on Trustworthy Systems and Their Applications, pp. 54–63 (2016)
10. Chen, Z., Ma, W., Lin, W., Chen, L., Li, Y., Xu, B.: A study on the changes of dynamic feature code when fixing bugs: towards the benefits and costs of Python dynamic features. Sci. China (Inf. Sci.) **61**(1), 012107 (2018)
11. Furr, M., An, J.D., Foster, J.S.: Profile-guided static typing for dynamic scripting languages. In: ACM SIGPLAN Notices, vol. 44, pp. 283–300. ACM (2009)
12. Furr, M., An, J.D., Foster, J.S., Hicks, M.: Static type inference for Ruby. In: Proceedings of the 2009 ACM Symposium on Applied Computing, pp. 1859–1866. ACM (2009)
13. Gorbovitski, M., Liu, Y.A., Stoller, S.D., Rothamel, T., Tekle, T.K.: Alias analysis for optimization of dynamic languages. ACM SIGPLAN Not. **45**(12), 27–42 (2010)
14. Holkner, A., Harland, J.: Evaluating the dynamic behaviour of Python applications. In: Proceedings of the Thirty-Second Australasian Conference on Computer Science, vol. 91, pp. 19–28. Australian Computer Society, Inc. (2009)
15. Jensen, S.H., Møller, A., Thiemann, P.: Type analysis for JavaScript. In: Palsberg, J., Su, Z. (eds.) SAS 2009. LNCS, vol. 5673, pp. 238–255. Springer, Heidelberg (2009). https://doi.org/10.1007/978-3-642-03237-0_17
16. Kneuss, E., Suter, P., Kuncak, V.: Runtime instrumentation for precise flow-sensitive type analysis. In: Barringer, H., et al. (eds.) RV 2010. LNCS, vol. 6418, pp. 300–314. Springer, Heidelberg (2010). https://doi.org/10.1007/978-3-642-16612-9_23
17. Richards, G., Lebresne, S., Burg, B., Vitek, J.: An analysis of the dynamic behavior of JavaScript programs. In: ACM SIGPLAN Notices, vol. 45, pp. 1–12. ACM (2010)
18. Salib, M.: Starkiller: a static type inferencer and compiler for Python. Ph.D. thesis. Massachusetts Institute of Technology (2004)
19. Sapra, S., Minea, M., Chaki, S., Gurfinkel, A., Clarke, E.M.: Finding errors in Python programs using dynamic symbolic execution. In: Yenigün, H., Yilmaz, C., Ulrich, A. (eds.) ICTSS 2013. LNCS, vol. 8254, pp. 283–289. Springer, Heidelberg (2013). https://doi.org/10.1007/978-3-642-41707-8_20

20. Åkerblom, B., Stendahl, J., Tumlin, M., Wrigstad, T.: Tracing dynamic features in Python programs. In: MSR, pp. 292–295 (2014)
21. Thiemann, P.: Towards a type system for analyzing JavaScript programs. In: Sagiv, M. (ed.) ESOP 2005. LNCS, vol. 3444, pp. 408–422. Springer, Heidelberg (2005). https://doi.org/10.1007/978-3-540-31987-0_28
22. Vitousek, M.M., Kent, A.M., Siek, J.G., Baker, J.: Design and evaluation of gradual typing for Python. In: ACM SIGPLAN Notices, vol. 50, pp. 45–56. ACM (2014)
23. Wang, B., Chen, L., Ma, W., Chen, Z., Xu, B.: An empirical study on the impact of Python dynamic features on change-proneness. In: The International Conference on Software Engineering and Knowledge Engineering, pp. 134–139 (2015)
24. Xu, Z., Zhang, X., Chen, L., Pei, K., Xu, B.: Python probabilistic type inference with natural language support. In: Proceedings of the 2016 24th ACM SIGSOFT International Symposium on Foundations of Software Engineering, pp. 607–618. ACM (2016)

Software Mining

What Strokes to Modify in the Painting? Code Changes Prediction for Object-Oriented Software

Dinan Zhang[1,2], Shizhan Chen[1,2], Qiang He[3(✉)], Zhiyong Feng[1,4],
and Keman Huang[5]

[1] Tianjin Key Laboratory of Cognitive Computing and Application,
Tianjin 300072, China
{dnzhang,shizhan,zyfeng}@tju.edu.cn

[2] School of Computer Science and Technology, Tianjin University,
Tianjin 300072, China

[3] School of Software and Electrical Engineering, Swinburne University of Technology,
Hawthorn, VIC 3783, Australia
qhe@swin.edu.au

[4] School of Computer Software, Tianjin University, Tianjin 300072, China

[5] Sloan School of Management, MIT, Cambridge, MA 02142, USA
keman@mit.edu

Abstract. Software systems shall evolve to fulfill users' increasingly various and sophisticated needs. As they become larger and more complex, the corresponding testing and maintenance have become a practical research challenge. In this paper, we employ an approach that can identify the change-proneness in the source code of new object-oriented software releases and predict the corresponding change sizes. We first define two metrics, namely Class Change Metric and Change Size Metric, to describe the features and sizes of code changes. A new software release may be based on several previous releases. Thus, we employ an Entropy Weight Method to calculate the best window size for determining the number of previous releases to use in the prediction of change-proneness in the new release. Based on a series of change evolution matrices, a code change prediction approach is proposed based on the Gauss Process Regression (GPR) algorithm. Experiments are conducted on 17 software systems collected from GitHub to evaluate our prediction approach. The results show that our approach outperforms three existing state-of-the-art approaches with significantly higher prediction accuracy.

Keywords: Change histories · Software evolution
Object-oriented software · Software metrics
Change-prone source code

1 Introduction

Software systems shall evolve to fulfill users' increasingly various and sophisticated needs. During the evolution, their instability often increases with the

© Springer Nature Switzerland AG 2018
L. Bu and Y. Xiong (Eds.): SATE 2018, LNCS 11293, pp. 103–119, 2018.
https://doi.org/10.1007/978-3-030-04272-1_7

addition of new method invocations. Efficient testing and maintenance of a software system have become an urgent demand and a tough challenge. Pareto's Law has been validated in software engineering - a great majority (around 80%) of code changes are rooted in a small proportion (around 20%) of classes [12]. Thus, predicting which classes will change in the next release is very important because it allows the change-prone parts of a system to be prioritized in testing and maintenance. An accurate prediction approach can effectively reduce the testing and maintenance overheads.

Some studies have been performed on the identification of change-prone classes for Object-oriented (OO) systems. There are three gaps that need to be addressed. First of all, some researchers use several structural metrics to describe the objective-oriented characteristics of classes [2–5, 14, 16, 22]. However, they ignore the effective information provided by the evolution history. From a different perspective, Elish and Al-Rahman Al-Khiaty [6] proposed evolution-based metrics that focus on the change history of the system, include the birth of a class, the birth of code changes, density of code changes, etc. However, those statistics are too coarse and do not describe some very important change and in classes and the change-size, e.g., whether a class has been added, deleted, changed compared with the last previous release. Second, some studies attempted to summarize the change history of a software in order to identify change-prone classes or assess the probability that a class will change in the next version [9,10]. However, their experiments are only conducted on the initial & final releases or a series of intermediate releases during release process of a software system. The information collected from those software releases do not suffice to describe the complete evolution process of the system. Third, traditional statistical techniques and machine learning techniques have been employed to identify change-prone classes in the forthcoming release of a software product [7,8,12,13]. However, these techniques can only classify classes into two categories, i.e., changed or not changed. This does not suffice to properly prioritize the predicted change-prone classes during software testing and maintenance, which requires the prediction of change size for each class.

To address the above issues, this paper proposes an approach for predicting change-prone classes and change sizes for OO systems. Two metrics, namely Class Change Metric (CCM) and Change Size Metric (CSM), are defined, the former for describing the changes in classes between two successive releases and the latter for measuring the sizes of code changes. Our approach marks each class of the target software with 22 metrics, including CCM, CSM, C&K [3,4], QMOOD [2], as well as some other metrics [11,19]. It then builds a series of change evolution matrices by integrating the changes in the source code between every two successive releases. These matrices are called *change evolution matrices* because they contain the information on class changes during the entire evolution process. After that, based on those matrices, the optimal window size, which determines the number of previous releases for prediction, is calculated based on the Information Entropy theory. Finally, our approach makes predictions based on the Gaussian Process Regression (GPR) model. The result is a list of the change-prone classes ranked according to their expected change sizes. The major contributions of this paper are:

- Two new metrics are proposed for describing the code changes in classes between successive software releases, and the corresponding change sizes. They are combined with other metrics to build change evolution matrices that contain information on class changes during the entire evolution process of an OO software.
- An approach is proposed for predicting the change-size of change-prone classes based on the GPR model. So, the classes in the top position of change-size ranking list can be tested firstly and intensely.
- Extensive experiments based on 17 real-world OO software systems were conducted to evaluate the prediction accuracy achieved by our approach.

The remainder of the paper is organized as follows. Section 2 reviews the related work. Section 3 presents the approach overall and each module in detail. Section 4 reports experimental results. Section 5 concludes the paper.

2 Related Work

Many researchers have attempted to identify change-prone classes in OO software systems. A number of metrics have been proposed to describe the structural information on the classes in an objective-oriented application. To name few, Chidamber et al. [3,4] developed and implemented the C&K metrics suite that consists of six metrics for describing object-oriented designs. Bansiya et al. [2] proposed the QMOOD metrics for evaluating the design properties of classes. Martin et al. [19] proposed afferent coupling (Ca) and efferent coupling (Ce) metrics.

Researchers have also used code history information to predict future changes in classes in object-oriented applications. Tsantalis et al. [20] evaluated the probability that each class of the system be affected when a new functionality is added or when an existing functionality is modified. For example, if a class has changed in one of four recent releases, the probability of changes in classes for the next release is 25%. Elish et al. [6] collected 16 evolution-based metrics of release 10 to predict the change-proneness of classes for release 11. The metrics used include the birth of a class, the first time changes occurred in classes, the last time changes occurred in classes, etc.

A few researchers have appealed to statistical techniques. Eski et al. [7] used the QMOOD and C&K metrics to calculate the classes' metric values. They combined each ordered list of metrics into a new list where the top 10% classes on the list are labelled as "change-prone classes". Machine learning techniques have also been employed to develop change prediction models for software applications. Amoui et al. [1] proposed a Neural Network-based Temporal Change Prediction (NNTCP) framework for predicting "when" changes are likely to happen. Giger et al. [8] used neural network models to predict the categories of changes. Malhotra et al. [17] analyzed and compared the predictive performance of five search-based techniques, five hybridized techniques, four widely used machine learning techniques and a statistical technique in the prediction of change-prone classes.

3   Change-Prone Classes Prediction

3.1   Framework Overview

Change-prone classes, by definition, are classes which are likely to change in the next release. Our approach aims to identify and rank change-prone classes in an OO software based on the sizes of their changes. To achieve this goal, we need to (1) collect effective historical changes and (2) construct a regression model to predict the change sizes of classes for the new software release. As illustrated in Fig. 1, our approach goes through five phases. The first phase is data collection, where historic version evolution data are collected through analyzing the previous releases. The second phase is data pre-processing. A series of change evolution matrices are built that contain information on class changes during the entire evolution process of an OO software. The third phase is feature selection. In this phase, a proper subset of metrics is selected. The last two phases are determination of the optimal window size and construction of the regression model. In the subsequent sections, we describe each of the five phases in detail.

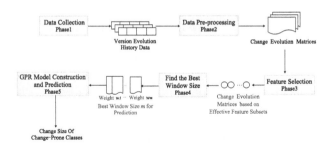

Fig. 1. The system framework.

3.2   Data Collection

The historic version evolution data need to be collected, including the software description, commit history and source code of all releases. Through the commit history, the additions, deletions and modifications at each level can be identified based on the location of the corresponding entity (file, class, method, etc.). Through the source code, we can calculate the code c in the each class between two successive releases. When a new version is released, the changes are often stated by developers. In our study, we collected the above required data from Github. As shown in Fig. 2, using the GitHub API, we wrote the scripts which could store the description and historical commits to a MySql database and download the source code files to the local.

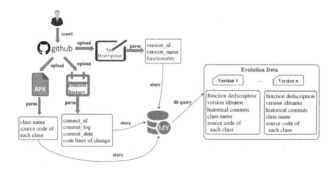

Fig. 2. Data crawling.

Fig. 3. Data pre-processing.

3.3   Data Pre-processing

In order to describe the changes in classes, we propose two new metrics, Class Change Metric (CCM) and Change Size Metric (CSM). All metrics measuring the changes of the source code in an OO software between every two successive releases are integrated to build a series of change evolution matrices. The evolution matrices are the basis for predicting the change-sizes of change-proneness of classes. Fig. 3 shows the procedure for pre-processing the collected data about the software sytem, and the procedure involve three steps. In the following subsections, the metrics we propose are introduced firstly, then we describe each of the three steps in detail.

Definitions of CCM and CSM. CCM is used to describe the addition, deletion, and modification of classes. CSM is proposed to measure the sizes of changes in classes.

Class Change Metric (CCM). This metric describes whether a class is added, deleted or modified in $version_{i+1}$ in comparison to $version_i$. It has three optional values: Added, Deleted, Modified, formally defined below.

- *Added.* It is a Boolean value that indicates whether the class has been newly added in $version_{i+1}$. If yes, there is $Added(i+1)_{classj} = 1$. Otherwise, there is $Added(i+1)_{classj} = 0$.
- *Deleted.* It is a Boolean value that indicates whether the class has been deleted from in $version_{i+1}$. If yes, there is $Deleted(i+1)_{classj} = 1$. Otherwise, there is $Deleted(i+1)_{classj} = 0$.

– *Modified.* It is a Boolean value that indicates whether the class has been changed $version_{i+1}$. If yes, there is $Modified(i+1)_{classj} = 1$. Otherwise, there is $Modified(i+1)_{classj} = 0$.

Change Size Metric (CSM). This metric describes the size of a change in the class between two successive releases. This way, the sizes of class changes are quantified. The value of this metric is calculated in two cases.

– *Common Classes:* Classes that exist in successive releases are called common classes. The source code of a common class is extracted from those releases. Suppose the source code of $class_j$ in $version_i$ is $source\,code(i)_{class_j}$, the source code of $class_j$ in $version_{i+1}$ is $source\,code(i+1)_{class_j}$. The similarity between $source\,code(i)_{class_j}$ and $source\,code(i+1)_{class_j}$ is calculated, represented by $similarity(i+1)_{class_j}$. The change size between $version_i$ and $version_{i+1}$ of $class_j$ is:

$$\text{change size}(i+1)_{class_j} = 1 - \text{similarity}(i+1)_{class_j} \qquad (1)$$

If the class is modified in the next release and the $similarity(i+1)_{class_j} = 0.8$, the *Change Size*$(i+1)_{class_j} = 1 - 0.8 = 0.2$.

– *Added or Deleted Classes:* If a class is added or deleted in the next release, its change size is assigned a fixed value of 1.

The similarity between the source codes of different software releases is measured with the Longest Common Subsequence (LCS) algorithm. Two source codes are converted to two strings, and the longest common subsequence of two strings is obtained.

Scanner Module. All the classes that appear since the first version until the last release are extracted and combined. This way, we can obtain all the classes during the entire evolution process. Assume that there is a $version_i$ in an OO software, the collection of classes is represented as:

$$Ci = \{\text{class}|\text{class} \in version_i\}(0 < i \le v) \qquad (2)$$

All classes that have participated in the software evolution are represented as:

$$C = C_1 \cup C_2 \dots \cup C_{v-1} \cup C_v \qquad (3)$$

Metric Extraction. Three types of metadata information for each class are extracted, involves CCM, CSM and OO metrics. Each class is marked with 22 metrics, the calculation of CCM and CSM have been described in the previous section, the calculation of OO metrics detailed as follow.

Object-Oriented Metrics. From the perspective of the object-oriented attributes of classes, the difference in object-oriented metrics is used to describe the code changes between two successive releases. In contrast to the previous

Table 1. Description of the object-oriented metrics (OOM)

No.	Metrics	Description	Characteristic	Metric suite
1	WMC	Weighted methods per class	Size	C&K
2	DIT	Depth of inheritance tree	Inheritance	C&K
3	NOC	Number of children	Inheritance	C&K
4	CBO	Coupling between object classes	Coupling	C&K
5	RFC	Response for a class	Coupling	C&K
6	LCOM	Lack of cohesion in methods	Cohesion	C&K
7	MOA	Measure of aggregation	Composition	QMOOD
8	DAM	Data access metric	Encapsulation	QMOOD
9	MFA	Measure of functional abstraction	Inheritance	QMOOD
10	NPM	Number of public methods for a class	Size	QMOOD
11	CAM	Cohesion among methods of class	Cohesion	QMOOD
12	Ca	Afferent coupling	Coupling	Other
13	Ce	Efferent coupling	Coupling	Other
14	AMC	Average method complexity	Size	Other
15	LOC	Lines of code	Size	Other
16	LCOM3	Lack of cohesion in methods Henderson-sellers version	Cohesion	Other
17	IC	Inheritance coupling	Coupling	Other
18	CBM	Coupling between methods	Coupling	Other

metrics, this allows changes in classes to be described in a more fine-grained manner. The CKJM tool[1] is employed to calculate the 18 metrics for each class, including C&K [3,4], QMOOD [2], Ca Ce [19] and those proposed in [11]. More details about those metrics can be found in Table 1. Then, the difference between two successive versions in each metric is measured. Here, the WMC metric of a $class_j$ in $version_i$ is denoted by $wmc(i)_{classj}$, the WMC metric of a $class_j$ in $version_{i+1}$ is denoted by $wmc(i+1)_{classj}$. The corresponding change in $class_j$ is calculated with formula 4:

$$\Delta wmc(i+1)_{class_j} = wmc(i+1)_{class_j} - wmc(i)_{class_j} \qquad (4)$$

Integrate and Store. Next, we build a change evolution matrix based on every two successive releases. For an OO software with m releases and n classes as an example, a total of $m-1$ matrices are built. In this matrix, each row represents one class of all classes in all the software releases. Each column contains one of the 22 metrics.

---

[1] http://gromit.iiar.pwr.wroc.pl/p_inf/ckjm.

3.4   Feature Selection

As discussed before, each class is marked with 22 metrics. However, there are correlations between these metrics. For example, some of those metrics measure the same properties of the class. Thus, it is not necessary to include all these 22 metrics in the identification of change-prone classes because overuse of those does not offer any new information and in fact might even have a negative impact on the prediction. Therefore, we need to certain metrics rather than all metrics to make predictions. To achieve this, we employ the Correlation-based Feature Selection (CFS) method. This method evaluates all possible combinations of the 22 metrics to find the optimal combination of metrics for prediction. An effective subset of metric is selected by considering the individual predictive ability of each metric and the degree of redundancy between the metrics. Finally, only the metrics that provide important information independent about classes are selected. The matrices are built by integrating the selected metrics of the classes.

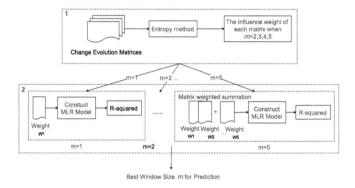

Fig. 4. Find the best window size m for prediction.

3.5   Find the Best Window Size m for Prediction

In this research, the window size for prediction is the number of previous releases used to predict class change-proneness. Similar to the weather forecast based on the weather in the last several days, the new release may be relevant to several previous releases. This parameter, denoted by m, is software-specific and needs to be specified experimentally. According to the information entropy theory, different window sizes have different impacts on the prediction. This section discusses how to select the optimal window size for prediction. This procedure is shown in Fig. 4.

Calculate the Weight of Matrix. Different previous releases may have different impacts on the change-proneness prediction for the next release. The most recent release usually has the greatest impact. However, the difference in the impacts of different releases are not necessarily significant. It is usually software-specific and needs to be investigated experimentally, as will be demonstrated in Sect. 4. In order to obtain more accurate prediction results, before the prediction, the weight of each change evolution matrix is determined by the degree of impact on the corresponding next release. When the predicted window size is different, we use the entropy weight method to calculate information entropy and obtain the weights of different matrices within the window.

Here, the weight is determined by the size of the index variability. A greater information entropy of a certain indicator offers more information. As a result, it has a greater impact on the software evolution. A greater weight is assigned. Following this methodology, the entropy weight method can be employed to determine the matrix weights. A matrix with a larger weight provides more information and have a greater impact on the prediction results. Suppose the software have n releases. A total of $n-1$ matrices can be obtained, i.e., $matrix_2$, $matrix_3, \ldots, matrix_n$. Figure 5 illustrates each indicator group extracted by the $n - 1$ matrices. The total effective change information contained in the $n - 1$ matrices, i.e., $x_1, x_2, \ldots, x_{n-1}$, are calculated and taken as the feature of the matrices. The effective change information is calculated by summing up all the non-zero added, deleted and modified metrics. It reflects the amount of information provided by the matrix for the prediction. Suppose that the window size is m. There are $n - m$ indicator groups. For example, if $m = 3$, prediction for release 5 is made based on version 2, 3, 4, prediction for release 6 with versions 3, 4, 5, etc. Thus, version 2, 3, 4/version 3, 4, 5/version 4, 5, 6, etc. are the indicator groups.

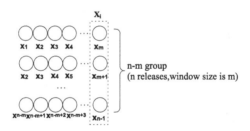

Fig. 5. Indicator groups.

Suppose the data set has n releases and the window size is m $(m = 2, 3, 4, 5)$. Following three steps, we can obtain the weight of each matrix when the window size m is different.

Step 1 Data-processing. Given a window size m, there are a total of m indicators, i.e., $X_1, X_2, \ldots X_m$, where $X_i = \{x_1, x_2, \ldots, x_{n-m}\}$, x_{ij} is the j_{th} element in the X_i collection. Here, we standardize these indicators:

$$Y_{ij} = \frac{x_{ij} - min\,(X_i)}{max\,(X_i) - min\,(X_i)} \tag{5}$$

where $i = 1, 2, \ldots, m$ and $j = 1, 2, \ldots, n - m$.

Step 2 Information entropy calculation. According to the definition of information entropy in information theory, the information entropy of a set of data, i.e., E_i, $i = 1, 2, \ldots, m$, is determined as follows:

$$E_i = -\ln(n-m)^{-1} \sum_{j=1}^{n-m} p_{ij} \ln p_{ij} \tag{6}$$

$$p_{ij} = \frac{Y_{ij}}{\sum_{j=1}^{n-m} Y_{ij}} \tag{7}$$

If $p_{ij} = 0$,

$$\lim_{p_{ij}=0} p_{ij} \ln p_{ij} = 0 \tag{8}$$

Using formulas (6)–(8), the information entropy of m matrices are determined.

Step 3 Determine the weight of each matrix. The weight of the m matrices are calculated through information entropy, formally

$$w_i = \frac{1 - E_i}{k - \sum E_i} \ (i = 1, 2, \ldots, m) \tag{9}$$

Determination of Optimal Window Size. The optimal window size m for prediction is calculated based on regression model. Using the evolutionary historical data, the regression models with different prediction window sizes are built to identify the change-prone classes. The fitting effect of these models determines the window size for prediction. Building a model requires the definition of independent variables and dependent variable.

The Independent Variable. When the window size $m = n$, according to the weights of different matrices in different window sizes, $w_1, w_2, w_3 \ldots, w_n$, there is $w_1 + w_2 + w_3 \ldots + w_n = 1$. The n matrices are combined as follows: $w_1 Matrix_1 + w_2 Matrix_2 + \ldots + w_n Matrix_n \rightarrow Matrix$. The line of the matrix is the union of all classes, let the value is A. The column of the matrix is the metrics that in the seleted metric suite, let the value is p. Expand the matrix into a vector, the $A * p$ dimension vector is the independent variable.

The Dependent Variable. It is a dichotomous variable that indicates whether a class was changed from the previous release to the current release. A class is considered changed when there is code addition, deletion or modification.

When m is different, the Multiple Logistic Regression (MLR) models are built for each class. Next, the R-squared of each model is calculated. Then, all the R-squared values are averaged. Next, we compare the cases with window sizes $m = 1, 2, 3, 4, 5$. The window size corresponding to the model that has the max average R-squared value is selected as the optimal window size for prediction.

3.6   GPR Model Construction and Prediction

The numbers of releases of different data sets vary significantly, from dozens to hundreds. And the number of classes in an OO software is usually very large.

Thus, the number of samples is small and the dimension of a matrix is large. The Gauss process can handle small samples with high dimensionality. Therefore, we construct our prediction model using the Gauss Process Regression (GPR) algorithm. According to the optimal window size m for prediction, m matrices are selected as independent variables, and the change-size of a class is taken as a dependent variable.

4 Experiment and Result

4.1 Data Sources

To conduct experiments for evaluating our prediction approach, we developed a web crawler to collect data sets from GitHub, an open-source software repository. The criteria for selecting the OO software sytems are:

- They must be written in Java.
- They must have a number of releases through their evolution history. This way, we can collect sufficient release-by-release evolution data.
- They must have different sizes and contain reasonably large number of classes to allow extraction of sufficient change-prone classes for evolution analysis.
- They must have different lifespans and they are long-lived to allow sufficient and representative sample data to be collected.
- They must be open-sourced to allow the collection of sufficient releases during the entire evolution process.

Table 2. Overview of examined projects

Software	Time frame	Versions	No. of classes	No. of changed classes
WordPress	2011-4-13~2017-11-14	254	7718	1282
V2ex-android	2015-07-06~2017-08-18	6	3443	144
Qksms	2015-09-01~2016-09-05	24	3751	700
TweetLanes	2013-02-23~2014-10-08	22	1986	829
Douya	2016-02-27~2017-07-15	8	6630	2858
POT-Droid	2012-01-30~2017-05-01	30	9768	3086
FaceSlim	2015-01-18~2017-09-27	44	3958	1911
MLManager	2015-05-26~2016-03-29	13	4066	814
Transdrone	2013-06-28~2017-03-17	24	3608	1332
AnySoft Keyboard	2012-4-25~2017-7-27	62	3841	2707
Zxing	2014-01-19~2017-10-25	23	448	299
Googlesamples	2015-07-06~2017-08-18	6	3889	1097
AppOpsx	2017-01-11~2017-09-30	12	7105	2288
Rpicheck	2014-8-29~2017-08-27	17	9560	3129
Reddit is fun	2011-11-27~2012-01-15	10	818	131
Financius	2014-10-18~2015-01-31	35	9233	2476
Openfoodfacts	2015-05-12~2017-03-24	25	9740	4320

We have collected the data about 17 software systems from GitHub. As shown in Table 2, they have long-lived lifespans, different functionalities, different percentage of changed classes and a sufficient number of releases as well as classes.

4.2 Metric Suite Selection

As explained in Section 3.4, we use the CFS method to select a subset of metrics for prediction. Some metrics are selected many times, while others are selected only a few times. Some metrics have even never been selected. Seven systems select CAM, DMP, which are QMOOD metrics. Four metrics have never been selected by any sytems, including NOC, DAM, IC and CBM. DAM measures the encapsulation characteristic, which is irrelevant to the prediction. IC, CBM and NOC measure coupling and inheritance characteristics respectively. These metrics may have the same dimension as some other metrics. Therefore, they are removed from the matrices. The *Class Change Metric and Change Size Metric* are selected by 12 out of systems, the most of all metrics. Thus, they are considered highly effective in describing the evolution process and predicting the change-proneness of classes.

4.3 Window Size Selection

According to Section 3.5, entropy weight method is used to calculate the weight of each matrix when the window size for prediction is different. The statistical results are shown in Table 3. It shows that the matrix has different weight when the window size is different. For a fixed window size, the sum of all matrix weights is 1. Some matrix have equivalent weights. For example, the two matrix weights are both 0.5 when the window size of Zxing is 2. Some matrix weights are slightly different. The three matrix weights are 0.31, 0.33, 0.34 when the m of Qkms is 3. Some matrix weights are significantly different. For example, the weights of Googlesamples with $m = 2$ are 0.4 and 0.6 respectively. The value with the largest weight is marked in bold. Previous matrices are used in prediction for the next software release. The last matrix is the closet to the next software release. Thus, the last matrix has the largest weight in almost all statistical results of different window sizes. It provides the most information for prediction and has the greatest impact on prediction.

The GPR model is constructed with weighted matrix according to different window sizes. The models' goodness of fit is summarised in Table 4 where the maximum value is marked in bold. Firstly, it can be observed that the highest average R-squared of 0.832 is obtained with $m = 2$. When $m = 1$ and $m = 2$, there are the most software systems with the maximum R-squared in different window sizes. This validates our methodology described before that uses the matrix closet to the publishing release to train the model for obtaining the best prediction results. Secondly, different data sets may manifest different characteristics. Thus, experiments need to be conducted with different window sizes and the window size that yields the highest R-squared is selected as the optimal

Table 3. The weight of each matrix when m is different

Window size	Weight on average
m = 2	0.471
	0.529
m = 3	0.291
	0.323
	0.386
m = 4	0.219
	0.213
	0.246
	0.322
m = 5	0.188
	0.186
	0.180
	0.214
	0.232

Table 4. R-squared of different window size m

Window size	R-quared on average
m = 1	0.79062
m = 2	**0.83174**
m = 3	0.78409
m = 4	0.77579
m = 5	0.72828

windows size. Take Table 4 for example. It shows that when $n = 2$ the maximum average R-quared is obtained for the example data set. Thus, the optimal window size in this case is 2.

4.4   Results of Prediction

In this section, we report the experimental results. The prediction accuracy achieved based on our model is compared with three representative models:

– *CEM:* Our model uses the change evolution matrices (based on the selected metric suite) as independent variables. It is referred to as CEM hereafter which is short for change evolution matrices.
– *PSM:* This probability estimation model uses the internal class probability of changes as independent variable [20].
– *QHC:* This model uses the evolution-based metrics as independent variables based on the quantifying historical changes model [6].
– *C&K:* This model uses the C&K metrics [3,4] as independent variables.

The Overview of Our Models' Prediction Results. We choose the top 80% versions of each project as training data, and the rest are as the test data. Table 5 overviews the results in our models goodness of fit: Residual Sum of Squares (RSS) and our model's prediction performance, including the classification accuracy and the average relative error. The classification accuracy, which is the ratio of the number of classes that were correctly classified (change or non-change) to the total number of classes. We use a threshold to determine whether the class is changed. If the change size is greater than 0.5, we think it is changed. On the contrary, we think that this class has not changed. It shows that our model fits these data sets properly.

Table 5. R-squared and RSS, classification accuracy, average relative error (ARE) on all data sets

	Residual sum of squares	Classification accuracy	Average relative error
Average	0.113	87.9%	0.048

Table 6. AUC, precision, and recall: all models

	CEM	PSM	QHC	C&K
Median AUC	**0.89**	0.71	0.79	0.81
Median precision	**0.88**	0.68	0.81	0.76
Median recall	**0.85**	0.76	0.81	0.83

The Robustness of Our Method. We use the area under the receiver operating characteristic (AOC) curve statistic (AUC), the median precision and recall values to evaluate these classification models [8]. When the difference between the change and non-change samples is large, the ROC curve can remain unchanged, so AUC is a robust measure to compare the performance of classifiers. We consider AUC values above 0.7 to have adequate classification power. As shown in Table 6, our model shows the best performance with a median AUC of 0.88, a median precision of 0.89, and a median recall of 0.85. This indicates the superiority of CEM model over other models.

The Change Size Ranking List Prediction. For the sake of space, Fig. 6 compare predicted change sizes of 19 classes in the last release of one project (V2ex-android) against the ground truth, i.e., the real number of classes that have been changed. It can be seen that the predicted sizes achieved by our approach are very similar to the ground truth. Given their change sizes, classes can be ordered by their predicted change sizes. The following ranking evaluation metrics are calculated to measure the performance of the change-size ranking list prediction.

– *Mean Average Precision (MAP):* MAP is used to calculate the average accuracy of the predicted ranking. It is calculated as follows:

$$MAP = \frac{\sum_{r=1}^{N}(\frac{r}{N_r}I_r)}{N_{used}} \tag{10}$$

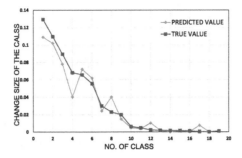

Fig. 6. Comparison between predicted value and true value. (Project: V2ex-android)

where N_r denotes the corresponding ranking of the top r changed classes in the new software release. I_r (0 or 1) indicates whether the changed class at ranked r is actually used. N_{used} represents the total number of changed classes in the new software release. A high MAP indicates a high predicted ranking of the changed class.

– *Normalized Discounted Cumulative Gain (NDCG):* When classes are ranked by their predicted change sizes, it will assign a lower weight to the big chang-size classes with a lower predicted ranking:

$$NDCG = \frac{1}{S_N} \sum_{j=1}^{N} \frac{(2^{r(j)} - 1)}{log_2^{(1+j)}} \tag{11}$$

where r_j is the relevant score (0 or 1) of the jth changed classes on the ranking list and S_N represents the ideal maximum score that all classes can reach.

Table 7 presents the MAP and NDCG for the four approaches. It shows that our model outperforms other models in both MAP and NDGC. The above analytical results indicate the superior performance of our model in class change-proneness prediction. It also indicates that the change evolution matrices built based on the proposed *Class Change Metric and Change Size Metric* are more suitable than the classic metric suites for code change-proneness prediction for OO software systems.

Table 7. Correlation and accuracy analysis

Index	CEM	PSM	QHC	C&K
MAP	**83.3%**	70.6%	75.8%	79.2%
NDCG	**88.2%**	75.1%	79.6%	82.5%

5   Conclusion

The testing and maintenance of object-oriented software have become an important challenge that needs to be attacked. One of the keys is to identify change-prone classes in a new software release and predict their change size. In this paper, we propose Class Change Metric & Change Size Metric for describing the changes made in classes between different software releases. Based on those metrics, a series of change evolution matrices can be built by analyzing the entire software evolution process. We also employ Entropy Weight Method for determining the optimal window size for prediction, with aim to achieve accurate prediction results. To the best knowledge of us, our model is the first attempt to predict the change size ranking list of change-prone classes. Our approach is experimentally evaluated on 17 real-world data sets collected from the Github. The results show that our model significantly outperforms three existing models.

Acknowledgment. This work is supported by the National Natural Science Foundation of China grants 61572350 and the National Key R&D Program of China grant NO.2017YF-B1401201.

References

1. Amoui, M., Salehie, M., Tahvildari, L.: Temporal software change prediction using neural networks. Int. J. Softw. Eng. Knowl. Eng. **19**(07), 995–1014 (2009)
2. Bansiya, J., Davis, C.G.: A hierarchical model for object-oriented design quality assessment. IEEE Trans. Softw. Eng. **28**(1), 4–17 (2002)
3. Chidamber, S.R., Kemerer, C.F.: Towards a metrics suite for object oriented design, vol. 26. ACM (1991)
4. Chidamber, S.R., Kemerer, C.F.: A metrics suite for object oriented design. IEEE Trans. Softw. Eng. **20**(6), 476–493 (1994)
5. D'Ambros, M., Lanza, M., Robbes, R.: On the relationship between change coupling and software defects. In: 16th Working Conference on Reverse Engineering, WCRE 2009, pp. 135–144. IEEE (2009)
6. Elish, M.O., Al-Rahman Al-Khiaty, M.: A suite of metrics for quantifying historical changes to predict future change-prone classes in object-oriented software. J. Softw. Evol. Process **25**(5), 407–437 (2013)
7. Eski, S., Buzluca, F.: An empirical study on object-oriented metrics and software evolution in order to reduce testing costs by predicting change-prone classes. In: 2011 IEEE Fourth International Conference on Software Testing, Verification and Validation Workshops (ICSTW), pp. 566–571. IEEE (2011)
8. Giger, E., Pinzger, M., Gall, H.C.: Can we predict types of code changes? An empirical analysis. In: 2012 9th IEEE Working Conference on Mining Software Repositories (MSR), pp. 217–226. IEEE (2012)
9. Girba, T., Ducasse, S., Lanza, M.: Yesterday's weather: guiding early reverse engineering efforts by summarizing the evolution of changes. In: Proceedings of 20th IEEE International Conference on Software Maintenance, pp. 40–49. IEEE (2004)
10. Graves, T.L., Karr, A.F., Marron, J.S., Siy, H.: Predicting fault incidence using software change history. IEEE Trans. Softw. Eng. **26**(7), 653–661 (2000)
11. Henderson-Sellers, B.: Object-Oriented Metrics: Measures of Complexity. Prentice-Hall, Inc., Upper Saddle River (1995)
12. Koru, A.G., Liu, H.: Identifying and characterizing change-prone classes in two large-scale open-source products. J. Syst. Softw. **80**(1), 63–73 (2007)
13. Koru, A.G., Tian, J.: Comparing high-change modules and modules with the highest measurement values in two large-scale open-source products. IEEE Trans. Softw. Eng. **31**(8), 625–642 (2005)

14. Lu, H., Zhou, Y., Xu, B., Leung, H., Chen, L.: The ability of object-oriented metrics to predict change-proneness: a meta-analysis. Empir. Softw. Eng. **17**(3), 200–242 (2012)
15. Malhotra, R., Khanna, M.: Inter project validation for change proneness prediction using object-oriented metrics. Softw. Eng.: Int. J. **3**(1), 21–31 (2013)
16. Malhotra, R., Khanna, M.: Investigation of relationship between object-oriented metrics and change proneness. Int. J. Mach. Learn. Cybern. **4**(4), 273–286 (2013)
17. Malhotra, R., Khanna, M.: An exploratory study for software change prediction in object-oriented systems using hybridized techniques. Autom. Softw. Eng. **24**(3), 673–717 (2017)
18. Malhotra, R., Khanna, M., Raje, R.R.: On the application of search-based techniques for software engineering predictive modeling: a systematic review and future directions. Swarm Evol. Comput. **32**, 85–109 (2017)
19. Martin, R.C.: Agile Software Development: Principles, Patterns, and Practices. Prentice Hall, Upper Saddle River (2002)
20. Tsantalis, N., Chatzigeorgiou, A., Stephanides, G.: Predicting the probability of change in object-oriented systems. IEEE Trans. Softw. Eng. **31**(7), 601–614 (2005)
21. Zhou, B., Neamtiu, I., Gupta, R.: A cross-platform analysis of bugs and bug-fixing in open source projects: desktop vs. android vs. iOS. In: Proceedings of the 19th International Conference on Evaluation and Assessment in Software Engineering, p. 7. ACM (2015)
22. Zhou, Y., Leung, H., Xu, B.: Examining the potentially confounding effect of class size on the associations between object-oriented metrics and change-proneness. IEEE Trans. Softw. Eng. **35**(5), 607–623 (2009)

How Reliable Is Your Outsourcing Service for Data Mining? A Metamorphic Method for Verifying the Result Integrity

Jiewei Zhang, Xiaoyuan Xie$^{(\boxtimes)}$, and Zhiyi Zhang

School of Computer Science, Wuhan University, Wuhan, China
{zhangjiewei,xxie,zhyzhang}@whu.edu.cn

Abstract. Association rules mining is an important and classic research topic in Data Mining, and has been widely applied in many real-life cases. The primary time and memory consumption in association rules mining is from its first step - frequent itemsets mining. With the development of cloud computing, outsourcing this task to third-party service providers will save efforts in system development, deployment, operation, etc. Outsourcing, however, actually brings risks and difficulties in verifying the results returned by these services. In this paper, we focus on verifying the integrity of the results returned by outsourcing services. We propose a metamorphic-based method, which is light-weight and requires not much complicated process. The key point of our method is the construction of a set of metamorphic relations (MRs). Through analysis and experimental research, we show that our approach delivers quite satisfactory results.

Keywords: Frequent itemsets mining · Outsourcing
Result integrity verification · Metamorphic-based method

1 Introduction

Association rules mining, which is inspired by the famous shopping basket problem [6,14], is an important and classic research topic in Data Mining, and has been widely applied in many real-life cases such as prediction of disease in the medical field [3], recommendation system [17], and so on [4]. In general, association rules mining techniques are mainly composed of two steps. First, they obtain the frequent itemsets from the users' specified minimum support threshold; secondly, they conclude the association rules from the users' specified minimum confidence threshold on the basis of the frequent itemsets obtained from the first step. The primary time and memory consumption in association rules mining is

This work is supported by National Key R&D Program of China (2018YFB1003901), the National Key Basic Research and Development Program of China (973 Program 2014CB340702), and the National Natural Science Foundation of China (61572375, 61772263).

L. Bu and Y. Xiong (Eds.): SATE 2018, LNCS 11293, pp. 120–136, 2018.
https://doi.org/10.1007/978-3-030-04272-1_8

from the first step. Therefore, studies in the field mainly focus on improving the performance of the frequent itemsets mining algorithms [1,2,7,13,23].

With many algorithms for more efficiently mining frequent itemsets being proposed and widely applied, people started to pay attention to the quality of the result returned by these algorithms. In particular, many frequent itemset mining processes have been performed by outsourcing services. This solution though can save efforts in system development, deployment, etc., actually brings risks and difficulties in verifying the results returned by these services. Specifically, the data integrity of the returned results is one of the most important aspects to be inspected. Wong et al. [19] defined data integrity as "completeness" and "correctness".

However, verifying the integrity is generally non-trivial. In practice, the amount of returned frequent itemsets can be very huge. There are some studies for verifying the integrity of the outsourced data mining process. Pang et al. introduce a scheme for users to verify whether the results are complete and authentic [16]. Xie et al. propose an integrity audit mechanism where they audit query integrity by inserting some fake tuples into the database [20]. However, [16,20] do not support aggregate queries. Wong et al. propose an "artificial itemset planting" (AIP) technology [19] to verify the integrity of the returned frequent itemsets. Dong et al. present a method which uses probability and determinism to check whether the server returns the correct and complete frequent itemsets [11]. However, [11,19] suffer from high cost issue.

Therefore, in this paper, we propose to introduce metamorphic testing for verifying the integrity of frequent itemsets obtained from the outsourcing services. The main contributions are as follows:

(1) We propose a light-weight method based on metamorphic testing to verify the integrity of returned frequent itemsets. We design six metamorphic relations for our method.
(2) We conduct a comprehensive experiment to investigate the effectiveness of our method.
(3) We study the differences of the effects among different metamorphic relations and further explored the key factors which influence the effect of metamorphic relations.

The structure of the paper is as follows. We discuss preliminaries in Sect. 2. We propose our approach, an metamorphic-based method in Sect. 3. We introduce our experiment setup intensively in Sect. 4. We show results and analysis of our approach in Sect. 5, and conclude in Sect. 6.

2 Preliminaries

2.1 Mining Frequent Itemsets

In this section, we first brief the frequent itemsets (referred to as FI) mining algorithms.

Definition 1. *Let $I = \{i_1, i_2, \cdots, i_m\}$ be a global set of items, and any subset of I is called an itemset. Let $D = \{T_1, T_2, \cdots, T_n\}$ be a transaction database, where each transaction T_k $(1 \leq k \leq n)$ is also a subset of I (i.e. $T_k \subseteq I$). An itemset X is said to be contained by transaction T if and only if $X \subseteq T$.*

Definition 2. *Let $Count(X)$ be the number of transactions in D that contain X. The support of X is defined as $Support(X) = \frac{Count(X)}{|D|}$. X is said to be a frequent itemset (FI) if $Support(X)$ is no less than a predefined minimal support threshold min_sup; and infrequent itemset (IFI) otherwise. In addition, X is called frequent k-itemset if $|X| = k$.*

Definition 3 (FI mining algorithm). *Given a set of items $I = \{i_1, i_2, \cdots, i_m\}$, a transaction database D and a minimum support threshold min_sup as the inputs, an FI mining algorithm outputs all frequent itemsets $\mathbb{F}$. In particular, this output can be written as $\mathbb{F} = \bigcup_{k=1}^{n} F_k$, where F_k denotes the set of all frequent k-itemsets. We denote the size of F_k as CF_k.*

Here we give a simple example to demonstrate the inputs and outputs of an FI mining algorithm. Given a $min\_sup = 2$ and a transaction database D as shown in Table 1, where all items are from a global set $I = \{i_1, i_2, i_3, i_4, i_5\}$. FI algorithm will output all itemsets with *Support* no less than $min\_sup = 2$, which are shown in Fig. 1. It can be found that in this example, we have 14 frequent itemsets in total, where $CF_1 = 5$ (i.e. there are five frequent 1-itemsets), $CK_2 = 6$, $CK_3 = 2$ and $CK_4 = 1$. There is no frequent k-itemset with k higher than 4.

There are many FI mining algorithms in the literature, such as Apriori [1,2], FP-growth [13], Eclat [23], etc. These algorithms differ from each other in terms of their time complexity and memory consumption, but deliver the same FI results. Since the focus of this paper is to verify the data integrity of the results,

Table 1. Transaction database example.

Tid	T1	T2	T3	T4	T5	T6	T7	T8	T9
Itemset	i_1, i_2, i_5	i_2, i_4	i_2, i_3	i_1, i_2, i_4	i_1, i_3	i_2, i_3	i_1, i_3	i_1, i_2, i_3, i_5	i_1, i_2, i_3

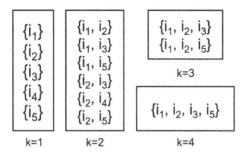

Fig. 1. Outputs of FI algorithm

rather than the efficiency, we will adopt the Apriori algorithm as a representative in our investigation[1].

2.2   Verifying the Data Integration of FI Mining Algorithms

Nowadays, the significantly increasing volume of big data brings great challenge to FI mining. Apart from efficient algorithms, FI mining process also requires high performance computing equipment, which brings great burden to data owners. A widely adopted solution is known as data-mining-as-a-service (DMaS) paradigm [11]. This paradigm outsources FI mining to third-party service providers (servers), which can save much efforts and cost for data owners (clients). However, this solution brings another concern to clients, that is, how to verify the data integrity of results returned by the third-party services. Based on [19], data integrity in frequent itemset mining is defined as follows.

- *Completeness*: All actual frequent itemsets are included in the result.
- *Correctness*: All returned frequent itemsets are actually frequent.

Assume the client owns a D. Service providers compute and return a set of FIs to the client. However, service providers may not be trusted and it is possible that server returns results with ill data integrity, due to malicious actions [19]. In this paper, we consider three types of malicious actions, namely, deletion, insertion and replacement, which will be detailed in Sect. 4.3.

The insertion and replacement damage the *correctness* while deletion will affect the *completeness*. However, verifying the integrity is not an easy task. As mentioned above, the amount of returned FIs can be very huge. For completeness, it could be infeasible to find out whether all actual FIs are included; for correctness, though the correctness of an arbitrary itemset can be determined, it could be very expensive to figure out the correctness for the large amount of FIs. In other words, such verification is suffering from oracle problem [5,18].

In order to address this problem, we propose a metamorphic-based method, to verify the data integrity returned by the third-party services.

2.3   Metamorphic Testing

As discussed above, verifying the data integrity suffers from oracle problem. To alleviate this problem, Chen et al. have developed the metamorphic testing approach [9], which has later been successfully applied in various application fields [8,10,15,21,22], etc.

Metamorphic testing (MT) uses existing test cases known as the source test case to generate subsequent test cases known as the follow-up test cases. The key component in MT is metamorphic relation (MR), which defines the relation among source and follow-up inputs, as well as source and follow-up outputs. Given a source test case t_i and an MR, we can construct follow-up test case t_i'

---

[1] Strictly speaking, Apriori consists of both FI and association rules mining. But since the FI mining takes up most of the resources, we focus on this step only.

accordingly. Let P denote the program under test. Then we check if t_i, $P(t_i)$, t_i' and $P(t_i')$ satisfy the relation defined by the MR. If the relation is not held, a violation is said to be found, which indicates faults in the program under testing.

3   Approach

In this paper, we propose a metamorphic-based method, to verify the data integrity of results returned by third-party services. Let us denote an input of an FI mining algorithm as a tuple $In=<I, D, min\_sup>$, and the corresponding output Out contains the overall $\mathbb{IF}$, as well as CF_k for each $F_k \in \mathbb{IF}$, where the I, D, min_sup, $\mathbb{IF}$, F_k and CF_k are defined in Sect. 2.1. Notice, in our method, we specify $min\_sup > 1/|D|$, where $|D|$ denotes the number of the transactions in the database D. We propose a series of metamorphic relations (MRs). Each MR will define a way to transform a source input (In) into a follow-up input (In'), by modifying one of more elements in the tuple. MR also defines the relation among the source output corresponds to In (denoted as Out) and follow-up output corresponds to In' (denoted as Out'). And we will give the proof of MR1 to MR3, while MR4 is a combination of MR2 and MR3 and the proof of MR5 and MR6 is very easy, so we will not prove them due to the limitation of page.

Moreover, let I, D, min_sup denote the **source global item set**, **source transaction database**, and **source minimum support threshold**, respectively. Let I', D', min'_sup denote the **follow-up global item set, follow-up transaction database**, and **follow-up minimum support threshold**, respectively. Let $\mathbb{IF}$ denote **the frequent itemsets of the source output**, and let CF_k denote **the number of the source frequent k-itemsets**; let $\mathbb{IF}'$ denote **the frequent itemsets of the follow-up output**, and let CF_k' denote **the number of the follow-up frequent k-itemsets**.

By comparing the actual outputs returned by an FI mining algorithm against the defined relation, we know that there exist errors if any one of the relations is not held. In the following sections, we will introduce our MRs that modifies input In from two perspectives.

3.1   MRs with Changes on Transaction Database D

In the first group, we introduce MRs that keep min_sup constant, but change the transaction database D and the number of the transactions in the source transaction database D is n.

(1) **MR1:** The follow-up global item set I' is constructed by inserting a new item a to I, where a is not in I. The follow-up database D' is constructed by adding a in each transaction T_i of D, where $i = 1, 2, \cdots, n$. Then, we have output relation: $\mathbb{IF} \subseteq \mathbb{IF}'$, $CF_k' = CF_k + CF_{k-1}$, where $CF_0 = 1$.
For this MR: Suppose source frequent 1-itemsets are $F_1 = \{i_1\}, \cdots, \{i_c\}$, then follow-up frequent 1-itemsets are $F_1' = \{i_1\}, \cdots, \{i_c\}, \{a\}$, thus $F_1 \subseteq F_1'$, and $CF_1' = CF_1 + CF_0$. Source frequent 2-itemsets are

$F_2 = \{i_1, i_2\}, \cdots, \{i_{c-1}, i_c\}$, and follow-up frequent 2-itemsets are $F_2' = \{i_1, i_2\}, \cdots, \{i_1, a\}, \cdots, \{i_c, a\}$, thus $F_2 \subseteq F_2'$, and $CF_2' = CF_2 + CF_1$. By inductive deduction, we can get that there is $F_k \subseteq F_k'$, i.e. $\mathbb{F} \subseteq \mathbb{F}'$, and $CF_k' = CF_k + CF_{k-1}$.

(2) **MR2:** I' is constructed by inserting some new items $i_{m+1}, i_{m+2}, \cdots, i_{m+k}$ to I, where $i_{m+1}, i_{m+2}, \cdots, i_{m+k}$ are not in I. D' is constructed by inserting a new transaction T_{n+1}' to D, where the itemset in T_{n+1}' is $\{i_{m+1}, i_{m+2}, \cdots, i_{m+k}\}$. Then, we have output relation: $\mathbb{F}' \subseteq \mathbb{F}$, $CF_k' \leq CF_k$.

For this MR: The support count of each item in T_{n+1}' is "1", *Support* of these items is $1/(|D| + 1)$, which is less than min_sup we specified ($min\_sup > 1/|D|$), so these items are infrequent 1-itemsets. The support count of each itemset in the original FIs is unchanged after D inserted to T_{n+1}', while $|D'| = |D| + 1$, so *Supports* of these items are decreased, thus they may be IFIs, and the "original infrequent 1-itemsets" are still IFIs. The analysis for frequent k-itemsets is the same as above. Thus, $\mathbb{F}' \subseteq \mathbb{F}$, $CF_k' \leq CF_k$.

(3) **MR3:** I' is constructed by removing items that are contained in infrequent 1-itemsets of source test case from I. We denote the set of these items as I_{IFI}. D' is constructed by removing all items in I_{IFI} from each transaction T_i of D, where $i = 1, 2, \cdots, n$. Then, we have output relation: $\mathbb{F}' = \mathbb{F}$, $CF_k' = CF_k$.

For this MR: D' is received by removing all items in I_{IFI} from D, then the support count of each itemset is not changed and $|D'| = |D|$, so the *Support* of each itemset is not changed. Thus frequent k-itemsets are not changed. Thus, $\mathbb{F}' = \mathbb{F}$, $CF_k' = CF_k$.

(4) **MR4:** I' is constructed by inserting some new items $i_{m+1}, i_{m+2}, \cdots, i_{m+k}$ to I (where $i_{m+1}, i_{m+2}, \cdots, i_{m+k}$ are not in I), and removing I_{IFI} from I. D' is constructed by inserting a new T_{n+1}' to D (where the itemset in T_{n+1}' is $\{i_{m+1}, i_{m+2}, \cdots, i_{m+k}\}$), and removing I_{IFI} from each T_i of D, where $i = 1, 2, \cdots, n$. Then we have output relation: $\mathbb{F}' \subseteq \mathbb{F}$, $CF_k' \leq CF_k$.

3.2   MRs with Changes on min_sup

In the second group, we introduce MRs that keep the transaction database constant, but change min_sup.

(1) **MR5:** $I' = I$, $D' = D$, $min'\_sup < min\_sup$, then $\mathbb{F} \subseteq \mathbb{F}'$, $CF_k \leq CF_k'$.
(2) **MR6:** $I' = I$, $D' = D$, $min'\_sup > min\_sup$, then $\mathbb{F}' \subseteq \mathbb{F}$, $CF_k' \leq CF_k$.

It is easy to find that our proposed method can detect errors in results returned by an FI algorithm. In the next two sections, we will perform a simulation, to evaluate the effectiveness of our proposed method.

4   Setup for Simulation

We choose five datasets to perform our experiment and get the corresponding source and follow-up outputs (including original and mutated outputs). In our method, the corresponding outputs are compared against MRs. If a violation can be found, the corresponding malicious action is said to be detected. Specific experimental details will be described in Sects. 4.1, 4.2 and 4.3.

In our simulation, we calculate the "killing rate" (kr) for each batch of experiment as follows.

$$kr = \frac{number\_of\_violation}{total\_number\_of\_tests}$$

It should be noted that the greater the "killing rate", the better the malicious actions detection ability of MRs.

Specifically, we are interested to answer the following research questions.

RQ1. How about the fault detection ability of our proposed method?

We are concerned about how well our method works to detect the malicious actions. We further investigate the effects of mutation strategies which are depicted in Sect. 4.3, including malicious actions and error ratio, on the killing rate.

RQ2. Will different MRs deliver different performance?

We want to investigate whether there is some similarity between different MRs' ability to detect malicious actions. Further, we study whether some MRs are sensitive to some kinds of malicious actions.

RQ3. What are the key factors to good performing MRs?

We want to know which factors are related to the ability of MRs to detect malicious actions and which factors are irrelevant. Factors include the input relations and output relations of MRs.

4.1   Experimental Datasets

We run experiments with Apriori algorithm on five datasets which exhibit different characteristics. Synthetic datasets - "c20d10k", "t20i6d100k", and "t25i10d10k". Real-life datasets - "accidents" and "mushrooms".

As we all know, in actual industrial production, min_sup is determined by the clients, what's more, it is constantly changing for different kinds of datasets and requirements of clients. Therefore, in this experiment, in order to obtain a *reasonable min_sup* for each dataset, we first conduct a pre-experiment for each dataset. *Reasonable min_sup* means the number of FIs which we get based on min_sup is not too large or too small. Through the pre-experiment, we find that for "c20d10k", "accidents" and "mushrooms", the reasonable min_sup is around 0.4 and for "t20i6d100k" and "t25i10d10k", min_sup is about 0.008. Therefore, according to the requirements of different MRs and the results of the pre-experiment, we set min_sup for each dataset as follows:

– For "c20d10k", "accidents" and "mushrooms", the min_sup of the source inputs is set as 0.4. According to Sect. 3, min_sup of follow-up inputs are set as 0.4 for MR1 to MR4, 0.3 for MR5 and 0.5 for MR6.
– For "t20i6d100k" and "t25i10d10k", the min_sup of the source inputs is set as 0.008. According to Sect. 3, min_sup of follow-up inputs are set as 0.008 for MR1 to MR4, 0.007 for MR5 and 0.009 for MR6.

4.2 Experimental Subject

We choose SPMF [12] to conduct our experiment. SPMF is an open-source data mining library written in Java, specialized in pattern mining. As explained in Sect. 2.1, different FI mining algorithms deliver the same FI results. So we choose Apriori algorithm to generate the original source outputs and follow-up outputs.

4.3 Simulating Malicious Actions in Outsourcing Services

In our simulation, source and follow-up inputs are fed into FI miner individually, and the actual outputs are collected. Then, we mutate the outputs via the various strategies to simulate the malicious actions. In this paper, we consider three types of malicious actions, namely, deletion, insertion and replacement.

Let $\mathbb{F}_{TR}$ be the true result of mining and $\mathbb{F}_{RE}$ be the actual results returned by the server. $\mathbb{F}_{RE}$ may not be equal to $\mathbb{F}_{TR}$ and server may have performed a series of the following malicious actions:

Deletion. Server excludes some FIs from the true results. Formally, server picks some itemsets $X_1, X_2, \cdots, X_k \in \mathbb{F}_{TR}$ and returns $\mathbb{F}_{RE} = \mathbb{F}_{TR} - X_1 - X_2 - \cdots - X_k$.

Insertion. Server includes some IFIs in the returned set of FIs and declares that these itemsets are frequent. Formally, server picks some itemsets $X_1 \notin \mathbb{F}_{TR}, X_2 \notin \mathbb{F}_{TR}, \cdots, X_k \notin \mathbb{F}_{TR}$ and returns $\mathbb{F}_{RE} = \mathbb{F}_{TR} \cup X_1 \cup X_2 \cup \cdots \cup X_k$.

Replacement. Server selects some FIs and replaces them with IFIs. Formally, $X_1, X_2, \cdots, X_k \in \mathbb{F}_{TR}$, $X_1', X_2', \cdots, X_k' \notin \mathbb{F}_{TR}$ and returns $\mathbb{F}_{RE} = (\mathbb{F}_{TR} - X_1 - X_2 - \cdots - X_k) \cup X_1' \cup X_2' \cup \cdots \cup X_k'$.

Normally these malicious actions will be performed on the source and/or follow-up outputs, to simulate the corresponding malicious actions in real applications of third-party services. In the following discussion, we also refer these malicious actions as "errors".

Our mutation strategies involve atomic and composition actions performed both unilaterally and bilaterally. The simulated malicious actions are depicted in Table 2. In Table 2, "unilateral" means that the malicious action(s) are performed on either source or follow-up outputs; and "bilateral" means that the malicious action(s) are performed on both the source and follow-up returned outputs. "Atomic action" means that there is one and only one malicious action performed on the returned FIs. The ratio of simulated errors are set as $0.1\%, 0.2\%, 0.3\%, 0.4\%, 0.5\%, 0.6\%, 0.7\%, 0.8\%, 0.9\%$ and 1.0%. "Composite

Table 2. Mutation strategies to simulated malicious actions.

Unilateral		Bilateral			
Atomic action	Composite actions	Identical		Non-identical	
		Atomic action	Composite actions	Atomic action	Composite actions

actions" means that there are multiple actions performed on the returned FIs. Our experiment considers "deletion + insertion", "deletion + replacement", "insertion + replacement", as well as "replacement + insertion + deletion", denoted as "d_i", "d_r", "i_d", and "r_i_d", respectively. And the error rates for "d_i", "d_r", "i_d" are set as $0.2\%, 0.4\%, 0.6\%, 0.8\%, 1.0\%, 1.2\%, 1.4\%, 1.6\%, 1.8\%$ and 2.0%. The error rates for "r_i_d" are set as $0.3\%, 0.6\%, 0.9\%, 1.2\%,$ $1.5\%, 1.8\%, 2.1\%, 2.4\%, 2.7\%,$ and 3.0%.

As a reminder, for "bilateral" setting, we have both "identical" and "non-identical". "Identical" means that the malicious actions and the corresponding error rates on the source and follow-up outputs are exactly the same; while "non-identical" does not have this restriction, which aims to simulate the most general scenarios in reality.

5   Results and Analysis

In the course of the experiment, we found that most of the results of the five datasets we selected were the same, when MRs and/or malicious actions were determined. In addition to the "bilateral non-identical atomic" level, MR5 and MR6 have slightly different killing rates for different datasets, but the difference is small. So in the following results show, we take the average killing rates of five datasets as the result of each MR (for certain malicious action) in the following tables.

5.1   Overall Results of Our Proposed Method

First, let us consider "atomic action" performed unilaterally. Table 3 gives the results, where "Ms_Of" and "Os_Mf" means that the malicious actions are performed on source outputs and follow-up outputs, respectively; "de", "in" and "re" indicate "deletion", "insertion" and "replacement", respectively. The percentage in each cell is the average killing rate of five datasets under the corresponding scenario.

Results for "unilateral composite actions" are presented in Table 4, where "d_i", "d_r", "i_r" and "r_i_d" are explained in Sect. 4.3. The symbol "Cms_Of" and "Os_Cmf" means the composite malicious actions are performed on source outputs and follow-up outputs, respectively.

And results for "bilateral atomic actions" and "bilateral composite actions" (identical cases) are shown in Tables 5 and 6, respectively. The symbol "Act" means the "malicious actions" performed on the returned FIs.

Finally, results for "bilateral atomic actions" and "bilateral composite actions" (non-identical cases) are shown in Tables 7 and 8, respectively. For "unilateral" and "bilateral (identical cases)" actions, we can determine which malicious action is performed on each output and the error rate for each malicious action. However, for "bilateral (non-identical cases)" actions, we are not sure what kind of malicious action we have performed on source and follow-up outputs. Therefore, the design of Tables 7 and 8 is different from other tables mentioned above.

Table 3. Average killing rate of unilateral atomic actions.

Type	Ms_Of			Os_Mf		
Action	de	in	re	de	in	re
MR1	100%	100%	100%	100%	100%	100%
MR2	100%	0%	100%	0%	100%	100%
MR3	100%	100%	100%	100%	100%	100%
MR4	100%	0%	100%	0%	100%	100%
MR5	0%	100%	100%	100%	0%	100%
MR6	100%	0%	100%	0%	100%	100%

Table 4. Average killing rate of unilateral composite actions.

Type	Cms_Of				Os_Cmf			
Action	d_i	d_r	i_r	r_i_d	d_i	d_r	i_r	r_i_d
MR1	100%	100%	100%	100%	100%	100%	100%	100%
MR2	100%	100%	100%	100%	100%	100%	100%	100%
MR3	100%	100%	100%	100%	100%	100%	100%	100%
MR4	100%	100%	100%	100%	100%	100%	100%	100%
MR5	100%	100%	100%	100%	100%	100%	100%	100%
MR6	100%	100%	100%	100%	100%	100%	100%	100%

Table 5. Average killing rate of bilateral atomic actions (identical).

kr\MR Act	MR1	MR2	MR3	MR4	MR5	MR6
de	100%	100%	100%	100%	100%	100%
in	100%	0%	0%	0%	0%	0%
re	100%	100%	100%	100%	100%	100%

Table 6. Average killing rate of bilateral composite actions (identical).

kr\MR Act	MR1	MR2	MR3	MR4	MR5	MR6
d_i	100%	100%	100%	100%	100%	100%
d_r	100%	100%	100%	100%	100%	100%
i_r	100%	100%	100%	100%	100%	100%
r_i_d	100%	100%	100%	100%	100%	100%

Table 7. Average killing rate of bilateral atomic actions (non-identical).

MR	MR1	MR2	MR3	MR4	MR5	MR6
kr	100%	82.78%	98.89%	82.78%	80.62%	80.07%

Table 8. Average killing rate of bilateral composite actions (non-identical).

MR	MR1	MR2	MR3	MR4	MR5	MR6
kr	100%	100%	100%	100%	100%	100%

5.2 Effectiveness of Our Proposed Method (RQ1)

From the above tables, we can find that our method delivers quite satisfactory results. As compared with previous studies: For [19], their experiment setup is that e ranges from 0.1% to 1% and v ranges from 0.5% to 3%, where e is the error ratio of certain malicious action and v is a fraction which is used to set the target sizes of AFI and AII, and one error ratio e corresponds to six vs. So for each error ratio e, we calculate the average value of its corresponding killing rates of six vs as the average killing rate of this error ratio. Therefore, the average killing rate is about 72% for $e = 0.1\%$, 91% for $e = 0.2\%$, 95% for $e = 0.3\%$, 98% for $e = 0.4\%$, 99% for $e = 0.5\%$, 100% for $e \geq 0.6\%$; for [11], the average killing rate for the completeness and correctness is higher than β_1 and β_2 respectively, where $\beta_1, \beta_2 \in [0.7, 0.9]$ for probabilistic approach, and the killing rate for the completeness and correctness is 100% for deterministic approach.

It should be noted that though we have tuned error ratios in the mutation process we do not find any difference in the killing rates. The results in Tables 3, 4, 5, 6, 7 and 8 are valid for all the error ratios we have tried. In other words, we have answered that **the killing rates are not affected by the error ratios added to the outputs, but only depend on the type of malicious action performed**.

Let's take MR5 as an example to analyze the causes of this phenomenon, and the analysis of this phenomenon for other MRs can be carried out in a similar way.

(1) Scenario 1: Only one party in the source and follow-up outputs is interpolated with 0.1% certain atomic malicious action. The output relations of MR5 require $\mathbb{F} \subseteq \mathbb{F}'$, $CF_k \leq CF'_k$. When the original source outputs are performed "deletion", MR5 cannot find such malicious action, obviously. Otherwise, when the original follow-up outputs are performed "deletion", MR5 can find such malicious action because though the source outputs are the subsets of the follow-up outputs, they are almost the same, therefore MR5 are sensitive to "deletion" performed on follow-up outputs even if the error ratio is 0.1%. Other error ratio cases and atomic malicious actions performed unilaterally can be analyzed in a similar way.

(2) Scenario 2: Both source and follow-up outputs are interpolated with 0.1% "deletion" malicious action. Because the line numbers of FIs which are going to be deleted are generated randomly and they cannot be the same, so the mutated outputs must not satisfy the output relations which are required by MR5. Therefore, MR5 can detect 0.1% "deletion" performed on the corresponding outputs. Other error ratio cases can be analyzed in a similar way.

(3) Scenario 3: Both source and follow-up outputs are interpolated with 0.1% "insertion" malicious action. Let FI_{ar} denote "artificial frequent itemsets" (which are not exist in the real FIs) and $|FI_{ar}|$ denote the number of FI_{ar}. Based on the number of the original FIs (denoted as $|\mathbb{F}|$) and error ratios (denoted as e), we calculate the required $|FI_{ar}|$, $|FI_{ar}| = |\mathbb{F}| \times e$. FI_{ar} are generated by the previous infrequent 1-itemsets. The process of producing FI_{ar} is: Original infrequent 1-itemsets are regarded as "artificial frequent 1-itemsets", then we use these "artificial frequent 1-itemsets" to constitute "artificial frequent 2-itemsets" and so on. According to $|FI_{ar}|$ required by the experiment, the "artificial frequent itemset" is taken from FI_{ar} to add to the original FIs one by one to generate the mutated outputs. From the idea

of the experiments, we can conclude that the mutated source and follow-up FIs still satisfy the output relations required by MR5. Therefore, MR5 cannot detect 0.1% "insertion". Other error ratio cases can be analyzed in a similar way.

(4) Scenario 4: Both source and follow-up outputs are interpolated with 0.1% "replacement" malicious action. We calculate the number of FIs (denoted as $|f|$) which are needed to be replaced according to the number of the original FIs (denoted as $|\mathbb{F}|$) and error ratios (denoted as e), and $|f| = |\mathbb{F}| \times e$, then we randomly generate the line numbers of FIs which are needed to be replaced. Because it is over a wide range of data randomly generated a very small number of line numbers, so the source and follow-up FIs performed by "replacement" must be detected by MR5 no matter what error ratio is.

(5) Scenario 5: Source and follow-up outputs are performed "composite" malicious actions on both parties or either party of them. From scenario 4, we know that "replacement" must be detected whatever error ratio is and for "composite" malicious actions which contain "replacement" must be detected whatever error ratio is. As for "deletion + insertion", we can find that either "deletion" or "insertion" can be detected by MR5 at atomic level, so "deletion + insertion" can be detected whatever error ratio is. Therefore, "composite" malicious actions must be detected by MR5 whatever error ratio is.

5.3 Comparison Among the Proposed MRs (RQ2)

We group the six MRs based on their performance in Tables 3, 4, 5, 6, 7 and 8.

- The top tier is MR1, who always deliver the same killing rate of 100% for all malicious actions.
- The second tier is MR3, who is only worse than the top tier under the "insertion" of "bilateral atomic actions (identical)" (see Table 5), and "bilateral atomic actions (non-identical)" (see Table 7) .
- The third tier consists of MR2, MR4, MR5, and MR6, where MR5 is slightly different from the others in "unilateral atomic actions" (see Table 3), and "bilateral atomic actions (non-identical)" (see Table 7), and MR6 is slightly different from the others in "bilateral atomic actions (non-identical)", too.

By further investigating killing rates, we summarize the malicious actions to which an MR is sensitive.

(1) **For "deletion" malicious action:** MR1 and MR3 are sensitive to "deletion" in all atomic actions; MR2, MR4, and MR6 are only sensitive to "deletion" in the cases Ms_Of and "bilateral atomic actions (identical)"; MR5 is only sensitive to "deletion" in the cases Os_Mf and "bilateral atomic actions (identical)".

(2) **For "insertion" malicious action:** MR1 is sensitive to "insertion" in all atomic actions; MR2, MR4, and MR6 are only sensitive to "insertion" in the case Os_Mf; MR3 is only sensitive to "insertion" in "unilateral atomic actions"; MR5 is only sensitive to "insertion" in the case Ms_Of.

(3) **For "replacement" malicious action:** All MRs are sensitive to "replacement" in all atomic actions.

(4) **For "composite" malicious actions:** All MRs are sensitive to "composite" in all composite actions.

5.4 Mining the Key Factors to Fault Detection Ability (RQ3)

By comparing the six MRs, we are interested to know the reason for the different performance. In this section, we address RQ3 by giving a list of observations.

1. **MRs with complex input relations are not necessary to good metamorphic testing performance.**
   As we can see that the input relations of MR4 are composed of the input relations of MR2 and MR3. MR1, MR2, MR3, MR5, and MR6 are atomic MRs. In other words, the input relations of MR4 are more complex than those of MR1, MR2, MR3, MR5, and MR6.
   (1) MR4 is composed of MR2 and MR3, while its killing rate is equal to MR2 and is lower than MR3. From the experiment results, we can see that the killing rate of MR2 is equal to MR4 for all malicious actions, while the killing rate of MR3 is 100%, 98.89% for "unilateral atomic action" and "bilateral atomic actions (non-identical)", espectively, which are higher than that of MR4 (see Tables 3 and 7). So we can conclude that the performance of MR4 is similar to MR2 and is worse than MR3.
   (2) As for MR5 and MR6, their input relations are the simplest, however, from Tables 3, 4, 5, 6, 7 and 8, we can find that the killing rate of MR5 and MR6 is similar to MR2 and MR4. So we can conclude that the performance of MR5 and MR6 is similar to MR2 and MR4.
   From the analysis above, we can draw a conclusion: MRs with complex input relations are not necessary to good metamorphic testing performance.

2. **MRs with tight output relations have higher killing rate than that with loose output relations.**
   (1) The output relations of MR1 is the tightest: $\mathbb{F} \subseteq \mathbb{F}'$, $CF'_k = CF_k + CF_{k-1}$. From the results, we can find that the killing rate of MR1 is 100% for all errors, which means that error detection ability of MR1 is the best. Because our mutation strategies is directed against the FIs, and the malicious actions performed on the outputs are random. Therefore, the output relation, $CF'_k = CF_k + CF_{k-1}$, required by MR1 cannot be satisfied if any malicious action is performed on FIs.
   (2) The second tightest requirement for output relations is MR3. It requires that $\mathbb{F}' = \mathbb{F}, CF'_k = CF_k$. The error detection ability of MR3 is slightly worse than that of MR1. The output relations for MR3 are requested to be **equal** which is a harsh condition, however, the killing rate of MR3 is 0% for "insertion" in "bilateral atomic action (identical)". MR3 is specific at this level, the original source and follow-up FIs are the same, so the "artificial FIs" which should be inserted to the original FIs are the

same according to our experimental ideas explained above, therefore the mutated source and follow-up FIs are the same, so MR3 cannot detect this malicious action.

(3) The loosest requirement for output relations is MR2, MR4, MR5, and MR6. They require that $\mathbb{F}' \subseteq \mathbb{F}$, $CF'_k \leq CF_k$ (for MR2, MR4, and MR6) or $\mathbb{F} \subseteq \mathbb{F}'$, $CF_k \leq CF'_k$ (for MR5). As shown in Tables 3 and 7, the error detection ability of them is worse than that of MR3.

From what have discussed above, we can conclude that MRs with tight output relations have higher killing rate than that with loose output relations.

5.5   Comparison with Previous Methods

An early study to verify the integrity of the results returned by outsourcing services is proposed by Wong et al. [19]. Their technique generates an artificial database based on AFI and AII to develop an audit environment to verify the integrity of the mining answer by the server. Dong et al. conduct follow-up studies by proposing a probabilistic method and a deterministic method to verify the correctness and completeness of the returned FI mining results [11].

However, the method [19] requires great extra effort in the verification. First, the client has to take extra time and space to construct and store AFI and AII, as well as the support counts of all itemsets in AFI and their subsets must also be computed and recorded. During the verification, the clients must (1) check whether there is any AII itemset returned as a FI by the service provider and (2) for all itemsets in AFI and the subsets thereof, compare the support counts given by the third-party service provider with the stored counts. Obviously, these actions could be very expensive. Secondly, to construct an audit environment, the authors proposed to decide the sizes of AFI and AII according to the number of frequent itemsets and the number of itemsets in the negative border of its database. However, to figure out the corresponding numbers requires prior knowledge to the dataset or a lot of extra work. More importantly, the dataset on the data owner side is constantly updated in very high frequency. As a consequence, the above numbers must also be updated accordingly, which is impractical. The method [11] improves Wong et al.'s method by eliminating some unrealistic assumptions, however, it is still suffering from high cost issue. First, the probabilistic approach requires a lot of pre-processing and post-processing, such as construction of evidence frequent itemsets, construction of evidence infrequent itemsets, removal of artificial frequent itemsets, and recovering missing real frequent itemsets. Secondly, the deterministic approach also requires a lot of pretreatment and the verification procedure of correctness and completeness is complex, such as setting intersection verification protocol, construction of authenticated data structure, and proof construction should be done at server side before verification at client side. As compared with previous works, our metamorphic-based method has some advantages: (1) Our method is based on metamorphic relations and the main task is to construct MRs and implement the proposed MRs. Hence, we do not need extra pre-processing, post-processing and complex techniques. In other words, our method is light-weight, without much complicated processes required. (2) As the experiment results shown in Tables 3, 4, 5, 6, 7 and 8, our method has high malicious actions detection ability. (3) Moreover, our method takes into account the "composite" actions, especially the "bilateral non-identical" malicious actions, which simulate the most general scenarios in reality and are not considered in previous studies.

Apart from the above advantages, our method actually requires more resources: (1) Because it is based on metamorphic relations, the number of follow-up datasets depends on the number of MRs we proposed, which means that our method requires extra storage for follow-up datasets, and the more the number of MRs, the more storage space it needs. However, as discussed above, the previous works not only require extra storage, but also they require extra time and processing and etc. (2) With extra follow-up datasets, our method requires more communication with the third-party services, which may lead to higher charges. However, we argue that these extra resources will not lead to much higher cost, because the third-party frequent itemsets mining services are usually charged based on the usage period (e.g. charge monthly), rather than the usage frequency.

6   Conclusions

This paper mainly verifies the integrity of the frequent itemsets received from the outsourcing services. Our contribution is a metamorphic-based method which is light-weight and requires not much complicated process compared with other previous works discussed above. And we propose a set of metamorphic relations for FI mining algorithms, and they have good performance to verify the integrity of the results returned by the outsourcing services. From the experiment results, we can draw the following conclusions:

(1) The implementation of our method is relatively simple, which does not need complex algorithms, complex prior knowledge, extra processing, and is much easier to be understood and applied in practice.
(2) We get several good performance MRs which delivers quite satisfactory results. And it should be noted that the killing rates are not affected by the error ratios added to the outputs, but only depend on the type of malicious actions we performed, for our method.
(3) For different malicious actions, "replacement" and "composite" are the easiest to be detected, and the killing rates of MRs for these two actions are 100%. Moreover, MR1 has the best error-checking ability, which can detect all kinds of malicious actions.
(4) MRs with complex input relations are not necessary to good metamorphic testing performance and MRs with tight output relations have higher killing rate than that with loose output relations.

This paper provides a pioneer study to verify the integrity of the frequent itemsets mining based on the idea of metamorphic testing. In our future work, we will propose more MRs, and conduct more comprehensive empirical analysis to investigate their effectiveness.

References

1. Agrawal, R., Imieliński, T., Swami, A.: Mining association rules between sets of items in large databases. In: Proceedings of the 1993 ACM SIGMOD International Conference on Management of Data, vol. 22, pp. 207–216. ACM (1993)
2. Agrawal, R., Mannila, H., Srikant, R., Toivonen, H., Verkamo, A.I., et al.: Fast discovery of association rules. Adv. Knowl. Discov. Data Min. **12**(1), 307–328 (1996)
3. Alwidian, J., Hammo, B.H., Obeid, N.: WCBA: weighted classification based on association rules algorithm for breast cancer disease. Appl. Soft Comput. **62**, 536–549 (2018)
4. Aravindhan, R., Shanmugalakshmi, R., Ramya, K.: Circumvention of nascent and potential Wi-Fi phishing threat using association rule mining. Wirel. Pers. Commun. **94**(4), 2331–2361 (2017)
5. Barr, E.T., Harman, M., McMinn, P., Shahbaz, M., Yoo, S.: The oracle problem in software testing: a survey. IEEE Trans. Softw. Eng. **41**(5), 507–525 (2015)
6. Berry, M.J., Linoff, G.: Data Mining Techniques: For Marketing, Sales, and Customer Support. Wiley, Hoboken (1997)
7. Borgelt, C.: Efficient implementations of Apriori and Eclat. In: 2003 Proceedings of the IEEE ICDM Workshop on Frequent Itemset Mining Implementations (2003)
8. Chan, W.K., Cheung, S.C., Leung, K.R.: A metamorphic testing approach for online testing of service-oriented software applications. Int. J. Web Serv. Res. **4**(2), 61–81 (2007)
9. Chen, T.Y., Cheung, S.C., Yiu, S.M.: Metamorphic testing: a new approach for generating next test cases. Technical report, Technical Report HKUST-CS98-01, Department of Computer Science, Hong Kong University of Science and Technology, Hong Kong (1998)
10. Chen, T.Y., Ho, J.W., Liu, H., Xie, X.: An innovative approach for testing bioinformatics programs using metamorphic testing. BMC Bioinformatics **10**(1), 24 (2009)
11. Dong, B., Liu, R., Wang, H.W.: Trust-but-verify: verifying result correctness of outsourced frequent itemset mining in data-mining-as-a-service paradigm. IEEE Trans. Serv. Comput. **9**(1), 18–32 (2016)
12. Fournier-Viger, P., Gomariz, A., Gueniche, T., Soltani, A., Wu., C., Tseng, V.S.: SPMF: a Java open-source pattern mining library (2016). http://www.philippe-fournier-viger.com/spmf/
13. Han, J., Pei, J., Yin, Y.: Mining frequent patterns without candidate generation. In: Proceedings of the 2000 ACM SIGMOD International Conference on Management of Data, vol. 29, pp. 1–12. ACM (2000)
14. Kotsiantis, S., Kanellopoulos, D.: Association rules mining: a recent overview. GESTS Int. Trans. Comput. Sci. Eng. **32**(1), 71–82 (2006)
15. Kuo, F.C., Chen, T.Y., Tam, W.K.: Testing embedded software by metamorphic testing: a wireless metering system case study. In: 2011 Proceedings of IEEE 36th Conference on Local Computer Networks, pp. 291–294. IEEE (2011)
16. Pang, H., Jain, A., Ramamritham, K., Tan, K.L.: Verifying completeness of relational query results in data publishing. In: 2005 Proceedings of the ACM SIGMOD International Conference on Management of Data, pp. 407–418. ACM (2005)
17. Rolfsnes, T., Moonen, L., Di Alesio, S., Behjati, R., Binkley, D.: Aggregating association rules to improve change recommendation. Empir. Softw. Eng. **23**(2), 987–1035 (2018)
18. Weyuker, E.J.: On testing non-testable programs. Comput. J. **25**(4), 465–470 (1982)

19. Wong, W.K., Cheung, D.W., Hung, E., Kao, B., Mamoulis, N.: An audit environment for outsourcing of frequent itemset mining. PVLDB **2**(1), 1162–1173 (2009)
20. Xie, M., Wang, H., Yin, J., Meng, X.: Integrity auditing of outsourced data. In: 2007 Proceedings of the 33rd International Conference on Very Large Data Bases, pp. 782–793. VLDB Endowment (2007)
21. Xie, X., Ho, J., Murphy, C., Kaiser, G., Xu, B., Chen, T.Y.: Application of metamorphic testing to supervised classifiers. In: 2009 Proceedings of the Ninth International Conference on Quality Software, pp. 135–144. IEEE (2009)
22. Xie, X., Ho, J.W., Murphy, C., Kaiser, G., Xu, B., Chen, T.Y.: Testing and validating machine learning classifiers by metamorphic testing. J. Syst. Softw. **84**(4), 544–558 (2011)
23. Zaki, M.J., Parthasarathy, S., Ogihara, M., Li, W., et al.: New algorithms for fast discovery of association rules. In: 1997 Proceedings of the Third International Conference on Knowledge Discovery and Data Mining, vol. 97, pp. 283–286 (1997)

CMSuggester: Method Change Suggestion to Complement Multi-entity Edits

Ye Wang[1(✉)], Na Meng[1], and Hao Zhong[2]

[1] Virginia Tech, Blacksburg, VA 24061, USA
{yewang16,nm8247}@vt.edu
[2] Shanghai Jiao Tong University, Shanghai 200240, China
zhonghao@sjtu.edu.cn

Abstract. Developers spend significant time and effort in maintaining software. In a maintenance task, developers sometimes have to simultaneously modify multiple program entities (*i.e.*, classes, methods, and fields). We refer to such complex changes as *multi-entity edits*. It is challenging for developers to apply multi-entity edits consistently and completely. Existing tools provide limited support for such edits, mainly because the co-changed entities usually contain diverse program contexts and experience different changes. This paper introduces CMSuggester, an automatic approach that suggests complementary changes for multi-entity edits. Given a multi-entity edit that adds a field and modifies one or more methods to access the field, CMSuggester suggests other methods to co-change for the new field access. CMSuggester is inspired by our previous empirical study, which reveals that *the methods co-changed to access a new field usually commonly access the same set of fields declared in the same class*. By extracting the fields accessed by the given changed method(s), CMSuggester identifies and recommends any unchanged method that also accesses those fields.

Our evaluation shows that CMSuggester recommends changes for 279 out of 408 suggestion tasks. With the recommended methods, CMSuggester achieves 73% F-score on average, while the widely used tool ROSE achieves 48% F-score. In most cases, as shown in our evaluation results, CMSuggester are useful for developers, since it recommend complete and correct multi-entity edits.

Keywords: Multi-entity edit · Common field access
Change suggestion

1 Introduction

Developers spend almost 70% of time and resources in maintenance to fix bugs, add features, or refactor code [11]. Due to the complexity of modern software systems, developers sometimes apply complex changes by modifying multiple program entities (*i.e.*, classes, methods, and fields) for one maintenance task. Herzig *et al.* [15] report that more than half of maintenance issues are related

© Springer Nature Switzerland AG 2018
L. Bu and Y. Xiong (Eds.): SATE 2018, LNCS 11293, pp. 137–153, 2018.
https://doi.org/10.1007/978-3-030-04272-1_9

to bug fixes, and Zhong and Su [32] report that developers fixed around 80% of real bugs by editing multiple program locations together. *A multi-entity edit is a program commit that simultaneously changes multiple entities.* It is challenging for developers to always apply multi-entity edits consistently and completely. Park et al. studied why some bug fixes failed to repair bugs [24], and observed that developers sometimes failed to identify all the edit locations relevant to a bug. For instance, they can forget to update the value initialization of a newly added field in certain methods.

Existing tools provide limited support for how to apply multi-entity edits [17, 22,30,33]. For instance, Zimmerman et al. [33] and Ying et al. [30] independently developed tools to mine the association rules between co-changed entities from software version histories, e.g., *"if method A is changed, method B is also changed"*. Based on such rules, when developers change method A, method B is automatically suggested as a likely change. However, the suggestion accuracy of these tools is low for two reasons. First, they do not observe any syntactic or semantic relationship among co-changed entities. If some entities are *accidentally* co-changed in history, the resulting inferred rules are incorrect, and can produce false positives (e.g., false alarms) when predicting changes. Second, if some entity pairs were never co-changed in history, these tools cannot infer or predict any potential co-change of the entities in the future, causing false negatives.

Another related tool is LSDiff [17]. Given a textual diff, LSDiff infers systematic structural differences as logic rules, and detects anomalies from systematic changes as exceptions to the inferred logic rules. One sample rule is *"All classes implementing type A have method B deleted except class C."* LSDiff mainly focuses on systematic entity additions and deletions, instead of entity changes (or updates). LASE infers a general program transformation from the exemplar edits in several similarly changed methods, and leverages the inferred transformation to (1) locate other methods for change and (2) suggest customized edits [22]. LASE is useful only when similar methods should be changed similarly; it does not help if distinct edits should be co-applied to dissimilar methods.

A recent study reveals a ***CM→AF** change pattern, which popularly exists in multi-entity edits [28]. **AF** means *Added Field*, while ***CM** represents one or more *Changed Methods*. The pattern shows that when one field is added, developers usually change multiple methods together to access the field. As the co-changed methods usually contain different program contexts and experience divergent changes, developers may forget to change *all* relevant methods to access the new field. This paper introduces a novel approach—CMSuggester— that suggests methods to co-change and helps developers completely apply such edits.Specifically, we first conducted a preliminary study (Sect. 3) to explore whether there is any syntactic or semantic relationship between the co-changed entities in ***CM→AF** edits. We found that the co-changed methods usually access common fields before an edit is applied. It indicates that **there are clusters of methods that access the same sets of fields**. If one or more methods in a cluster are changed to access a new field, the other methods from the same cluster are likely to be co-changed for the new field access.

Based on the observation, we developed CMSuggester to suggest complementary changes for *CM→AF multi-entity edits (Sect. 4). Specifically, given an added field (f_n) and one or more changed methods, CMSuggester first extracts existing fields accessed by the changed methods. If some of such fields (i) have the same naming pattern as f_n, and (ii) are accessed in the same way as f_n (*i.e.*, purely read, purely written, or read-written), CMSuggester considers them as the *peer fields* of f_n. CMSuggester then locates any unchanged method that accesses the peer fields, and suggests those methods as candidate change locations.

In this paper, we made the following contributions:

- We designed and implemented a novel approach CMSuggester that suggests complementary changes for *CM→AF edits.
  The approach is based on our empirical study [28], which reveals that the co-changed methods for an added field usually access existing fields in common. CMSuggester can be integrated to Integrated Development Environment (IDE) or version control systems to help developers completely apply multi-entity changes.
- We compared CMSuggester with a widely used tool ROSE [33], in terms of their change suggestion capability. We leveraged 106 real multi-entity edits from 4 open source projects to construct 408 change suggestion tasks. Within each task, a tool is given one added field and one related changed method as input to predict likely changes. CMSuggester recommends changes for 279 of these tasks. Among the 279 cases, CMSuggester's recommendation obtains 75% precision, 72% recall, and 73% F-score on average. Meanwhile, ROSE suggests changes in only 117 cases, obtaining 41% precision, 58% recall, and 48% F-score. The results indicate that CMSuggester effectively complements ROSE when suggesting changes for *CM→AF edits.
- We defined two filters in CMSuggester to ensure accurate method change suggestion. By disabling the filters, we implemented three variants of CMSuggester, and the evaluation results on these variants show our filters improve our f-scores by about 10%. Especially, the naming-based filter achieves a better trade-off between precision and recall than the access-based filter.

2   Motivating Example

Developers can fail to fully apply changes in tasks requiring multi-entity edits. Figure 1 shows a simplified program revision to Derby [4]—a Java-based relational database. The added code is colored with **blue** and marked with "**+**". In this revision, developers added a field _clobValue (line 5) and modified 12 methods in different ways to access the field (e.g., changing getLength() at lines 8–9). However, developers forgot to also change restoreToNull() (lines 15–20). Consequently, the multi-entity edit is incomplete. The inadvertently "*missed change*" remained in the software for more than two years, until developers finally inserted a statement _clobValue = null; to restoreToNull() [7].

It is challenging for developers to examine or ensure the completeness of such multi-entity edits. When a method fails to be changed to access a new field, compilation error are often not triggered, neither can any well-known bug detector reveal the problem. In this example, the missing field access in `restoreToNull()` did not introduce any compilation errors, and was identified two years after it was first introduced.

In this paper, we developed CMSuggester, a tool that identifies complementary changes and helps developers avoid incomplete multi-entity edits. For this example, given the added field `_clobValue` and the changed method `getLength()`, CMSuggester identifies two existing fields accessed by `getLength()`: `rawLength` and `stream`. Similar to `_clobValue`, these fields are *purely read* by the method. Thus, CMSuggester considers both fields as *peers* of the new field. CMSuggester then searches for any method that accesses the peer fields but has not been changed to access the new field. In this way, CMSuggester finds `restoreToNull()`—

```
1  public class SQLChar extends
2       DataType implements
3       StringDataValue, StreamStorable{
4  ...
5 + protected Clob _clobValue;
6  public int getLength() throws
7       StandardException{
8 +   if ( _clobValue != null ) {
9 +     return getClobLength(); }
10    if (rawLength != -1)
11      return rawLength;
12    if (stream != null) {
13  ...
14  }
15  public void restoreToNull() {
16    value = null;
17    stream = null;
18    rawLength = -1;
19    cKey = null;
20 }}
```

Fig. 1. A program revision requires 1 field addition and 13 method-level changes. However, developers changed only 12 of the 13 methods, ignoring `restoreToNull()` for change [6]. (Color figure online)

which accesses the peer fields in the same *"pure write"* mode—and recommends the method for change. With CMSuggester, developers can identify the change locations that they may otherwise miss when applying multi-entity edits.

3 Our Empirical Finding

In our prior study [28], we analyzed 2,854 bug fixes from four popular open source projects to explore multi-entity edits, including Aries [2], Cassandra [3], Derby [4], and Mahout [5]. Our study shows that recurring change patterns commonly exist in all the projects. In particular, ***CM→AF** is one of the most popular patterns. Therefore, in this paper, we sampled five such commits in each project to manually analyze the co-changed methods for any newly added field.

Table 1 presents our inspection results. For each added field, there are 2–5 methods co-changed to access the field. We manually compared co-changed methods to identify any commonality between them. We found that **in 15 of the 20 examined revisions, the co-changed methods commonly access existing field(s) before the edits are applied.** Among the other five program commits, two commits have co-changed methods to commonly invoke certain method(s), while the remaining ones have no commonality among them. Our finding shows that when one or more methods in a cluster are changed to access a new field, the other methods from the same cluster are likely to be co-changed

Table 1. Commonality inspection of 20 ***CM→AF** multi-entity edits

Project	Commits	Added field	# of changed methods	Commonality
Aries	3d072a4	monitor	2	Field access
	50ca3da	properties	2	Field access
	5d334d7	BEAN	2	Method invocation
	95766a2	NS_AUTHZ	2	None
	9586d78	enlisted	3	Field access
Cassandra	0792766	validBufferBytes	3	Field access
	0963469	isStopped	2	Field access
	0d1d3bc	componentIndex	3	Field access
	1c9c47d	nextFlags	2	Field access
	266e94f	STREAMING_SUBDIR	2	Method invocation
Derby	f578f070	stateHoldability	2	Field access
	6eb5042	outputPrecision	2	Field access
	2f41733	MAX_OVERFLOW_ONLY_REC_SIZE	3	None
	099e28f	XML_NAME	3	Field access
	81b9853	activation	5	Field access
Mahout	0be2ea4	LOG	2	Field access
	0fe6a49	FLAG_SPARSE_ROW	2	Field access
	22d7d31	namedVector	2	Field access
	29af4d7	normalizer	2	Field access
	2f7f0dc	NUM_GROUPS_DEFAULT	2	None

for the new field access. This finding is consistent with the Object Oriented (OO) paradigm, since OO emphasizes to group related data in the same structure to ease modification and understanding [25].

4   Approach

Section 3 shows *it is promising to suggest methods for change based on the accessed fields by already-changed methods.* Inspired by that, we developed CMSuggester with the hypothesis that *similar field usage indicates methods' co-change relationship*.

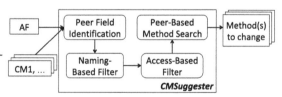

Fig. 2. CMSuggester's overview

Figure 2 shows the overview of the approach. Given an edit that adds a field and changes one or more methods to access the field, CMSuggester extracts peer fields from the changed method(s) (Sect. 4.1), filters the fields based on naming patterns and access modes (Sects. 4.2 and 4.3), and searches for any unchanged method with the refined fields for change suggestion (Sect. 4.4).

4.1   Peer Field Identification

Based on our finding in Sect. 3, we believe that when a cluster of methods need to commonly access a cluster of fields to implement relevant functionalities, the fields are more likely to be defined in the same class. Given a newly added field f_n, we use **peer fields** to denote the existing fields that are (1) declared in the same class as f_n, and (2) accessed by one or more changed methods that also access f_n. For our motivating example, the newly added field is _clobValue, and we identify that in the method getLength(), rawLength and stream are its peer fields. CMSuggester traverses the AST of each changed method's old version to extract the accessed existing fields, obtaining a peer field set $P = \{p_1, p_2, \ldots\}$.

4.2   Naming-Based Filtering

We notice that peer fields may have diverse powers to indicate the usage of f_n. To ensure CMSuggester's accuracy when suggesting methods for change, we refined the peer fields P with two intuitive filters. The first filter leverages the heuristic that *similarly named fields are more likely to be used similarly than other fields*. This filter compares peer fields with f_n, and removes any field whose naming pattern is different from f_n's. We observed **two naming patterns** that developers usually followed when defining fields.

- **Pattern 1:** The names of constant fields (e.g., static final) capitalize all involved letters, such as MAX_OVERFLOW_ONLY_REC_SIZE.
- **Pattern 2:** The names of variable fields use lowercase or a combination of lowercase and uppercase letters, such as outputPrecision.

We rely on the naming patterns to classify fields as variables or constants. If f_n is a variable, it is likely to be similarly used to existing variable fields, so we filter out the constant peers in P. Similarly, if f_n is a constant, we can use the constant peers to suggest f_n's usage, and remove variable peers from P.

4.3   Access-Based Filtering

This filter implements another heuristic that *similarly accessed fields are more likely to have similar usage*. For each method, we classify the accessed fields into three access modes: **pure read**, **pure write**, and **read-write**, depending on how each field is accessed. For instance, if a method reads and writes a field, we put the field into the *"read-write"* category of that method. To implement the filter, CMSuggester scans the internal representation (IR) of each CM's old version created by WALA [10], and checks if an accessed field serves as a left or right value of each IR instruction. If the field serves as a right value, it is read by an instruction; otherwise, it is written. When a field's access mode is distinct from that of f_n, CMSuggester removes the field from P.

4.4   Peer-Based Method Search

With the refined fields, CMSuggester searches for methods to co-change by identifying any unchanged method that accesses at least two refined fields. In the search, CMSuggester scans a large portion of code, because a program revision usually changes a small portion of code while keeping the majority code unchanged [32]. To improve the search efficiency, we leveraged the access modifiers of f_n to reduce search space. Specifically, if f_n is a `private` field, only the methods declared by f_n's declaring class C are analyzed because f_n is not visible to any method outside C. Similarly, if f_n is a `protected` field, only the methods declared in C and C's subclasses are analyzed. In the worst case, when a field f_n is a `public` field, it is visible to any method in the whole project; thus, we cannot reduce the search space, but instead scan all unchanged methods.

5   Evaluation

This section explains our data set (Sect. 5.1) and presents our defined metrics to evaluate CMSuggester's effectiveness (Sect. 5.2). The experiments discussed in Sects. 5.3 and 5.4 were designed to explore the following two research questions:

- **RQ1:** What is CMSuggester's effectiveness to predict methods for change, and how does it compare with ROSE?
- **RQ2:** How does CMSuggester's effectiveness vary with the two used filters?

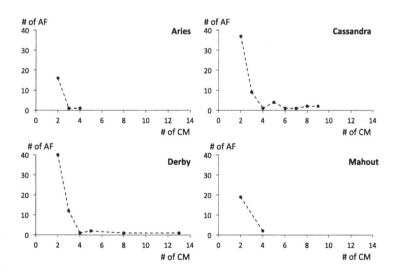

Fig. 3. The distribution of AFs based on the number of corresponding CMs

5.1 Data Set

We created an evaluation data set based on the data of our prior work [28]. We searched for any ***CM→AF** edit that (1) contains at least two methods co-changed for an added field, and (2) has each changed method accessing at least two existing fields. In this way, we found 10 commits, 45 commits, 42 commits, and 9 commits separately in the revision data of Aries, Cassandra, Derby, and Mahout, among which each commit contains one or more ***CM→AF** edits. Figure 3 shows the distribution of added fields (AFs) based on the number of changed methods (CMs) corresponding to them. Each commit has one or more added AFs, in which each AF is related to 2–13 CMs. In particular, among the 9 commits from Mahout, there are 21 AFs applied. 19 of these AFs have 2 CMs co-applied; while each of the other 2 AFs are co-applied with 4 CMs.

For each AF, we constructed suggestion tasks by providing the AF and some of its co-applied CMs to CMSuggester as input, and using the remaining part as the oracle to evaluate CMSuggester's output. For instance, suppose that a commit has one added field f_n and two changed methods $M = \{m_1, m_2\}$. In one task, we provide f_n and m_1 to CMSuggester, and check whether CMSuggester suggests m_2 for change. Alternatively, we can provide f_n and m_2 to CMSuggester, and check whether CMSuggester's output is m_1. In this way, if a ***CM→AF** edit has one AF and n CMs ($n \geq 2$), we can create n **one-AF-one-CM (1A1C)** tasks based on the edit. In each task, only one AF and one CM are provided as input, and all the other CM(s) is/are treated as the expected output. Similarly, we can create **one-AF-two-CM (1A2C)** and **one-AF-three-CM (1A3C)** tasks. As the majority of AFs in our data set correspond to 2–4 CMs, our experiments mainly focus on 1A1C, 1A2C, and 1A3C tasks, as shown in Table 2.

Table 2. Evaluation data set

	Aries	Cassandra	Derby	Mahout	Total #
# of program commits	10	45	42	9	106
# of 1A1C suggestion tasks	39	172	151	46	408
# of 1A2C suggestion tasks	9	237	168	12	426
# of 1A3C suggestion tasks	4	379	366	8	757

5.2 Metrics

We defined and used four metrics to measure a tool's capability of suggesting methods for change: coverage, precision, recall, and F-score. We also defined the weighted average to measure a tool's overall effectiveness among all subject projects for each of the metrics mentioned above.

Coverage (C) measures the percentage of tasks for which a tool is able to provide suggestion. Given a task, a tool may or may not suggest any change to complement the already-applied edit, so this metric assesses a tool's applicability.

$$C = \frac{\# \text{ of tasks with a tool's suggestion}}{\text{Total } \# \text{ of tasks}} * 100\% \tag{1}$$

Intuitively, if a tool always suggests something given a task, its coverage is 100%, and thus the tool is widely applicable. All our later evaluations for precision, recall, and F-score are limited to the tasks covered by a tool. For instance, suppose that given 100 tasks, a tool can suggest changes for 8 tasks. Then the tool's coverage is $8/100 = 8\%$, and the evaluations for other metrics are based on these 8 tasks instead of the original 100 tasks.

Precision (P) measures among all methods suggested by a tool, how many of them are correct:

$$P = \frac{\# \text{ of correct suggestions}}{\text{Total } \# \text{ of suggestions by a tool}} * 100\% \tag{2}$$

This metric evaluates how precisely a tool suggests changes. If all suggestions by a tool are contained by the oracle or expected output, the precision is 100%.

Recall (R) measures among all the expected suggestions, how many of them are actually reported by a tool:

$$R = \frac{\# \text{ of correct suggestions by a tool}}{\text{Total } \# \text{ of expected suggestions}} * 100\% \tag{3}$$

This metric assesses how effectively a tool retrieves the expected outcome. Intuitively, if all expected suggestions are reported by a tool, the recall is 100%.

F-score (F) measures the accuracy of a tool's suggestion:

$$F = \frac{2 * P * R}{P + R} * 100\% \tag{4}$$

F-score is the harmonic mean of precision and recall. Its value varies within [0%, 100%]. The higher F values are desirable, as they demonstrate better trade-offs between the precision and recall rates.

Weighted Average (WA) measures a tool's **overall effectiveness** among all experimented data in terms of coverage, precision, recall, and F-score:

$$\Gamma_{overall} = \frac{\sum_{i=1}^{4} \Gamma_i * n_i}{\sum_{i=1}^{4} n_i}. \tag{5}$$

In the formula, i varies from 1 to 4, representing Aries, Cassandra, Derby, and Mahout in sequence. n_i represents the number of tasks built from the ith project. Γ_i represents any measurement value of the ith project for coverage, precision, recall, or F-score. By combining such measurement values of all projects in a weighted way, we are able to assess a tool's overall effectiveness $\Gamma_{overall}$.

5.3   Comparison with ROSE

To assess CMSuggester's capability of suggesting complementary changes, we used CMSuggester to complete the tasks mentioned in Table 2 (*i.e.*, 1A1C, 1A2C, and 1A3C). To understand how CMSuggester is compared with prior work, we also executed the state-of-the-art co-change suggestion tool, ROSE [33], for the same tasks. ROSE mines the association rules between co-changed entities from software version histories. Below presents an exemplar rule mined by ROSE [33]:

$$\{(\_Qdmodule.c, func, GrafObj\_getattr())\} \Rightarrow \\ \{(qdsupport.py, func, outputGetattrHook()).\} \tag{6}$$

This rule means that whenever the function `GrafObj_getattr()` in a file _Qdmodule.c is changed, the function `outputGetattrHook()` in another file qdsupport.py should also be changed. We configured ROSE with support=1, confidence=0.1, because the paper [33] mentioned this setting more often than other settings.

Table 3 shows the results of CMSuggester and ROSE for 1A1C tasks. Overall, CMSuggester obtained higher measurement values for all the projects than ROSE. Particularly for Mahout, CMSuggester predicted likely changes for 72% of the tasks, while ROSE provided predictions for 13% of the tasks. Among the generated suggestions, CMSuggester achieved 72% precision, 68% recall, and 70% F-score; while ROSE obtained 5% precision, 33% recall, and 9% F-score. CMSuggester's weighted average values for coverage, precision, recall, and F-score are 68%, 75%, 72%, and 73%, while ROSE's corresponding weighted average values are 29%, 41%, 58%, and 48%.

Table 3. CMSuggester vs. ROSE for 1A1C tasks (%)

Project	CMSuggester				ROSE			
	C	P	R	F	C	P	R	F
Aries	51	68	85	76	31	35	39	37
Cassandra	69	81	75	78	38	53	71	61
Derby	71	71	68	69	22	25	42	31
Mahout	72	72	68	70	13	5	33	9
WA	**68**	**75**	**72**	**73**	**29**	**41**	**58**	**48**

Two major reasons can explain why CMSuggester outperformed ROSE. First, ROSE uses the co-changed entities in version histories to predict likely changes. When the history data are incomplete or some entities were never co-changed before, ROSE lacks the evidence to predict some

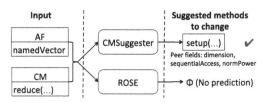

Fig. 4. A task for which CMSuggester outperformed ROSE

co-changes, obtaining lower coverage and recall rates. Second, ROSE does not leverage any syntactic or semantic relation between the co-changed entities. ROSE can infer incorrect rules from co-changed but unrelated entities, achieving lower precision.

Figure 4 presents a task for which CMSuggester outperformed ROSE. This task is extracted from the commit 22d7d31 [9] of Mahout. In the task, there is one AF `PartialVectorMergeReducer.namedVector` and one CM `PartialVectorMergeReducer.reduce(...)` provided as input, and another CM provided as the expected output. CMSuggester succesfully predicted `PartialVec-torMergeReducer. setup(...)` based on the three peer fields extracted from the given CM. However, ROSE could not predict any method, because the version history did not manifest any association rule between `reduce(...)` and `setup(...)`.

Figure 5 shows a task for which ROSE worked better than CMSuggester. This task is from the commit f06e1d6 [1] of Cassandra. It provides one AF `Session.compactionStrategy` and one CM `Session.Session(...)` as input, and includes another CM as the oracle. CMSuggester predicted nothing, because the

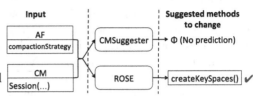

Fig. 5. A task for which ROSE outperformed CMSuggester

identified peer fields in `Session(...)` are not commonly used by any unchanged method. However, ROSE correctly suggested one method `Session.createKeySpaces(...)`. Our results show that CMSuggester can complement ROSE by suggesting co-changes in a different way.

Finding 1: *CMSuggester outperformed ROSE in many 1A1C tasks. This means that CMSuggester complements ROSE by inferring co-changes from methods' common field accesses instead of from the history.*

In addition to 1A1C tasks, we also compared CMSuggester with ROSE for 1A2C and 1A3C tasks, as shown in Tables 4 and 5. The tools have similar F-scores. For 1A2C tasks, CMSuggester obtained 61% F-score, while ROSE achieved 62%. For 1A3C tasks, the F-score comparison is 61% vs. 60%. More importantly, CMSuggester obtained much higher coverage rates than ROSE for both types of tasks. In Table 4, the coverage compar-

Table 4. CMSuggester vs. ROSE for 1A2C tasks (%)

Project	CMSuggester				ROSE			
	C	P	R	F	C	P	R	F
Aries	89	35	50	41	0	-	-	-
Cassandra	76	65	66	65	31	63	69	66
Derby	96	65	55	60	3	7	15	10
Mahout	100	35	39	37	0	-	-	-
WA	**85**	**63**	**60**	**61**	**8**	**59**	**66**	**62**

ison is 85% vs. 8%. For Aries and Mahout, CMSuggester achieved 89% and 100%, meaning that it predicted changes for the majority of tasks. However, ROSE predicted nothing for either project. In Table 5, CMSuggester's coverage is 88%, while ROSE's is 17%. Especially for Aries, Derby, and Mahout, CMSuggester achieved 100% coverage, while ROSE covered 0% of the tasks.

The coverage comparisons in Tables 3, 4, and 5 show that given an arbitrary task, CMSuggester is more likely to provide suggestions than ROSE, and the suggestion accuracy is at least comparable to ROSE's. Two reasons can explain it. First, ROSE is limited by the available historical co-change data. If certain methods have never been changed together in history, ROSE can not find potential co-

Table 5. CMSuggester vs. ROSE for 1A3C tasks (%)

Project	CMSuggester				ROSE			
	C	P	R	F	C	P	R	F
Aries	100	12	25	16	0	-	-	-
Cassandra	75	56	62	59	33	57	64	60
Derby	100	66	61	63	0	0	0	-
Mahout	100	21	25	23	0	-	-	-
WA	**88**	**61**	**61**	**61**	17	57	63	60

changes between the methods. Second, when more CMs are provided, CMSuggester can detect more peer fields from more methods, and leverage the fields to predict more. Suppose CMSuggester can predict changes $M1 = \{m_{1a}, m_{1b}, \ldots\}$ based on CM1, and predict changes $M2 = \{m_{2a}, m_{2b}, \ldots\}$ based on CM2. Given CM1 and CM2, CMSuggester predicts the joint set of M1 and M2 by outputting $M_s = \{m_{1a}, m_{2a}, m_{1b}, m_{2b}, \ldots\}$. However, ROSE always intersects the prediction sets of individual CMs to ensure its prediction precision. Thus, with the CM1 and CM2, ROSE outputs $M_r = M1 \cap M2$, which covers less methods than M_s.

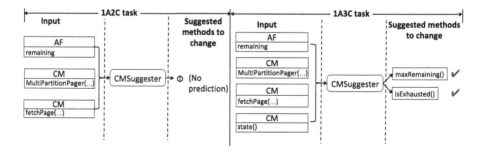

Fig. 6. CMSuggester predicts better when more CMs are provided as input

Figure 6 presents two tasks from Cassandra, showing that when more CMs are provided as input, CMSuggester can predict better. These tasks are from the commit 7c32ffb [8], in which one AF and five CMs were applied by developers. For the 1A2C task, CMSuggester was given one AF and two CMs. Since CMSuggester could not identify enough peer fields from the methods to predict changes, it predicted nothing. In contrast, when CMSuggester was given one more CM in the 1A3C setting, it was able to identify enough peer fields from the third method `MultiPartitionPager.state()` and correctly suggested two methods.

> **Finding 2:** *For 1A2C and 1A3C tasks, when multiple CMs were provided as input, CMSuggester outperforms ROSE by achieving better coverage and at least comparable accuracy. Overall, CMSuggester works better than ROSE when suggesting complementary changes for *CM→AF edits.*

5.4   Sensitivity to Filter Settings

Two filters were used in CMSuggester to refine the peer fields. To understand how each filter affects CMSuggester's effectiveness, we built three variant approaches:

- CMSuggester$_o$: We disabled both filters, and leveraged all detected peer fields in the input CM(s) to predict changes.
- CMSuggester$_n$: We only used the naming-based filter to refine peer fields but disabled the access-based filter.
- CMSuggester$_a$: We refined peer fields only with the access-based filter while turning off the naming-based filter.

Table 6. CMSuggester vs. its three variant approaches with filters on or off (%)

Project	CMSuggester				CMSuggester$_o$				CMSuggester$_n$				CMSuggester$_a$			
	C	P	R	F	C	P	R	F	C	P	R	F	C	P	R	F
Aries	51	68	85	76	77	70	83	76	72	70	86	77	56	67	86	75
Cassandra	69	81	75	78	88	78	76	77	80	81	74	77	75	79	76	77
Derby	71	71	68	69	97	63	60	61	94	66	63	64	73	67	64	65
Mahout	72	72	68	70	96	6	57	56	74	72	68	70	93	56	57	56
WA	**68**	**75**	**72**	**73**	**91**	**69**	**68**	**68**	**84**	**73**	**70**	**71**	**75**	**71**	**70**	**70**

We applied all three variants to the 1A1C tasks. Table 6 presents the effectiveness comparison between CMSuggester and the variants. According to this table, CMSuggester obtained the lowest overall coverage (68%), but the highest overall precision (75%), recall (72%), and F-score (73%). This is as expected, because CMSuggester applied two filters to refine the detected fields as much as possible. As a result, fewer fields passed both filters and suggested fewer but more accurate changes. CMSuggester$_o$ achieved the highest coverage (91%) but lowest F-score (68%). Since it did not refine peer fields before predicting changes, some of the included peer fields are used less similarly to the newly added fields, causing incorrect suggestions.

Compared with CMSuggester$_a$, CMSuggester$_n$ obtained better coverage (84% vs. 75%), better precision (73% vs. 71%), equal recall (both 70%), and better F-score (71% vs. 70%). This is out of our expectation. Although the naming-based filter seems more intuitive and is easier to implement than the access-mode filter, it obtained a better trade-off among coverage, precision, and recall. This may indicate that developers usually name fields in meaningful ways. Thus, the similarity in fields' names can more effectively indicate methods' co-change relationship than the similarity in access modes. When some fields are named similarly, even though they are accessed divergently by one or more CMs, the fields' co-occurrence can still effectively predict methods for change.

> **Finding 3:** *Both filters used in CMSuggester effected to improve F-score at the cost of coverage. Especially, the naming-based filter achieved a better balance between F-score and coverage than the access-based filter.*

6   Threats to Validity

Threats to External Validity. Our evaluation results show that CMSuggester outperforms ROSE, as far as only one change pattern is concerned. However, as our prior work [28] found more patterns, it is feasible to extend CMSuggester, and we believe that CMSuggester can outperform ROSE in more cases. Furthermore, based on our manual inspection, we believe that our patterns are not specific to only Apache projects, so CMSuggester can outperform ROSE, even if we select projects from other open source communities as the subjects. In the future, we will support more patterns and evaluate the tools on subjects from more software repositories. We also plan to develop a hybrid approach of ROSE and CMSuggester. By relating methods based on common field accesses and historic co-change relationship, the hybrid approach is guaranteed to suggest changes when either tool predicts something, and may provide more precise suggestions if both tools' outputs can cross-validate each other.

Threats to Construct Validity. When we prepared the golden standards, we constructed suggestion tasks from manual fixes. Yin *et al.* [29] show that a bug fix can be not fully correct, which can lose useful co-changes. It is possible that developers made mistakes when making some multi-entity edits. Therefore, the imperfect evaluation data set based on developers' edits may affect our assessment for both CMSuggester and ROSE. We share this limitation with prior work [22,27,33]. In the future, we plan to mitigate the problem by conducting user studies with developers. By carefully going through the edits made by developers and the complementary changes suggested by CMSuggester or other tools, we can further evaluate the usefulness of different tools' suggestions.

7   Related Work

Our research is related to co-change mining, automatic change recommendation, and automatic program repair.

Co-change Mining. Tools were built to mine version histories for co-change patterns [12,13,26,30,33]. Specifically, Gall et al. mined release data for the co-change relationship between subsystems [12] and classes [13]. Shirabad et al. trained a machine-learning model to predict whether two given files should be changed together [26]. However, none of these approaches analyze any syntactic or semantic relationship between co-changed modules. Hassan et al. created a framework to predict change propagation based on the historical co-changes, caller-callee relationship of methods, def-use relationship of fields, and/or entities' co-occurrence in the same file [14]. They found that the historic co-changes had better prediction capability than other types of information. Instead of mining software repositories, CMSuggester identifies co-changed methods based on the commonly accessed fields, and complemented above-mentioned approaches when the revision history is limited or unavailable.

Change Recommendation Systems. Researchers built tools to recommend code changes [17,19,22,23]. For instance, PR-Miner was created to mine the implicit API invocation rules (e.g., `lock()` and `unlock` should be called together), to detect any code violating the rules, and to suggest changes that complement existing API invocations [19]. Clever is a tool tracking all clone groups in software and monitoring for edits on clones [23]. If one clone is detected to be updated, Clever lists all its clone peers, and recommends relevant changes. These approaches recommend changes based on either the co-occurrence of APIs or code similarity. In comparison, CMSuggester recommends changes based on the common field accesses between methods.

Automatic Program Repair (APR). There are tools proposed to generate candidate patches for certain bugs, and automatically check patch correctness using compilation and testing [16,18,20,21,31]. For example, GenProg [18] generated candidate patches by replicating, mutating, or deleting code randomly from the existing programs. Genesis trained a machine-learning model by extracting features from existing bug fixes, and suggesting candidate patches accordingly [20]. CMSuggester is different from APR in two aspects. First, CMSuggester focuses on multi-entity changes by suggesting method changes to complement already-applied edits. However, APR focuses on single-entity changes by creating single-method updates from scratch. Second, CMSuggester locates methods to change, while APR approaches generate concrete and applicable statement-level changes as a candidate fix. We believe that CMSuggester is valuable because it is challenging to locate places to change in large codebases, and it needs to locate such places, before APR tools can generate changes.

8 Conclusion

When developers change multiple entities simultaneously for one maintenance task, it can be challenging for them to identify all relevant entities to edit. This paper presents CMSuggester, a novel approach that suggests complementary changes for multi-entity edits. Different from prior work that relates co-changed methods based on their historic co-change relationship or similar program contexts, CMSuggester takes a different perspective by modeling the common field accesses between methods. Our evaluation shows that CMSuggester outperforms ROSE when suggesting complementary changes for ***CM→AF** edits—a type of frequently applied complex changes. Since ROSE can work well in certain scenarios where CMSuggester does not suggest changes, we plan to explore a hybrid approach between the tools in the future. To better characterize the strengthens and weaknesses of different tools, we will also apply CMSuggester and other tools to suggest changes for more types of multi-entity edits.

Acknowledgment. We thank anonymous reviewers for their valuable comments on our earlier version of the paper. This work was supported by NSF Grant CCF-1565827, National Basic Research Program of China (973 Program) No. 2015CB352203, the National Nature Science Foundation of China No. 61572313, and the grant of Science and Technology Commission of Shanghai Municipality No. 15DZ1100305.

References

1. Support of compaction strategy option for stress.java. https://github.com/apache/cassandra/commit/f06e1d63a2006aa95d36636c56561158c8758a3c
2. Apache Aries (2018). http://aries.apache.org
3. apache/cassandra (2018). https://github.com/apache/cassandra
4. apache/derby (2018). https://github.com/apache/derby
5. apache/mahout (2018). https://github.com/apache/mahout
6. DERBY-2201: Allow scalar functions to return LOBs (2018). https://github.com/apache/derby/commit/638f1b48afc27c094c7f34a6254778c1a4ad9608
7. DERBY-5162: Null out the wrapped Clob when resetting a SQLClob to NULL (2018). https://github.com/apache/derby/commit/e9737b6
8. Fix infinite loop when paging queries with IN (2018). https://github.com/apache/cassandra/commit/7c32ffb
9. MAHOUT-401: Use NamedVector in seq2sparse (2018). https://github.com/apache/mahout/commit/22d7d31
10. WALA (2018). http://wala.sourceforge.net/wiki/index.php/Main_Page
11. Christa, S., Madhusudhan, V., Suma, V., Rao, J.J.: Software maintenance: from the perspective of effort and cost requirement. In: Satapathy, S., Bhateja, V., Joshi, A. (eds.) Proceedings of the International Conference on Data Engineering and Communication Technology, vol. 469, pp. 759–768. Springer, Singapore (2017). https://doi.org/10.1007/978-981-10-1678-3_73
12. Gall, H., Hajek, K., Jazayeri, M.: Detection of logical coupling based on product release history. In: Proceedings of ICSM, pp. 190–198 (1998)
13. Gall, H., Jazayeri, M., Krajewski, J.: CVS release history data for detecting logical couplings. In: Proceedings of IWPSE, pp. 13–23 (2003)
14. Hassan, A.E., Holt, R.C.: Predicting change propagation in software systems. In: Proceedings of ICSM, pp. 284–293 (2004)
15. Herzig, K., Just, S., Zeller, A.: It's not a bug, it's a feature: how misclassification impacts bug prediction. In: Proceedings of ICSE, pp. 392–401 (2013)
16. Kim, D., Nam, J., Song, J., Kim, S.: Automatic patch generation learned from human-written patches. In: Proceedings of ICSE, pp. 802–811 (2013)

17. Kim, M., Notkin, D.: Discovering and representing systematic code changes. In: Proceedings of ICSE, pp. 309–319 (2009)
18. Le Goues, C., Nguyen, T., Forrest, S., Weimer, W.: Genprog: a generic method for automatic software repair. IEEE Trans. Softw. Eng. **38**(1), 54 (2012)
19. Li, Z., Zhou, Y.: PR-Miner: automatically extracting implicit programming rules and detecting violations in large software code. In: Proceedings of ESEC/FSE, pp. 306–315 (2005)
20. Long, F., Amidon, P., Rinard, M.: Automatic inference of code transforms for patch generation. In: Proceedings of ESEC/FSE, pp. 727–739 (2017)
21. Long, F., Rinard, M.: Automatic patch generation by learning correct code. In: Proceedings of POPL, pp. 298–312 (2016)
22. Meng, N., Kim, M., McKinley, K.: LASE: locating and applying systematic edits. In: Proceedings of ICSE, pp. 502–511 (2013)
23. Nguyen, T.T., Nguyen, H.A., Pham, N.H., Al-Kofahi, J.M., Nguyen, T.N.: Clone-aware configuration management. In: Proceedings of ASE, pp. 123–134 (2009)
24. Park, J., Kim, M., Ray, B., Bae, D.H.: An empirical study of supplementary bug fixes. In: Proceedings of MSR, pp. 40–49 (2012)
25. Rumbaugh, J., Blaha, M., Premerlani, W., Eddy, F., Lorensen, W.: Object-Oriented Modeling and Design. Prentice-Hall Inc., Upper Saddle River (1991)
26. Shirabad, J.S., Lethbridge, T.C., Matwin, S.: Mining the maintenance history of a legacy software system. In: Proceedings of ICSM, pp. 95–104 (2003)
27. Tan, M.: Online defect prediction for imbalanced data. Master's thesis, University of Waterloo (2015)
28. Wang, Y., Meng, N., Zhong, H.: An empirical study of multi-entity changes in real bug fixes. In: Proceedings of ICSME (2018)
29. Yin, Z., Yuan, D., Zhou, Y., Pasupathy, S., Bairavasundaram, L.: How do fixes become bugs? In: Proceedings of ESEC/FSE, pp. 26–36 (2011)
30. Ying, A.T.T., Murphy, G.C., Ng, R.T., Chu-Carroll, M.: Predicting source code changes by mining change history. IEEE Trans. Softw. Eng. **30**(9), 574–586 (2004)
31. Zhong, H., Mei, H.: Mining repair model for exception-related bug. J. Syst. Softw. **141**, 16–31 (2018)
32. Zhong, H., Su, Z.: An empirical study on real bug fixes. In: Proceedings of ICSE, pp. 913–923 (2015)
33. Zimmermann, T., Weisgerber, P., Diehl, S., Zeller, A.: Mining version histories to guide software changes. In: Proceedings of ICSE, pp. 563–572 (2004)

Mining Function Call Sequence Patterns Across Different Versions of the Project for Defect Detection

Zhanqi Cui[1(✉)], Xiang Chen[2], Yongmin Mu[1], Zhihua Zhang[1], and Xu Ma[1]

[1] Computer School, Beijing Information Science and Technology University, Beijing, China
{czq,yongminmu,zhang_zh}@bistu.edu.cn, maxu@mail.bistu.edu.cn
[2] School of Computer Science and Technology, Nantong University, Nantong, China
xchencs@ntu.edu.cn

Abstract. Large scale programs usually imply many programming rules, which are missing from specification documents. However, if programmers violate these rules in the process of programming, they may introduce software defects. Mining programming rules for detecting defect is an effective way to alleviate this problem. However, previous works suffer from a large number of candidate rules and suspicious defects which need manual validation. This issue affects the applicability and scalability of these previously proposed approaches. This paper proposes a novel approach to detect defects based on programming rules mined from different versions of a project. Firstly, it mines function call sequence patterns from the version under analysis and a previous stable version; secondly, it filters useful function call sequence patterns based on the patterns contained in the previous version; thirdly, the programs are automatically checked against filtered patterns for detecting suspicious defects. Experiments are carried out on three open source projects varies from 12k to 142k LOC to evaluate the effectiveness of our proposed approach. The experiment results show that the approach can improve the efficiency of defect detection by reducing 55% suspicious defects for the three projects without comprising the defect detection capability.

Keywords: Programming rules · Version history · Defect detection

1 Introduction

A large number of programming rules are implied in programs. Due to the limitation of developing time and schedule, many of the rules are missing from proper specifications. For instance, Saied et al. [1] carried out an observational

This work is supported by the National Natural Science Foundation of China (Grant No. 61702041), and the Science and Technology Project of Beijing Municipal Education Commission (Grant No. KM201811232016).

L. Bu and Y. Xiong (Eds.): SATE 2018, LNCS 11293, pp. 154–169, 2018.
https://doi.org/10.1007/978-3-030-04272-1_10

study on API usage constraints and their documentations, the results show that three out of four constraint types, from 79% to 88% usage constraints are non-documented. In addition, some of the rules hide deeply, and software engineers are even not aware of their existence. As a result, traditional approaches, like code review, cannot find defects violating these rules. If these rules are violated in some way, when programming, defects would be introduced into the software. Defect mining is an effective way to alleviate this kind of defects [2]. In defect mining, models are constructed from related data, such as code and documents, then they are used to mine defect patterns or programming rules. Defect mining approaches can be automated to a large extent. Recently, a large body of successful applications of defect mining are conducted [3,4].

However, one of the most important problems, which restrict the scalability and applicability of defect mining, is the huge number of programming rules and suspicious defects reported. For instance, PR-Miner [5] found 32283 program candidate rules, and reported 1447 suspicious defects after inter-procedural analysis; Legunsen et al. [6] carried out experiments on 200 open-source projects, the results found 97.89% of 200 suspicious defects which violate automatically mined specifications are false positives. The process of validating suspicious defects manually could consume a lot of time and efforts, and highly depended on the experience and expertise of the engineers. Moreover, this process is hard to automate and error prone.

In addition, with the widespread of modern software engineering methods, such as agile methods, and the rapid development of mobile Internet, the characteristics of iterative development lead to frequent updates. This produces a large number of historical versions. For example, the Today's Headline, which is one of the most popular mobile news applications in China, released 4 versions for Android platform in July 2018. Almost one new version is released every week. A lot of information could be contained in so many historical versions of the program.

Proposed Solution. In order to improve the efficiency of defect detection by mining programming rules, we propose a novel approach to mine programming rules for defect detection by utilizing the historical version information. Firstly, it obtains function call information from different versions of a program to mine function call sequence patterns; secondly, it checks the consistence between the two set of programming patterns, filters out patterns according to the change of confidence; thirdly, it checks for suspicious defects, which violate the filtered patterns. In the experimental study, we evaluate this approach in terms of time costs, the number of reported candidate rules and suspicious defects. After experimental results analysis, we find that a large portion of function call sequence patterns are contained across different versions. The experimental results show that by utilizing the historical version information, the number of suspicious defects can be dramatically reduced without comprising the defect detection capability.

Contributions. The main contributions of this paper are summarized as follows:

- propose an approach of mining function call sequence patterns from different versions of a project and the patterns are used to find defects. This approach improves the efficiency of detecting defects by filtering patterns and reduces the number of suspicious defects by utilizing the information of the historical version.
- a prototype tool is implemented based on above approach, and experiments are carried on a series of open source projects to evaluate the effectiveness of the approach.

The rest of the paper is organized as follows. Section 2 discusses how to mine function call sequence patterns from two different versions and how to detect defects with the filtered patterns. Section 3 presents the experimental design and evaluation. Section 4 reviews related work. Finally, we conclude this paper and discuss the future work in Sect. 5.

2   Our Approach

In this paper, we propose a novel approach to mine implied function call sequence patterns across different versions of a project, and the patterns are used to find defects. Suppose there is a stable version V_α being used by the users and a new version V_β under analysis for next release. The flowchart of the approach is described in Fig. 1. At first, it obtains function call information from the two versions of the program and mines for function call sequence patterns, respectively; then, it filters out programming rules of the new version according to the confidence change of the rules with respect to the stable version; finally, it checks for suspicious defects in the new version which violate the rules filtered out.

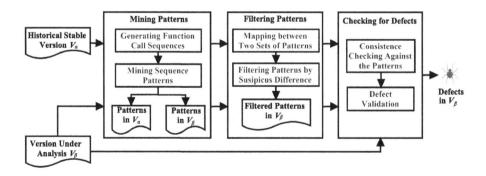

Fig. 1. The flow chart of our approach.

2.1   Mining Function Call Sequence Patterns

Functions are basic functional modules, which compose a program. A version of a program V which is composed by n functions can be expressed as a set $\{FD_1, FD_2, \cdots, FD_n\}$. The definition of a function, which is composed by m statements, can be expressed as $FD_i = \{s_{i,1}, s_{i,2}, \cdots, s_{i,m}\}$. Statements in the program can be categorized as variable define/use, conditional branch, function call etc. The control flow, data flow, point-to information can be obtained by static analysis [7,8]. The function call statement is a kind of statements which call other methods to complete the expected feature of a method. The function call statements in the body of a method FD_i is a sequence $FC_i = \langle fc_{i,1}, fc_{i,2}, \cdots, fc_{i,j}, \cdots \rangle (fc_{i,j} \in FD_i)$, according to the order of their appearance. This sequence can express the function call relationship in some extent. For simplicity, the function call statements are processed as a sequence, the control and data flows are not analyzed in this paper.

Suppose $I = \{i_1, i_2, \cdots, i_o\}$ is the set of all the items, D is a database of sequences. An itemset is a non-empty set of items in I, while a sequence is an ordered list of itemsets $\langle is_1, is_2, \cdots, is_p \rangle$. An element is_u in the sequence is a set of items, which can be denoted as $(x_1, x_2, \cdots, x_q)$. The elements in a sequence are ordered, when $u < v$, is_u happens before is_v. While the items in an itemset are unordered. A sequence $s_a = \langle a_1, a_2, \cdots, a_x \rangle$ is a subsequence of another sequence $s_b = \langle b_1, b_2, \cdots, b_y \rangle$ if and only if there exist integers $1 \le i_1 < i_2 < i_x \le y$, where $a_1 \subseteq b_{i_1}, a_2 \subseteq b_{i_2}, \cdots, a_x \subseteq b_{i_x}$. In other words, s_b contains s_a in this case. Mining sequential patterns is to find frequent sequence patterns in D with user specified minimum support, where the support count of a sequence is the number of data sequences that contain the sequence.

For a version of a program under analysis, the dataset of sequences is $V = \{FC_1, FC_2, \cdots, FC_n\}$. FC_i is a sequence composed by function call statements which are items. Suppose a sequence s, the support count of s is the number of sequences in V which contain s. *Support* is the rate of sequences, which contain s in the database, which is defined as Eq. (1).

$$support(s, V) = \frac{supCount(s, V)}{|V|} \tag{1}$$

Support is used to measure the commonness of a sequence pattern. A threshold value *minSup* is set as a lower bound. The sequence patterns with *support* no less than *minSup* are called frequent sequence patterns. The frequent function call sequence patterns of a program are denoted as a set *FCS*, which is adopted for the following analysis.

GSP algorithm [9] is taken to mine frequent function call sequence patterns in programs. On the basis of AprioriAll [10], GSP introduces maximum and minimum gaps between adjacent elements of the sequential pattern as time constraints. In mining function call patterns, when the distance of function call statements in a pattern is large, the likelihood of existing associations between them is low, and it is probably a false pattern. In this approach, we mine frequent function call patterns in both version V_α and V_β to generate two pattern sets FCS_α and FCS_β, respectively. The details of mining function call sequence patterns can be found in [11].

2.2 Filtering Sequence Patterns by Analyzing the Historical Version

In order to improve the efficiency of detecting defects, the patterns across different versions are utilized. Many implied programming rules can be found as frequent patterns in both version V_α and V_β, while other patterns are only frequent or even only exist in one version. As illustrated in Fig. 2, considering the function call sequence patterns of V_β, six cases may arise with respect to function call sequences of V_α.

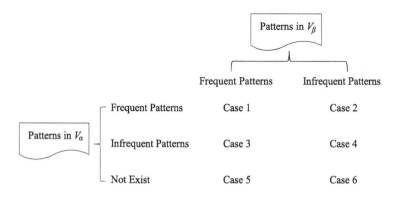

Fig. 2. Six cases of function call sequence patterns between two different versions.

Function call sequence patterns in case 1, 2, 3 and 4 are related to function calls both contained in V_α and V_β, while patterns in case 5 and 6 are related to new functions or libraries introduced in V_β as updates. Patterns in case 1, 3 and 5 are chosen as candidate patterns.

To evaluate the certainty of a sequence pattern, we define its *confidence* as the proportion of function call sequences which contain the pattern out of the sum of function call sequences either contain or violate the pattern in the program. For a sequence pattern s and a version of the program V, the *confidence* of s with respect to V is defined as Eq. (2). The definition of violating will be further explained in Subsect. 2.3. We set $minConf$ as a threshold value for confidence, if the confidence of a pattern is smaller than $minConf$, it probably a false pattern. The sequence patterns are measured by *confidence* to reflect the certainty of the rule.

$$confidence(s, V) = \begin{cases} \frac{supCount(s,V)}{supCount(s,V)+vioCount(s,V)} & , if\, supCount(seq, V) > 0 \\ 1 & , if\, supCount(seq, V) = 0 \end{cases}$$

$$(2)$$

For a stable version V_α and a new version V_β, the *confidence* change of a sequence pattern s is defined as Eq. (3).

$$\delta_{conf}(s, V_\alpha, V_\beta) = confidence(V_\beta, s) - confidence(V_\alpha, s) \qquad (3)$$

Because V_α has been thoroughly tested and used by users for a period of time, we gain more confidence on V_α than V_β. If the confidence of a pattern decreases, which means new places violating the rule are found in V_β. In this case, new defects probably are introduced in V_β. Otherwise, the confidence remaining the same or increasing means there is no new defects related to this rule are introduced in V_β. We assume that the programmer writes correct code in most of the time and only makes mistakes occasionally. As a result, if the confidence of a pattern increases or decreases too much, it may be a false pattern as well. δ_{max} is set as a threshold value for δ_{conf}, patterns with $|\delta_{conf}|$ greater than δ_{max} are considered to be false positives.

Based on the above heuristic intuitions, the function call sequence candidate patterns can be filtered from three facets: (1) rule out candidate patterns with confidence less than $minConf$; (2) rule out candidate patterns with δ_{conf} greater than or equal to 0; (3) rule out candidate patterns with $|\delta_{conf}|$ greater than δ_{max}. The process of filtering candidate patterns is described in Algorithm 1.

Algorithm 1. Filtering function call sequence pattern candidates

Input:
    Program: V_α and V_β //*two versions of a program*
    Set: FCS_α and FCS_β
    //*two sets of corresponding function call sequence pattern candidates of V_α and V_β*
Output:
    Set: FCS_β'//*sequence patterns of V_β filtered out from FCS_β*
1: **for** each s_i in FCS_β **do**
2:     // *rule out patterns with low confidences*
3:     **if** *confidence* $(seq_i, V_\beta) \geq minConf$ **then**
4:         // *s_i is also a sequence pattern in V_α*
5:         **if** $s_i \in FCS_\alpha$ **then**
6:             $\delta_{conf}=$ *confidence* $(s_i, V_\beta) - confidence$ (s_i, V_α)
7:             **if** $\delta_{conf} < 0$ and $|\delta_{conf}| \leq \delta_{max}$ **then**
8:                 FCS_β'.add(s_i)
9:             **end if**
10:        **else**
11:            // *s_i is not a sequence pattern in V_α*
12:            FCS_β'.add(s_i)
13:        **end if**
14:     **end if**
15: **end for**
16: **return** FCS_β'

2.3 Checking Program Against the Sequence Patterns for Defects

After the function call sequence patterns are filtered out, the program is scanned to find code segments which violate the patterns as suspicious defects.

A function call sequence FC of a function definition, which not including a function call sequence pattern $s = \langle fcs_1, fcs_2, \cdots, fcs_k \rangle$ is called a *violation* when FC includes a subsequence s' of s, $s' = \langle fcs_1, \cdots, fcs_{i-1}, fcs_{i+1} \cdots, fcs_k \rangle$, but a function call statement $fcs_i (1 < i \le k)$ is not included in FC.

A violation means the function definition violates a function call sequence pattern, and a suspicious defect is detected. To measure certainty of a reported defect quantitatively, we define the *suspicious* of a defect as Eq. (4).

$$suspicious(s, V_\alpha, V_\beta) = \begin{cases} 1 + \delta_{conf}(s, V_\alpha, V_\beta) \,, if \delta_{conf}(s, V_\alpha, V_\beta) < 0 \\ 0 \qquad\qquad\qquad , if \delta_{conf}(s, V_\alpha, V_\beta) \ge 0 \end{cases} \quad (4)$$

To control the cost of validating suspicious defects, the reported potential defects are further reduced by the value of *suspicious*. A threshold value *minSus* is set as a lower bound, only violations with *suspicious* no less than *minSus* are reported as suspicious defects, since we assume programmers only make mistakes occasionally.

The process of checking program against function call sequence patterns is described in Algorithm 2. However, the generated rules are potential function usage sequence patterns in statistics sense, the suspicious defects still need to be manually checked for validation.

Algorithm 2. Checking program against function call sequence patterns

---

Input:
    Program: V_α and V_β //*two versions of a program*
    Set: FCS_β' //*filtered function call sequence patterns of* V_β
Output:
    Set: *bugList*//*a set of suspicious defects reported for manually validating*
1: **for** each s_i in FCS_β' **do**
2:    // *rule out patterns with low suspicious*
3:    **if** $suspicious(s_i, V_\alpha, V_\beta) \ge minSus$ **then**
4:      **for** each FD_j in V_β **do**
5:        $FC_j \leftarrow$ the sequence of function call statement in FD_j
6:        **if** FC_j is a violation of s_i **then**
7:          $bugList$.add(FC_j)
8:        **end if**
9:      **end for**
10:    **end if**
11: **end for**
12: **return** *bugList*

---

3 Experiments and Evaluation

3.1 Tool Implementation

We implemented a prototype tool CV-Miner to evaluate the effectiveness of our approach. The development and experiments are carried on Intel i7 2.3 GHz CPU and 8 GB memory hardware platform, pycparser 2.14, Ubuntu 16.04 and Python 3.5 software platform.

The tool is composed by two main modules. **The program analysis module** generates function call sequences in both two versions of the program, then uses Rapidminer 7.2.1[1] to mine function call sequence patterns, respectively. **The defect detection module** filters out the patterns by synthesizing the two sets of patterns, then the version under analysis is checked against the filtered patterns to find function definitions which violate the patterns, then reports the positions as suspicious defects.

3.2 Experimental Design

In our evaluation, we would like to answer these research questions:

RQ1. Is it common that many programming rules across different versions of a project are the same?

RQ2. Can historical versions improve the efficiency of detecting defects by filtering programming rules?

RQ3. Can this approach comprise the capability of defects detection?

To answer these questions and evaluate the effectiveness of our approach, we compare CV-Miner with our previous work [11] on mining sequence patterns for detecting defects (called Seq-Miner for simplifying in this paper). We conducted experiments on a series of open source projects and compare the two methods from three facets: time costs, the number of reported function call sequence patterns and suspicious defects.

To facilitate the comparison, we follow the experiment subjects in [11], which include memory database Redis[2], cross-platform scripting language Lua[3], and embedded database Sqlite[4]. These projects are selected from a blog of Open Source China, which recommends 10 excellent open source projects written in C for programmers to read and study[5]. The size of the different versions of the three projects varies from 12k to 142k LOC.

The statistical information of the three projects is shown in Table 1. The "Versions" column lists the version of the projects, the upper one is the β version under analysis, and the lower one is the α version which is the last stable

---

[1] Rapidminer: https://rapidminer.com/.
[2] Redis: https://redis.io/.
[3] Lua: http://www.lua.org/.
[4] Sqlite: https://www.sqlite.org/.
[5] 10 Open Source Projects in C, https://my.oschina.net/zhoukuo/blog/335788.

version being used for a while. For Redis, which uses a standard practice for its versioning: major.minor.patchlevel. An even minor marks a stable release, while odd minors are used for unstable releases. For example 2.9.x releases are unstable versions, which will be Redis 3.0 once stable. According to the version history, the latest version is 4.0.10, which is released on Jun 13, 2018, and the last stable version is 3.2.12. For Lua, the releases of Lua are numbered $x.y.z$, where $x.y$ is the version and z is the release. According to the version history, the latest version is 5.4.0, which is released on Jun 18, 2018, and the last stable version is 5.3.5. For Sqlite, according to the version history, the latest version is 3.24.0, which is released on Apr 10, 2018, and the last stable version is 3.23.1.

The ".c files" and "LOC" columns are the number of C files and lines of code (without empty lines and comments) in the projects. The "Function Definitions (Sequence)" column indicates the number of functions which are defined in each project, which is also the number of sequences to be mined for patterns. The "Function Calls" column is the number of function call statements in each project.

Table 1. The statistical information of the projects.

Projects	Versions	.c files	LOC	Function definitions (sequences)	Function calls
Redis	4.0.10	75	47887	1854	11629
	3.2.12	61	40223	1488	9641
Lua	5.4.0	34	16340	984	2984
	5.3.5	35	14610	900	2756
Sqlite	3.24.0	2	142713	2251	13265
	3.23.1	2	141320	2224	13090

3.3   Experimental Results and Analysis

In the experiments, the parameters are set as: $minSup = 0.01$, $minConf = 0.8$, $maxGap = 10$, $minSus = 0.9$ by following the parameters in [11,16]. δ_{max} is set to 0.1 with respect to the value of $minSus$.

Table 2 compares the time costs of the methods. As the column "Method" shows, the method in this paper is named as CV-Miner, and the pervious method in [11] is named as Seq-Miner. The column "Total time" is the sum of time to generate function call sequence pattern candidates and time to check for suspicious defects. The time costs for mining frequent sequence patterns with Rapidminer and validate the reported defects manually are not included in this table. In the table, CV-Miner costs more time than Seq-Miner in all the projects. On average, CV-Miner takes 91% more time costs than Seq-Miner. This is because CV-Miner mine patterns from an extra historical version and additional time are cost to filtering pattern candidates. However, the process of preprocessing source code, mining patterns, filtering patterns and checking programs against the patterns for suspicious defects are fully automated, which will not cause extra manual costs.

Table 2. Comparison between the 2 methods in terms of execution times (unit ms).

Projects	Method	Time to generate sequence patterns	Time to check for suspicious defects	Total time
Redis	Seq-Miner	26781	52	26834
	CV-Miner	46828	44	46872
Lua	Seq-Miner	7683	29	7712
	CV-Miner	15441	28	15470
Sqlite	Seq-Miner	15264	50	15314
	CV-Miner	30227	43	30270

Table 3 compares function call sequence patterns generated between version V_α and V_β. V_β is the version under analysis for detecting defects, and V_α is the last stable version has been used. The column "Only in V_α" and "Only in V_β" are the number of function call sequence patterns only contained in V_α and V_β, respectively. The middle column is the number of patterns exist in both of the two versions, which is further categorized into three types according to the change of *confidence*. In Table 3, 85% of 13 patterns in the α versions of the three projects are also contained in the β versions, while all the 11 patterns in the β versions are also contained in the α versions. For the 11 patterns both are contained in the two versions, the confidence of 4 sequence patterns remains the same, the confidence of 2 sequence patterns decreases, and confidence of 5 sequence pattern increases.

Table 3. Rule candidates across the 2 versions.

Projects	Only in V_α	confidence in V_β − confidence in V_α (exist in both V_α and V_β)			Only in V_β	Total in V_α	Total in V_β
		$\delta_{conf} < 0$	$\delta_{conf} = 0$	$\delta_{conf} > 0$			
Redis	2	2	0	5	0	9	7
Lua	0	0	1	0	0	1	1
Sqlite	0	0	3	0	0	3	3
SUM	2	2	4	5	0	13	11

Thus, our **answer for RQ1 is that "a large number same function call sequence patterns are contained in different versions of a project".** Furthermore, the *confidence* of a large portion of the common patterns remain unchanged. Only a small portion of common patterns decease *confidence*, and only these patterns are filtered our for checking defects.

To evaluate the effectiveness of the approach, we seed some defects in the projects by fault injection techniques. For function call sequence patterns, two mutation operators can be used to inject faults: remove a function call statement, change the order of two function call statements. We randomly select one function call sequence pattern in each projects as: $\langle dictNext(), dictReleaseIterator()\rangle$, $\langle luaL\_buffinit(), luaL\_pushresult()\rangle$ and $\langle sqlite3\_mutex\_enter(), sqlite3\_mutex\_le$ $ave()\rangle$. Then, the two mutation operators are applied to inject 6 faults as Table 4 described.

Table 4. The faults injected in the three projects.

Projects	Fault ID	Files	Faults injected
Redis	1	server.c	Remove the function statement $dictReleaseIterator()$ in method $resetCommandTaleStats()$
	2	pubsub.c	Change the order of function call statements $dictReleaseIterator()$ and $dictNext()$ in method $pubsubUnsubscribeAllChannels()$
Lua	3	lstrlib.c	Remove the function statement $luaL\_pushresult()$ in method $str\_pack()$
	4	ltablib.c	Change the order of function call statements $luaL\_buffinit()$ and $luaL\_pushresult()$ in method $tconcat()$
Sqlite	5	sqlite3.c	Remove the function statement $sqlite3\_mutex\_leave()$ in method $sqlite3\_db\_status()$
	6	sqlite3.c	Change the order of function call statements $sqlite3\_mutex\_enter()$ and $sqlite3\_mutex\_leave()$ in method $sqlite3\_soft\_heap\_limit64()$

Table 5 is the results of run CV-Miner and Seq-Miner on the injected version of the three projects. The column "Patterns" is the number of patterns used for checking violates. The column "Suspicious defects reported" is the number of defects reported by the two methods. The column "Bugs" is the number of detected injected faults.

As the result shows, the suspicious defects reported by CV-Miner is 17 in total, while the Seq-Miner method report 38 suspicious defects in total. The method reduces 55% of suspicious defects for the 3 projects. In addition, the number of the function call sequence patterns used by Seq-Miner is 11, which is 3.7 times of CV-Miner. Since validating programming patterns and suspicious defects depend on reviewing code manually, fewer programming patterns and suspicious defects means less human resource costs. Thus, our **answer for RQ2 is that "the historical version can improve the efficiency of detecting defects based on programming rules by reducing the programming** patterns and the suspicious defects, which need to be manually validated".

In Table 5, the number of injected bugs detected by the two method are both 6, respectively. Thus, our **answer for RQ3 is that "the CV-Miner method does not obviously comprise the capability of detecting defects, which violate function call sequence patterns"**.

Table 5. Comparison between patterns and defects reported by the 2 methods.

Projects	Method	Patterns	Suspicious defects reported	Bugs
Redis	Seq-Miner	7	19	2
	CV-Miner	1	6	2
Lua	Seq-Miner	1	3	2
	CV-Miner	1	3	2
Sqlite	Seq-Miner	3	16	2
	CV-Miner	1	8	2
SUM	Seq-Miner	11	38	6
	CV-Miner	3	17	6

3.4 Threats to Validity

The experiments and implementation of the tools have been double checked. However, there still could be some errors that we have not noticed. Moreover, to guarantee the correctness of extracting program information and mining frequent sequence patterns, mature third-party tools are used, such as pycparser and Rapidminer.

The experiments are carried out on three open source projects, in which the largest project size is 142k lines of code, the scalability of our approach still need to be verified in more projects. In this section, we compare our approach with the Seq-Miner approach, but the effectiveness of our approach would to be further validated by comparing with other public available function call patterns mining benchmarks and tools.

This approach assumes the version under analysis is not a complete change to the previous version. Otherwise, the portion of programming rules contains in both of the two versions is small. Under the circumstances, the approach will be degraded to previous approaches without historical version information. Also, this approach cannot be used for initial version, because there is no previous version available in this case.

4   Related Work

Mining implied programming rules in programs for detecting defects is one of the joint hot topics in software engineering and machine learning. In 2001, in order to improve the accuracy of static analysis, Engler et al. [12] extracted a set of rule templates, and categorized them into MUST and MAY rules. Then the program under test was checked against those rules. After then, lots of research works are dedicated to mine useful programming rules for finding bugs in programs [3,4], such as frequent itemsets, sequence patterns, state machines, frequent subgraphs, condition contracts and so on.

Frequent Itemsets. PR-Miner [5] mined association rules between program elements always appear together. It can find rules between both variables and functions. To improve the precision of specification mining, AntMiner [13] employed the program slicing technique to decompose the original source repository into independent sub-repositories to exclude statements irrelevant to critical operations. To reduce false positives, Thummalapenta and Xie [14] developed Alattin for mining alternative patterns in the form of "P_1 or P_2", where P_1 and P_2 are alternative rules such as checking conditions of method arguments or return values for API calls. To reduce the impact of noises in code corpus, Murali et al. [15] constructed a Bayesian model that correlates specifications and observed behaviors of the implementation. To address the problem of exploiting the program path information to improve the precision of mining defects related to function call patterns, Cui et al. [16] proposed an approach PSP-Finder which mines path-sensitive function call correlation patterns for detecting defects.

Sequence Patterns. To reduce false positives produced by these mining approaches, Kagdi et al. [17] took into consideration the syntactical context of where the calls occur in the source code to mine sequential patterns. To scale to large programs and work effectively, Perracotta [18] described an dynamic approximate inference algorithm, which reduced the large set of inferred temporal properties to a smaller set of interesting properties.

State Machines. To address the drawback of mined specifications are large and the states are unlabeled, ADABU [19] observed program executions to construct object behavior models as state machines that summarize object behaviors. The models generated by ADABU tended to be small and easily understandable. To improve the scalability of mining specifications, Pradel and Gross [20] only focused on collaborations of selected objects, and analyzed the collaboration of each object separately to generate the finite state machines (FSA).

Frequent Subgraphs. Zhong et al. [21]. proposed the program rule graph (PRG) in the form of directed graph to represent the rules that should be followed and implemented a prototype named Java Rule Finder (JRF) to infer specifications from Java source code of API libraries. Nguyen et al. [22] proposed a graph-based approach GrouMiner to mine the usage patterns of multiple objects. In GrouMiner, the usage of objects in a scenario was modeled by a labeled directed acyclic graph (DAG), the usage pattern was detected as the subgraph which frequently appears in the usage graphs of objects.

Condition Contracts. To provide programmers with relevant, non-trivial invariant contracts, Wei et al. [23] proposed an automated tool AutoInfer to take advantage of the simple contracts written by programmers in the code to infer sophisticated postconditions of commands as contracts. In order to help developers correctly use APIs, Nguyen et al. [24] proposed an approach that integrated control dependency analysis and source code mining techniques for large scale open-source repositories to find the preconditions for API methods in libraries and frameworks.

In this paper we only focus on the function call sequence patterns. However, this approach can also be adapted to other types of programming rules, like association rules, frequent subgraphs, and can also be adapted to programming rules between other program elements, such as conditions and variables.

In previous work [11], we proposed a defects detection approach based on mining function call sequence patterns. Different from our previous work, to reduce suspicious defects and false positives, we filter function call sequence patterns for detecting defects by using previous versions of the program. To the best of our knowledge, the approach proposed this paper is the first attempt to mining implied programming rules for defect detection across different versions.

5 Conclusions and Future Work

To address the problem of exploiting the information of historical versions to improve the efficiency of mining programming rules for detect detection, this paper proposes a defect detection technique across different versions of the project based on function call sequence patterns. The approach mines function call sequence patterns for the version under analysis and last stable version of the project, then filters out sequence patterns base on the two sets of candidate patterns and finds suspicious defects which violate the patterns. Based on this approach, experiments are carried out on a series of open source projects, the results show that the programming rules between versions are similar and this approach can improve the efficiency of detecting defects by reducing suspicious defects without obviously comprise the defect detection capability. As a result, the costs for manual validating suspected defects are also reduced.

In this approach, only the last stable version is utilized to improve the efficiency of mining defects. In the future, we plan to introduce incremental mining techniques to use all the versions of a project in the software repository and explore the possibility of using implied programming rules across projects.

References

1. Saied, M.A., Sahraoui, H., Dufour, B.: An observational study on API usage constraints and their documentation. In: 22nd IEEE International Conference on Software Analysis, Evolution and Reengineering, pp. 33–42 (2015)
2. Li, M., Huo, X.: Software defect mining based on semi-supervised learning. J. Data Acquis. Process. **31**(1), 56–64 (2016). (in Chinese)

3. Li, Z., Wu, J., Li, M.: Study on key issues about API usage. J. Softw. **29**(06), 1716–1738 (2018). (in Chinese)

4. Robillard, M.P., Bodden, E., Kawrykow, D., Mezini, M., Ratchford, T.: Automated API property inference techniques. IEEE Trans. Softw. Eng. **39**(5), 613–637 (2013)

5. Li, Z., Zhou, Y.: PR-Miner: automatically extracting implicit programming rules and detecting violations in large software code. In: 10th European Software Engineering Conference Held Jointly with 13th ACM SIGSOFT International Symposium on Foundations of Software Engineering, pp. 306–315 (2005)

6. Legunsen, O., Hassan, W.U., Xu, X., Roşu, G., Marinov, D.: How good are the specs? A study of the bug-finding effectiveness of existing java API specifications. In: 31st IEEE/ACM International Conference on Automated Software Engineering, pp. 602–613 (2016)

7. Mei, H., Wang, Q.X., Zhang, L., Wang, J.: Software analysis: a road map. Chin. J. Comput. **32**(9), 1697–1710 (2009). (in Chinese)

8. Young, M., Pezze, M.: Software Testing and Analysis: Process Principles and Techniques. Wiley, Hoboken (2005)

9. Srikant, R., Agrawal, R.: Mining sequential patterns: generalizations and performance improvements. In: Apers, P., Bouzeghoub, M., Gardarin, G. (eds.) EDBT 1996. LNCS, vol. 1057, pp. 1–17. Springer, Heidelberg (1996). https://doi.org/10.1007/BFb0014140

10. Agrawal, R., Srikant, R.: Mining sequential patterns. In: 11th IEEE International Conference on Data Engineering, pp. 3–14 (1995)

11. Cui, Z., Mu, Y., Zhang, Z., Wang, W.: Defects detection based on mining function call sequence patterns. Comput. Sci. (SATE 2016) **44**(11), 226–231 (2017). (in Chinese)

12. Engler, D., Chen, D.Y., Hallem, S., Chou, A., Chelf, B.: Bugs as deviant behavior: a general approach to inferring errors in systems code. In: 8th ACM Symposium on Operating Systems Principles, pp. 57–72 (2001)

13. Liang, B, Bian, P., Zhang, Y., Shi, W., You, W., Cai, Y.: AntMiner: mining more bugs by reducing noise interference. In: 38th IEEE/ACM International Conference on Software Engineering, pp. 333–344 (2016)

14. Thummalapenta, S., Xie, T.: Alattin: mining alternative patterns for detecting neglected conditions. In: 24th IEEE/ACM International Conference on Automated Software Engineering, pp. 283–294 (2009)

15. Murali, V., Chaudhuri, S., Jermaine, C.: Bayesian specification learning for finding API usage errors. In: 11th ACM Joint Meeting on Foundations of Software Engineering, pp. 151–162 (2017)

16. Cui, Z., Chen, X., Mu, Y., Pan, M., Wang, R.: PSP-Finder: a defect detection method based on mining correlations from function call paths. Chin. J. Electron. **27**(04), 776–782 (2018)

17. Kagdi, H., Collard, M.L., Maletic, J.I.: An approach to mining call-usage patterns with syntactic context. In: 22nd IEEE/ACM International Conference on Automated Software Engineering, pp. 457–460 (2007)

18. Yang, J., Evans, D., Bhardwaj, D., Bhat, T., Das, M.: Perracotta: mining temporal API rules from imperfect traces. In: 28th IEEE/ACM International Conference on Software Engineering, pp. 282–291 (2006)

19. Dallmeier, V., Lindig, C., Wasylkowski, A., Zeller, A.: Mining object behavior with ADABU. In: International Workshop on Dynamic Systems Analysis, pp. 17–24 (2006)

20. Pradel, M., Gross, T.R.: Automatic generation of object usage specifications from large method traces. In: 24th IEEE/ACM International Conference on Automated Software Engineering, pp. 371–382 (2009)
21. Zhong, H., Zhang, L., Mei, H.: Inferring specifications of object oriented APIs from API source code. In: 15th Asia-Pacific Software Engineering Conference, pp. 221–228 (2008)
22. Nguyen, T.T., Nguyen, H.A., Pham, N.H., Al-Kofahi, J.M., Nguyen T.N.: Graph-based mining of multiple object usage patterns. In: 7th Joint Meeting of the European Software Engineering Conference and the ACM SIGSOFT Symposium on the Foundations of Software Engineering, pp. 383–392 (2009)
23. Wei, Y., Furia, C.A., Kazmin, N., Meyer, B.: Inferring better contracts. In: 33rd IEEE/ACM International Conference on Software Engineering, pp. 191–200 (2011)
24. Nguyen, H.A., Dyer, R., Nguyen, T.N., Rajan, H.: Mining preconditions of APIs in large-scale code corpus. In: 22nd ACM SIGSOFT International Symposium on Foundations of Software Engineering, pp. 166–177 (2014)

Testing and Monitoring

Parallel Reachability Testing Based on Hadoop MapReduce

Xiaofang Qi$^{(\boxtimes)}$ and Yueran Li

School of Computer Science and Engineering, Southeast University,
Nanjing 211189, China
xfqi@seu.edu.cn, lyrsee333@163.com

Abstract. Reachability testing is an important approach to testing concurrent programs. It generates and executes all the possible sequences of a concurrent program automatically with a given input while not saving any sequences that have already been executed. However, for a large and complex concurrent program, the number of synchronization sequences that are exercised is too large. It will take too long time to perform reachability testing, which limits its application. In this paper, we propose a parallel reachability testing approach based on Hadoop MapReduce called PRT, aiming to improve its performance. PRT adopts the framework of Hadoop MapReduce with a heuristic strategy to realize dynamic loading balance. We present the algorithms used in PRT, and reports the results of five concurrent Java programs that were conducted to evaluate the speed-up with respect to the sequential execution of reachability testing. Experimental results demonstrate that our PRT is an effective approach to parallelizing reachability testing.

Keywords: Reachability testing · Hadoop · MapReduce · Software testing
Concurrent programming

1 Introduction

Concurrent programs are becoming increasingly pervasive and important with the wide-spread use of multi-core processors and the support for concurrent programming in modern languages, like C++, Java, Ada and Python [1]. Concurrent programming increases computational efficiency significantly and solves many inherently concurrent problems in a natural way [1, 2]. Despite these advantages, concurrent programs are difficult to test due to their nondeterministic behaviors.

There are two testing strategies to handle nondeterministic behaviors of concurrent programs, namely non-deterministic testing and deterministic testing [2, 3]. During non-deterministic testing, a concurrent program with a given input is executed many times without any control in order that different sequences of synchronization events (SYN-sequences) could be chosen and more faults could be exposed. This approach is easy to carry out, but it is inefficient and insufficient. In contrast, deterministic testing is more efficient and sufficient since the execution of a concurrent program is controlled to perform a specific synchronization sequence. However, these synchronization sequences are often generated from some static model of the program, which is inaccurate in most cases.

© Springer Nature Switzerland AG 2018
L. Bu and Y. Xiong (Eds.): SATE 2018, LNCS 11293, pp. 173–184, 2018.
https://doi.org/10.1007/978-3-030-04272-1_11

Reachability testing combines the strengths of non-deterministic and deterministic testing. It generates and exercises synchronization sequences automatically and on-the-fly without saving any test history [4, 5]. During reachability testing, every partially-ordered synchronization sequence of a concurrent program is exercised exactly once. Reachability testing is valuable in theory, but it is impractical for large and/or complex concurrent programs because of the state explosion problem [4]. Parallelization may be an ideal way to improve its performance since reachability testing is parallelizable. There is no synchronization or communication between different synchronization sequences that are exercised in reachability testing. Furthermore, no synchronization sequences among computing nodes are duplicated if parallelization is adopted.

Hadoop is an open source distributed computing and big data processing platform, used widely in the industry and academia [6–8]. It implements common modules for developing distributed programs and offers users to develop and run distributed programs. Developers can focus on their business logic implementations without knowing the underlying details of distributed systems. MapReduce is the core technique of Hadoop and provides a software framework for easily developing applications which process vast amounts of data in parallel on large clusters of computing nodes [7]. Hadoop exploits a distributed file system called the Hadoop Distributed File System (HDFS) to store data. The high fault tolerance and scalability of HDFS allow users to deploy Hadoop in ordinary commercial hardware. Hadoop is well supported to work not only on clusters, but also in the cloud. It provides a good solution for parallelizing reachability testing.

In this paper, we present the design and implementation of a parallel reachability testing approach based on Hadoop MapReduce, called PRT. Our work is the first attempt to propose and implement a parallel reachability testing approach based on Hadoop MapReduce. PRT adopted the framework of MapReduce and used a heuristic strategy to perform dynamic load balancing. Although it was implemented on a workstation cluster, it is easy to extend to the cloud computing environment.

The main contributions of this paper are as follows: First, we propose a parallel reachability testing approach based on Hadoop MapReduce. The key ingredient of our approach is a heuristic dynamic load balancing strategy. Second, we implement our approach, which significantly improve the performance of reachability testing. Third, we conduct an empirical study on five concurrent Java programs to evaluate the speedup with respect to the sequential execution of reachability testing. The results show that our approach is an effective one to parallelizing reachability testing.

The rest of the paper is organized as follows. Section 2 presents an overview of reachability testing process. Section 3 describes the design and implementation of PRT. Section 4 evaluates the effectiveness of PRT and reports the experimental results. Section 5 briefly surveys the related work. Section 6 provides concluding remarks and our plan for future work.

2   Overview of Reachability Testing

Reachability testing uses a general execution model that allows it to be applied to several commonly used synchronization constructs [4, 9]. In the general model, a *send* or *call* event is referred to as a *sending* event, and a *receive*, *completion* or *entry* event is referred to as a *receiving* event. A semaphore or monitor is generally referred to as a synchronization object. Due to space constraints, we illustrate the reachability testing process with a monitor-based program.

Figure 1 shows an example program. The program consists of three threads, which interact with each other by accessing monitor object M. When a thread T calls a synchronization method of M, i.e., *setL()* or *setW()*, a monitor *call* event occurs on T_i, and we refer to the calling as a *sending event*. When T finally enters M, a monitor *entry* event occurs on M, and we refer to the entry as a *receiving event*. If a called monitor method is entered, we say that the *sending event s* is synchronized with the receiving event r and $<s, r>$ is a synchronization pair. In this case, we say that s is the sending part of r, and r is the receiving part of s.

```
1. public class Test{
2.     public static void main(String args[]){
3.         Rectangle M=new Rectangle ();
4.         Thread1 T1=new T1(M);
5.         Thread2 T2=new T2(M);
6.         Thread3 T3=new T3(M);
7.         T1.start();
8.         T2.start();
9.         T3.start();
        }
    }

10. class Rectangle{
11.     private int length, width;
12.     public synchronized void SetL(int length) {this.length=length;}
13.     public synchronized void SetW(int width) {this.width=width;}
        }

14. class Thread1 extends Thread{
15.     private Rectangle rect;
16.     public Thread1(Rectangle r) {this.rect=r;}
17.     public void run() {rect.setL(2);}
        }

19. class Thread2 extends Thread{
20.     private Rectangle rect;
21.     public Thread2(Rectangle r) {this.rect=r;}
22.     public void run() {rect.setL(4);}
        }

23. class Thread3 extends Thread{
24.     private Rectangle rect;
25.     public Thread3(Rectangle r) {this.rect=r;}
26.     public void run() {rect.setW(3);}
        }
```

Fig. 1. An example program

Given an execution of a concurrent program, a SYN-sequence, short for synchronization sequence, is defined to be a totally ordered sequence of sending and receiving events that occurred on a thread or a synchronization object, as well as the synchronization pairs exercised in the execution. A SYN-sequence is usually represented as a space-time diagram, in which a vertical line represents a thread or monitor, and a horizontal solid arrow from a sending event to a receiving event represents a synchronization pair between them. Figure 2 shows six SYN-sequences, namely, Q_0, Q_1, Q_2, Q_3, Q_4 and Q_5. As illustrated in Q_0, $s_1 \rightarrow r_1$ represents a synchronization pair, in which s_1 is a sending event indicating that T_1 call $rec.setL()$, r_1 is a receiving event indicating that T_1 enters M.

Let s be a sending event, r be a receiving event. s is synchronized with r in a SYN-sequence Q. Let s' be another sending event in Q. If s' could be synchronized with r in a different execution Q', we say there exists a race between s and s' with respect to r. Note that all the events that happen before s' or r in Q, and the synchronizations between these events are the same as in Q' [4]. The happen before relation is the usual one defined as in [4]. Lei et al. presented a method to compute the race set [4]. As shown in Fig. 2, $<s_1, r_1>$ in Q_0 is a synchronization pair, and there exists a race between s_1 and s_3 with respect to r_1 because $<s_3, r_1>$ is also a synchronization pair in another SYN-sequence Q_3. The race set of r, denoted as $race\_set(r)$, is the set of sending events that have a race with s w.r.t r. For example, in Q_0, $race\_set(r_1)$ is $\{s_2, s_3\}$, $race\_set(r_2)$ is $\{s_3\}$, and $race\_set(r_3)$ is empty.

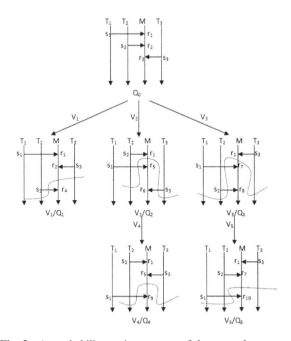

Fig. 2. A reachability testing process of the example program

A race variant V of a SYN-sequence Q is a prefix of Q by changing the sending event of one or more receiving events in Q while satisfying the following constraints for any one of these receiving events. Suppose that r is a receiving event that is synchronized with a sending event s in Q, and the sending part of r is changed to be s' in V. Then, (1) s' must be in the race set of r in Q; and (2) an event e in Q must be removed from V if and only if this change will affect the existence of e. The second constraint guarantees the feasibility of race variant V, i.e., there exists at least one program execution in which the sequence in V can be exercised. For a SYN-sequence Q, one approach to generating race variants is to build a race table. Details on building a race table can be found in [1].

Reachability testing begins by executing a program non-deterministically. For the example program, we assume it exercises SYN-sequence Q_0 in Fig. 1. Then, the race set of each receiving event in Q_0 is computed to derive the variants of Q_0, namely V_1, V_2, and V_3. Each variant is used to perform a prefix-based test run, in which the events and the synchronizations in the variant are controlled to be replayed. Thereafter, the test run continues non-deterministically again without controlling which SYN-sequence is exercised until it ends. As shown in Fig. 2, prefix-based testing with V_1, V_2 and V_3 exercises complete sequences Q_1, Q_2, and Q_3, respectively. In Fig. 2, the sequence Q_i and the variant V_i that is used to exercise it is depicted in the same space-time diagram. The events in the variant are those above the dashed line. Next, new variant V_4 and V_5 are derived from Q_2 and Q_3 respectively. Similarly, prefix-based testing with V_4 and V_5 exercise complete sequences Q_4 and Q_5 respectively. Finally, no new variants can be derived, so the reachability testing process ends.

3   Parallel Reachability Testing Based on Hadoop MapReduce

Hadoop divides the input data into fixed size pieces called input split, each of which is assigned to a MapReduce job [10]. A MapReduce job has two distinct functions, namely map and reduce. The map function performs parallelization while reduce function is responsible for collecting and handling the results. Each map task produces a set of intermediate key/value pairs. For each key, the user-defined reduce function is invoked. Then one or more reduce tasks will group together all the intermediate values associated to the same key and generate the final results, which are written into HDFS.

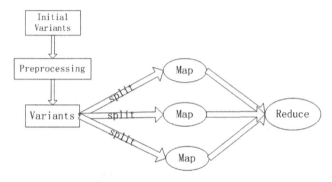

Fig. 3. The architecture of PRT

As mentioned before, reachability testing is naturally parallelizable. All the generated variants can be executed concurrently by different computing node without any synchronization. The underlying idea of our parallel reachability testing approach based on Hadoop MapReduce (PRT) is to use several *map* tasks to execute race variants in parallel and use a *reduce* task to collect the results. Figure 3 shows the architecture of our PRT, which is composed by an *Initial Variants* Generation, a *Preprocessing*, several *map* tasks for executing *variants,* and a *reduce* task for collecting results.

The execution time for reachability testing consists of the time to compute variants and the time to execute variants. The overall overhead is dominated by the time for executing variants. The execution time of each variant is roughly the same. For a given variant *V*, we say that the descendent sequences of *V* include the SYN-sequence *Q* collected from executing *V*, and all the sequences collected from executing the variants of *Q*, and so on. It is difficult to predict the number of descendent sequences of the initial variants in each *map* task. We cannot estimate the amount of work performed by each map task, thus dynamic load balancing is needed. In this paper, we exploit a heuristic strategy for dynamic load balancing, which is implemented by the *preprocessing* component in Fig. 3.

```
PRT(N){
 1.  Variants =GetInitialVariants( );
 2.  Variants =Preprocessing(N, Variants)
 3.  Create a new MRJob2 Job2;
 4.  Execute  Job2 with Variants as its input;
 5. }


GetInitialVariants( ){
 6.  Collect a sequence Q₀ by executing CP with input X
     non-deterministically;
 7.  Variants=GenerateVariants(Q₀);
 8.  return Variants;
 9. }

Preprocessing(N, Variants){
10.  while(iteration<=N) {
11.     Create a new MRJob1 Job1;
12.     Execute  Job1 with Variants as its input;
13.  }
14.  return Variants;
15. }
```

Fig. 4. The algorithm in PRT

Figure 4 describes the pseudo-code for the algorithm in our PRT. N is the iteration number of MapReduce jobs in *preprocessing*. First, PRT uses the *GetInitialVariants* function to generate initial race variants batches (line 1). Then, the *Preprocessing* function is called to preprocess the initial race variants for dynamic load balancing (line

2). In this function, N *MRJob1* jobs are created and executed. *MRJob1* performs prefix-based testing for *CP* with the initial race variants in parallel and generates their descendent race variants (line 10–12). Finally, an *MRJob2* job is created to perform parallel reachability testing, which executes the current race variants and their descendent race variants in parallel (lines 3–4).

Initial Race Variants. PRT calls *GetInitialVariants()* to generate initial race variants. This component first executes a concurrent program with a given input non-deterministically, and collects the SYN-sequence Q only once. Then it computes the race variants of Q and divides the initial set of race variants into several equal batches. The number of batches is the number of available worker nodes in Hadoop cluster. These batches were written into the specified directory in HDFS as the input data of *preprocessing* module.

Preprocessing. *Preprocessing* component tries to minimize the difference in the numbers of the initial variants in each *map* task in parallel reachability testing, i.e., the *MRJob2* job. It is implemented by another MapReduce job, i.e., the *MRJob1* job, which is encapsulated in a loop (Line 11). The number of iterations in the loop is set by users. The new race variants generated during each iteration, are divided into several equal batches, each of which is the input data of a map task in the next iteration. The race variants generated by the last iteration are the input data of the *MRJob2* job.

```
Map1(){
1.   let Variants and Sequences be an empty set;
2.   Variants = initial variants from HDFS;
3.   while(Variants is not empty){
4.       withdraw a variant V from Variants;
5.       collect a SYN-sequence Q by conducting a prefix-based
         test run with V;
6.       put Q in Sequences;
7.   }
8.   reurn Sequences;
9.}
```

Fig. 5. The *map* task in *MRJob1*

Figures 5 and 6 describe the pseudo-codes for the *map* and *reduce* task in *MRJob1* respectively. To reduce the overhead of reachability testing, *MRJob1* uses the *setup* function of each *map* task to read all variants into the memory one time. And it uses the user-defined *FileInputFormat* class to make the *map* function called for each variant batch. The *map* function performs prefix-based testing for CP with the variant batches in parallel and collects the SYN-sequences exercised by CP. Note that each *map* function only executes current variants, It does not generate and execute the descendent variants. Once the execution is completed, each *map* function generates a new pair <key, value>, where *value* is a list of SYN-sequences generated by itself. The generated *key* is the same for each SYN-sequence.

```
Reduce1( ){
  1.  let new_variants be an empty set;
  2.  while(Sequences is not empty){
  3.      withdraw a sequence Q from Sequences;
  4.      new_variants=new_variants ∪GenerateVariants(Q);
  5.  }
  6.  divide the new_variants into several equal batches and
      write them into HDFS;
  7. }
```

Fig. 6. The *reduce* task in *MRJob1*

MRJob1 uses a *reduce* task to compute the race variants of SYN-Sequences generated from the *map* tasks. When all new race variants are generated, the number of variants is calculated. Then the new variants are divided into several equal batches, which are written into HDFS as the input data of next job. Figure 6 reports the pseudo-code for the *reduce* task in *MRJob1*. To reduce the difference between the workload of each *map* task in *MRJob2*, *MRJob1* job can be executed many times. However, as the number of iterations increases, more and more race variants are generated. In *MRJob1*, since all variants must be read into the memory to be executed and divided, the iteration number N is not able to be too large. Otherwise, the memory will be used up, leading to an *OutOfMemoryError* error.

Race Variant Execution. PRT uses an *MRJob2* job to perform parallel reachability testing. Each *map* task reads all variants of the input that is split into the memory one time, and then the *map* function is called. The *map* tasks in *MRJob2* execute not only the current variants, but also their descendent sequences. Figure 7 shows the pseudo-codes for the *map* task in *MRJob2*. Each *map* task uses a *map* function to perform the prefix-based testing with the variant batches, collects the SYN-sequences exercised, computes the variants of SYN-Sequences, and repeats this process until no more new variants are generated. All *map* tasks are performed in parallel. The *reduce* task is responsible to compute the total number of SYN-sequences exercised by all *map* tasks.

```
Map2( ){
  1.  let Variants and Sequences be an empty set;
  2.  Variants = initial variants from HDFS;
  3.  while(Variants is not empty) {
  4.      withdraw a variant V from Variants;
  5.      collect a SYN-sequence Q by conducting a prefix-based   test
          run with V;
  6.      Variants=Variants∪GenerateVariants(Q);
  7.  }
  8.}
```

Fig. 7. The *map* task in *MRJob2*

4   Empirical Results

The goal of our experiment was to evaluate the effectiveness of our parallel reachability testing approach based on Hadoop MapReduce (PRT) in terms of the execution time. The speedup is calculated by dividing the overall time of the sequential reachability testing (SRT) by the overall time of PRT.

4.1   Subject

The SRT and PRT were applied to the following five Java programs:

RW-SC: a solution to the reader-writer problem using SC monitor for synchronization. RW-SC has three readers and three writers [11].

RW-SU: a solution to the reader-writer problem using SU monitors for synchronization. RW-SU has three readers and three writers [11].

PC-SC: a solution to the producer-consumer problem where the buffer is protected using SC monitors. PC-SC has four producers and four consumers and a buffer with two slots [11].

PC-SU: a solution to the producer-consumer problem where the buffer is protected using SU monitor. PC-SU has six producers and five consumers and a buffer with two slots [11].

Account: Account is a program in Contest benchmark suite. It has a bank thread and five account threads. The bank manages accounts and the account thread represents the actual behavior of account in the bank [12].

In the above five programs, if SC (Signal-and-Continue) monitor is used, the signaling thread continues executing in the monitor and the signaled thread has to compete with other threads to reenter the monitor. If SU (Signal-and-Urgent-Wait) monitor is used, the signaling thread exits the monitor and the signaled thread reenters the monitor immediately.

4.2   Experimental Setup

In the experiment, we used a small Hadoop cluster of four nodes. Among the nodes, one node is the master and the rest nodes are workers. We exploited three map tasks and one reduce task to conduct PRT. Our experiments were performed on a Linux computer cluster with 4 workstation nodes and 100 Mbit/s Ethernet. Each workstation has Intel Core i5 CPU with 4 GB memory running under Ubuntu11.10. The employed version of Hadoop was 1.04. SRT was executed on one node.

4.3   Results

Table 1 reports the execution time (column "Time") and the number of SYN-sequences (column "Num") in the sequential reachability testing (SRT). The number of SYN-sequences indicates the complexity of a concurrent program. Table 1 shows that the execution time approximately coincides with the number of SYN-sequences. As the number of SYN-sequences increases, the execution time exercised by SRT increases correspondingly.

Table 1. The execution time of SRT and the number of exercised SYN-sequences

Subject	Time (Min)	Num
RW-SC	2,462	2,442,348
RW-SU	213	236,016
PC-SC	856	16,511,040
PC-SU	1,422	39,906,800
Account	720	1,247,400

Table 2 shows that the execution time (column "T") and the speedup (column "S") of PRT. X in T-X and S-X represents the iteration number of $MRJob_1$ job executed in the *preprocessing*. PRT with different iteration number of $MRJob_1$ job uses the same initial race variants. Table 2 demonstrates that the total execution time is highly reduced with parallelization. T-3 takes the least execution time, then T-2, T-1 and T-0. This indicates that the *preprocessing* plays an important role in load balancing. Moreover, as the iteration number increases, the execution time of PRT decreases. The better speedup is achieved with more iterations of *MRJob1*.

Table 3 shows the execution time of *preprocessing*. X in PRT-X represents the iteration number of $MRJob_1$ job executed in the *preprocessing*. The time taken by *preprocessing* is so short that can be ignored, compared with the execution time taken by PRT. Yet *preprocessing* improves the initial load unbalance significantly. Table 3 also demonstrates that the iteration number should not be too large. Otherwise, *MRJob1* was not capable of reading all variants into the memory. In our experiment, PRT executed *MRJob1* no more than three times.

Table 2. The execution time (Min) and the speedup of PRT

Subject	T-0	S-0	T-1	S-1	T-2	S-2	T-3	S-3
RW-SC	1,345	1.83	1,289	1.91	1,140	2.16	1,080	2.28
RW-SU	124	1.72	113	1.88	101	2.10	98	2.18
PC-SC	559	1.53	473	1.81	440	1.95	382	2.24
PC-SU	857	1.66	773	1.84	687	2.07	649	2.19
Account	387	1.86	358	2.01	344	2.09	332	2.17

Table 3. The execution time of preprocessing (Sec) in PRT

Subject	PRT-1	PRT-2	PRT-3
RW-SC	49	106	341
RW-SU	40	84	353
PC-SC	37	82	166
PC-SU	42	97	179
Account	41	85	192

5 Related Work

There are only a few studies on improving the performance of reachability testing. To address the explosion problem in reachability testing, combinatorial strategies are leveraged to reduce synchronization sequences [13, 14]. The strategy adopts the dynamic framework of reachability testing, but it exercises SYN-sequences selectively, not exhaustively. In addition, Lei and Carver proposed a distributed reachability testing algorithm on a cluster of workstations [5].

T-way reachability testing uses a t-way combinatorial strategy to select and then exercise a subset of synchronization sequences [13]. Variable strength combinatorial strategy is also employed to reachability testing since uniform interactions between parameters do not often exist in concurrent systems [14]. Exhaustive reachability testing derives race variants which cover all possible combinations of the race outcome changes that can be made in a SYN-sequence. In contrast, reachability testing with combinatorial strategies derives race variants to cover combinations of the race outcome changes. S.R.S. Souza combined coverage criteria with reachability testing, in which merely race variants that contain uncovered synchronizations are selected to be executed [15]. As such modified reachability testing cannot exercise all possible SYN-sequences, its capability of fault detection is reduced.

The distributed reachability testing algorithm allows different SYN-sequences to be exercised concurrently by different workstations without any synchronization [5]. To handle the load unbalance in the initial allocation, it uses a round-based, randomized work-stealing protocol for dynamic load balancing. Compared with the sequential reachability testing, the distributed reachability testing significantly reduces the execution time. However, the algorithm is implemented only in common clusters, but not suitable in the modern cloud computing environment.

Some researchers have studied parallelization on software testing based on Hadoop [16, 17]. Hadoop is often used to solve complex and time-consuming problems. Geronimo presented a Parallel Genetic Algorithm for automatic generation of test suites based on Hadoop MapReduce [16]. Experimental results show that using PGA can save over the 50% of time. Parveen proposed a distributed execution framework for Junit test cases, called HadoopUnit [17]. Preliminary results indicate that HadoopUnit reduces test execution time significantly.

6 Conclusions

In this paper, we present the design and implementation of a parallel reachability testing approach based on Hadoop MapReduce (PRT). PRT adopts the framework of MapReduce and performs dynamic loading balance with a heuristic strategy. Experimental results show that PRT reduces the execution time of reachability testing significantly, compared with the sequential reachability testing. It is an effective approach to parallelizing reachability testing. While it is implemented on a workstation cluster, it is easy to extend to the cloud environment. In the future, we will extend our work on parallel reachability testing on the cloud.

Acknowledgements. This work is supported by the National Science Foundation of China under Grant No. 61472076 and No. 61472077.

References

1. Burns, A., Wellings, A.: Real-Time Systems and Programming Languages, 3rd edn. Addison Wesley Longman, Boston (2001)
2. Edelstein, O., Farchi, E., et al.: Multithread Java program test generation. J. IBM Syst. **41**(1), 111–125 (2002)
3. Taylor, R.N., Levine, D.L., Kelly, C.D.: Structural testing of concurrent programs. IEEE Trans. Softw. Eng. **18**(3), 206–214 (1992)
4. Lei, Y., Carver, R.H.: Reachability testing of concurrent programs. IEEE Trans. Softw. Eng. **32**(6), 382–403 (2006)
5. Carver, R.H., Lei, Y.: Distributed reachability testing of concurrent programs. Concurrency Comput.: Practice Exp. **22**(18), 2445–2466 (2010)
6. Apache Hadoop. http://hadoop.apache.org/. Accessed 28 June 2018
7. Li, R., Hu, H., et al.: MapReduce parallel programming model: a state-of-the-art survey. Int. J. Parallel Program. **44**(4), 832–866 (2016)
8. Amazon Elastic Compute Cloud. http://aws.amazon.com/ec2/. Accessed 28 June 2018
9. Carver, R.H., Lei, Y.: A general model for reachability testing of concurrent programs. In: Davies, J., Schulte, W., Barnett, M. (eds.) ICFEM 2004. LNCS, vol. 3308, pp. 76–98. Springer, Heidelberg (2004). https://doi.org/10.1007/978-3-540-30482-1_14
10. White, T.: Hadoop: The Definitive Guide, 3rd edn. O'Reilly Media, Sebastopol (2012)
11. Carver, R.H., Tai, K.C.: Modern Multithreading. Wiley, New Jersey (2005)
12. Edelstein, Y., Havelund, K., et al.: Towards a multi-threaded programs. Concurrency Comput.: Practice Exp. **19**(3), 267–279 (2007)
13. Lei, Y., Carver, R.H., Kacker, R., et al.: A combinatorial testing strategy for concurrent programs. Softw. Test. Verif. Reliab. **17**(4), 207–225 (2007)
14. Qi, X., He, J., et al.: Variable strength combinatorial testing of concurrent programs. Front. Comput. Sci. **10**(4), 631–643 (2016)
15. Souza, S.R.S., Souza, P.S.L., et al.: Using coverage and reachability testing to improve concurrent program testing quality. In: 23rd International Conference on Software Engineering and Knowledge Engineering (SEKE), pp. 207–212. Knowledge Systems Institute, Miami, U.S.A. (2011)
16. Geronimo, D., Ferrucci, F., Murolo, A., et al.: A parallel genetic algorithm based on hadoop mapreduce for the automatic generation of junit test suites. In: 5th IEEE International Conference on Software Testing, Verification and Validation (ICST), pp. 785–793. IEEE Computer Society, Montreal Canada (2012)
17. Parveen, T., Tilley, S., Daley, N., et al.: Towards a distributed execution framework for JUnit test cases. In: 25th IEEE International Conference on Software Maintenance (ICSM), pp. 425–428. IEEE Computer Society, Alberta (2009)

An Automated Test Suite Generating Approach for Stateful Web Services

Yin Li[✉], Zhi-Guang Sun, and Ting-Ting Jiang

Jiangsu Automation Research Institute, Lianyungang 215006, China
leein121999@126.com

Abstract. Web Services are the W3C-endorsed realization of the Service-Oriented Architecture (SOA). How to automatically generate effective test suites is a key problem in Web services testing. At present, the existing testing methods may cause the redundancy of test suite and the decrease of fault detecting ability. So this paper proposes an automated test suite generation approach based on EFSM (Extended Finite State Machine) model and operation interface contract. The operation tree model is firstly constructed according to the standard WSDL (Web Services Description Language) document. By appending semantic annotation to standard WSDL, the EFSM model is then built to generate operation sequences automatically. Finally, the optimal test suite can be obtained according to the operation interface contract. Moreover, the experiment shows that the proposed approach can generate reasonable test suites for stateful Web services effectively, while enhancing the fault detection ability and optimality on the size of existing approach.

Keywords: Web services · Operation tree model · Behavior information
Operation interface contract · Extended Finite State Machine

1 Introduction

As the corner stone technology of SOA (Service Oriented Architecture), Web service has widely been adopted in academic and industry communities. In order to guarantee the quality and improve the credibility of Web services, it needs a systematic and comprehensive testing. Due to the complexity of Web services technical specification, the network distribution of application deployment and the variability of operation state, the traditional software testing technology cannot afford the development of Web services. Moreover, Web services only provide little information and don't have graphical user interface, which makes test cases mainly based on interface designing and implementing. In order to test Web services carefully and comprehensively, an automated testing method is introduced.

© Springer Nature Switzerland AG 2018
L. Bu and Y. Xiong (Eds.): SATE 2018, LNCS 11293, pp. 185–201, 2018.
https://doi.org/10.1007/978-3-030-04272-1_12

The testers can perform the black box testing using the data description information based on standard XML specification document for a single Web service. At present, enormous efforts have been made to generate test cases through the description of service operation parameters and types in WSDL document, but there is lack of researches focusing on operation sequences in an individual service while WSDL documents analysis is confined to only on data type. Thus, the generated test cases cannot cover the service test paths while ignoring that there are strong coupling relationship between statuses of various operations in stateful Web services. The global state modified by an operation in Web services may have the influence on the execution for another operation. Hence, some special operation sequences are not taken into account in the development process, which may cause the service quality defects, and bring the risk to the reliable operations of the Web services.

In this study, we therefore aim to generate test suites automatically for operation sequence paths in stateful Web services by integrating EFSM (Extended Finite State Machine) and interface contract model. We first reconstruct operation tree model based on WSDL documents and extend the documents by means of semantic annotation. Here, the EFSM model based on operation sequence is constructed according to the state division. Through operation interface contract model, the operation sequence test data are then selected and generated. Finally, we can obtain the operation sequence paths for stateful Web services with the optimal test case converge.

2 Background and Related Work

With the wide application of SOA (Service Oriented Architecture), there is a higher requirement of quality and correctness for Web services. Therefore, how to guarantee the quality and reliability of Web services has become an urgent need in the field of software engineering. At present, Web services testing still mainly relies on the manual design, which leads to low efficiency with certain of blindness and tendency of generated test data. Therefore, improving the automation of test data generation and execution is the issue that needs to be addressed urgently [1–4].

Web services are divided into two types: stateless and stateful [5–7]. Moreover, Web services testing is divided into three levels according to the considering priorities of different levels of Web services [8]: testing for single operation in stateless Web services, testing for operation sequences in stateful Web services and testing for service composition based on BPEL (Business Process Execution Language). Stateful Web services contain multiple operations, while different combinations of operation sequence will lead Web services into different data states. Hence, testing operation sequences is more important than inspecting service state for stateful Web services.

In single operation testing for stateless Web services area, users can obtain the WSDL documents containing Web service interface information, such as service name and the parameter type, which can be adopted to execute testing using black box approach based on specification [9]. As clearly reported by Tsai et al., the WSDL document can be extended to form 4 aspects (input-output dependency, invocation sequences, concurrent sequences, and hierarchical functional description), in order to enhance the ability of description and improve the testability of Web services [10]. In the following years, Xu and Hanna transform WSDL documents into the form of DOM tree, and then construct the formal tree abstract model, generate test data randomly for simple and complex types in Web services using boundary value analysis and equivalence partitioning method [11, 12] and followed by Ma et al., demonstrates an approach based on additional description of complex data structure type and puts forward a more visualizing and intelligibility formal tree model which further refines the constraint relations between data and described the test case generation process more formally [13]. Besides, Sibilini and Mansour explore the testing single Web service through the mutation test, and analyze the test results through the service response [14].

Focusing on operation sequence generation for stateful Web services, there are some reports on operation sequence testing for stateful Web services by describing the expected behavior of the system. Because the lack of behavior information (input and output pre - and post -conditions IOPE), enormous efforts have been carried out. Bai et al. analyzes the WSDL document with semantic analysis, presents a test suite generation workflow from test data generation, test operation generation operation flow generation and test specification using DOM (Document Object Model) [15]. Later, a schema special tree model is imported by Li et al. generates operation sequences by analyzing the exchange of data between the operations [16]. However, this approach is restricted to deal with simple data type and lack of specific data generation methods and application, which has some limitations. Antonia Bertolino et al. proposed service providers should upload protocol state machine for operation sequences [17] and followed by Heckel et al. also presents service provider should describe behavior information of Web services by uploading GT rules (graph transformation rules) [18]. But this approach cannot actually get used while lacking of the corresponding standard and increasing the difficulty of the service development. Besides, there are several studies for test data generation which converts the semantic WSDL document into event sequence diagram model, IOPE graph model, EFSM and SXM model [19–24]. While most of these models need the additional semantic information, and cannot generate test data automatically [25, 26].

Focusing on the studies mentioned above, our study hereby construct the operation tree model based WSDL document and extend it by semantic annotations, EFSM modeling is performed automatically based on the extended semantic WSDL document. In a new perspective of testing, we demonstrate a concept of operation sequence paths generation combing interface contract model between the relationship of operations and data partition, which ultimately intend to improve the automation and efficiency of the test.

3 Model and Definitions

3.1 Operation Model Tree Based WSDL Description

Web services describe themselves to external services using WSDL, which is a XML-based language adhere to the W3C [27, 28]. Concerning on the stateful Web services, this paper proposes an operation tree model according to the references [16, 29], which formalizes the operation part in WSDL document for a single Web service into a logical tree structure, as shown in Fig. 1, where the root nodes correspond to the WSDL document, the nodes in layer 2 represent the included service operations, divided into operation input and output, the nodes in layer 3 represent the input/output data which are called by operations and the nodes in layer 4 represent the relationship between the input/output parameters. Compared with the previous works, it combines the Web service operations relationship with the single operation formal tree.

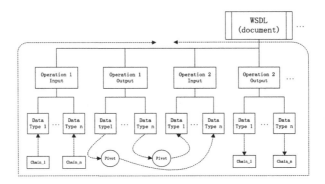

Fig. 1. Operation tree model

Definition 1. Web services operation tree model

Let $O = (Input(O), Output(O))$ denotes the operation elements for the WSDL document, where:

Input (O) = {M|M denotes an input message for operation O}.

Output (O) = {M|M denotes an output message for operation O}.

M = {P|P denote the part where M describes O}.

P = {G|G denote the XML definition related to P}.

According to Definition 1, the operation tree model construction algorithm is presented as follow:

Algorithm 1 operation tree model construction algorithm

```
Input: WSDL document;
Output: operation tree model O formed by operation ele-
ments in WSDL document.
CurLevelNode,NextLevelNode;
int level=0;
Root=build_node(Schema,Tree,0)
for each node Root.childNode( )
  CurLevelNode=NextLevelNode;
  Level++;
  Transform_node(node,Tree.Root);
end forTransform_node(Node,Root){
if(node.classtype==Element||node.classtype==
TYPE|| node.classtype==VALUE) {
  Bulid(Node,Root);}
else{
  New_Root=Root;}
for each node in Node.children

    Transform_node(node,New_Root);
end for; }
Build_node(Node,Root,level){
{ Child=new tree node;
  Child.set_attributes(Node,level);
  Root.children+=child;
  Retun child;  }
```

3.2   Semantic Annotation

The widely used WSDL documents are still lack of the behavior information (operation pre-conditions and results), however, it is difficult for testers to accomplish operation sequences testing only according to the standard WSDL. In order to enhance the descriptive ability of WSDL language in existing Web services standards, the WSDL-S is used to add the semantic information based on references [30–32], and adopt SWRL (semantic Web Rule Language) [33] in semantic annotation of WSDL document.

Add semantic tags to the operator using WSDL-S which contains the following 2 elements:

- "Behavior" tag is used to describe the operation behavior. The obtained results with the corresponding class in the ontology can be pointed out using behavior tag, which is described by effect tag in WSDL-S document.
- "Constraint" tag is used to describe the state. The entry condition of operation is described to ensure the implement of the operations, which is described by pre-condition tag in WSDL-S document.

3.3   EFSM (Extended Finite State Machine) Model

Stateful Web services testing is similar to traditional object-oriented software behavior testing, behavioral state contains the control state (operation sequences) and the data state (data variable value). This paper describes the interaction between the operation sequences based on the transformation of state in EFSM model according to the literature [7, 23], to assist the test path generation. The EFSM model for Web services testing is presented as follow:

Definition 2. EFSM model for Web services testing
It is a 6-tuple $(Q, \Sigma, \phi, q_0, F, QC)$ model, where:

Let Q denotes the state set, a finite set, each state represents historical record or condition judgment in a sequence of interactions.

Let Σ denotes the alphabet set, a finite set; it is the Cartesian collection of $O \times I$.

Let I denotes the input variable, O denotes the input variable.

Let $\phi : Q \times \Sigma \times QC \to Q$ denotes the Transfer function, ϕ denotes the next state, namely given a state, EFSM can transfer to another state according to input/output parameter conditions.

Let $q_0 \in Q$ denotes the initial state.

Let $F \subseteq Q$ denotes the receiving state set, namely the interaction state of users and Web service.

Let QC denotes the state condition set, the condition is composed of the state and the propositional logic formula.

According to the section B of this method, the extended WSDL document contains the semantic relations of Web services, so the conditional set of the state is represented by the semantic rule language SWRL.

3.4   Operation Interface Contract Model

This paper improves the model proposed by Hou [34] and Li [16], formalizes the information in single operation into a 5 tuple operation interface contract model, intend to capture the dependencies between the operations, the definition is as follows:

Definition 3. Operation interface contract model

$$Operation < Spec, Inputs, Outputs,$$
$$Control-Dependence, Data-Dependence > \quad , \text{ where:}$$

- Let $Spec : <ID, Name, Description>$ denotes the basic information for the operation (operation number, operation name and operation function description).
- Let $Inputs := \{data_i\}$ denotes the input parameter set.
- Let $Outputs := \{data_i\}$ denotes the output parameter set.
- Let $Control - Dependence := \{<ID, Dependence_i>\}$ denotes the control dependencies between operations, include Sequence constraints, temporal constraint and define the execution order of various constraint conditions.
- Let $Data - Dependence := \{<ID, Dependence_i>\}$ defines the data constrains between operations.

Definition 4. Data dependencies

$\exists d_1, d_2, O_1, O_2$ and $d_1 \in O_1 \cdot Inputs \bigcup O_2 \cdot Outputs, d_2 \in O_2 \cdot Inputs \bigcup O_2 \cdot Outputs$. If there exists function F, make $d_2 = F(d_1)$, then there is data dependencies between operation O_1 and O_2.

- If $d_1 \in O_1 \cdot Inputs$ and $d_2 \in O_2 \cdot Inputs$, then there is input dependencies between operation O_1 and O_2, denotes $IND(O_1, O_2)$.
- If $d_1 \in O_1 \cdot Outputs$ and $d_2 \in O_2 \cdot Outputs$, then there is output dependencies between operation O_1 and O_2, denotes $OUTD(O_1, O_2)$.

If $d_1 \in O_1 \cdot Outputs$ and $d_2 \in O_2 \cdot Outputs$, then there is input/output dependencies between operation O_1 and O_2, denotes $INOUTD(O_1, O_2)$.

4 Operation Sequence Test Path Generation

4.1 Operation Sequecnce Testing Workflow

Stateful Web services contain multiple operations which interact with each other through messages; however, testing single operation is not sufficient. The existing approaches used to construct the models relies on human experience, which results in test data deviation and low test efficiency. So we brought an operation sequence test path generate approach combing the EFSM model and interface contract model, as shown in Fig. 2.

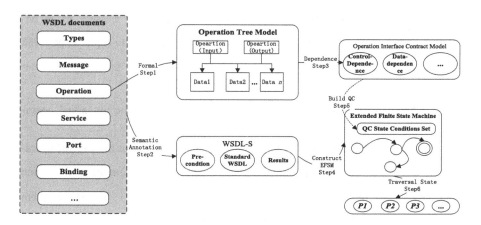

Fig. 2. Testing process of operation sequence

The path generation process is as follows:

Step 1. At first, operation tree model is constructed through the description information such as input/output parameters which was obtained by standard WSDL.

Step 2. Annotate the semantic information (pre-conditions and results) to operation in Web services according to the approach presented in Sect. 3.B.

Step 3. Operation interface contract model is constructed by the dependence relation between operations which is obtained based operation tree model according to Step 1(see Sect. 4.B).

Step 4. Construct EFSM model for Web services based on extended WSDL document with semantic annotation.

Step 5. Establish the condition set QC using the control dependencies in the interface contract model.

Step 6. Generate operation paths by traversing the EFSM constructed by Step 5.

4.2 Build Operation Dependencies

According to 3 rules definite in the literature [16], match the operation dependencies, the generation algorithm are as follows:

Algorithm 2 Operation dependencies generation algorithm

Input: WSDL documents;

Output: Control 、 data dependencies set between operations $Control\_Dependence, Data-Dependence$;

Initialize: $Un\,cov\,Operation = \varnothing$

① According to Figure 1, obtain operation set $Operation$, set a unmarked operation $o_i \in Operation$ as current operation, $UncovOperation = Opeartion - o_i$.

② Compare input message of operation o_1 with the output message of an unmarked operation $o_j \in Operation$, determine whether there are input/output data dependencies $INOUTD(o_i, o_j)$, if exist, add them into set $Control - Dependence, Data - Dependence$.

③ While($UncovOperation = \varnothing$),repeat step 2, until all the unmarked operations have been compared.

④ Set $Un\,cov\,Operation = Opeartion - o_i$,compare output message of operation o_i and input message of an unmarked operation $o_j \in Operation$,determine whether there are input/output data dependencies $INOUTD(o_j, o_i)$, if exist, add them into set $Control - Dependence, Data - Dependence$.

⑤While($UncovOperation = \varnothing$) , repeat step 4, until all the unmarked operations have been compared.

⑥ Mark current operation $mark(o_i)$.

⑦ Repeat step ①~⑥ until all operations have been marked.

4.3   EFSM Systematic Construction Algorithm

Based on the EFSM model proposed in Sect. 3.C, the obtained semantic WSDL and the interface contract model, this section proposed a systematic approach for EFSM construction, shown as follows:

Step 1. Build the behavior information table for Web services based on WSDL document.

Definition 5. Behavior information table

Build behavior information table $T \subseteq O \times A \times \{'I', 'S', ' '\}$, let O denote the set of the operations and A denote the set of the internal data variables in Web services. $\forall o \in O, \forall a \in A, (o, a, ' ') \in T$ or $(o, a, 'I') \in T$ or $(o, a, 'S') \in T, \forall o \in O$, where: ' ': denotes the operation does not access or access but the corresponding data variables are not modified. 'I': denotes the data variables are initialized by operation. 'S': The operation changes the corresponding data variables. Each data variable is required to have the initialization operation. $I(o) = \{a \in A|(o, a, 'I') \in T\}$ denotes the set of data variables initialized by the operation o. $S(o) = \{a \in A|(o, a, 'S') \in T\}$ denotes the set of data variables changed by operation o.

Step 2. Constructing the operating mode of Web services and its value domain based on the above behavioral information table.

Definition 6. Operation mode

Operation mode is an abstract variable e_k formed by the set $[a_{k1}, a_{k2}, \ldots, a_{ks}]$ of a number of data variables. Let behavior information table have m rows and n columns. Operations respectively are: $o_1, o_2, \ldots, o_m$ data variables are $a_1, a_2, \ldots, a_n$. If the set $e_k = [a_{k1}, a_{k2}, \ldots, a_{ks}]$ of s data variables constitute operation mode $\{a_{k1}, a_{k2}, \ldots, a_{ks}\}$, where $1 \leq s \leq n$, $1 \leq k1 \leq k2 \ldots \leq ks \leq n$, then the following conditions must be met: $\exists o \in O$, Conditions (1) and (2) are true.

(1) $\forall i(1 \leq i \leq s), (o, a_{ki}, ' ') \notin T$;
(2) $\forall a_j \notin \{a_{k1}, a_{k2}, \ldots, a_{ks}\}, 1 \leq j \leq n$.

By the above definition, operation mode is an abstract variable e_k formed by the set $OE = \{oe_1, oe_2, \ldots oe_s\}$ of a number of data variables. For operation mode e_k, the operations set satisfying conditions (1), (2) is called operation equivalence class of mode e_k, and describe the results through the SWRL with semantic information.

Step 3. Obtain the attributes of mode value.

Let the operation mode $e_k = [a_{k1}, a_{k2}, \ldots, a_{ks}]$ and the value of e_k be V_k, definition of mode value attributes is shown as below:

Definition 7. Mode value

$v : O_u$ is the set of operations where the current mode value cannot satisfy its preconditions of the corresponding operations.

$v : O_n$ denotes when mode e_k has valid value v. Let the set of operations be O, then $O = v : O_u \cup v : O_n$.

$v : O_c$ denotes when e_k has valid value v, the set of the operation which change v to other value in e_k value domain.

Mode value transition function η: If operation o_i changes v of mode e_k to w, where $o_i \in v : O_c$, then the mode value transition function $\eta(o_i, v, precondition) = w$, where $w \in V_k$ and precondition is the precondition of operation o_i.

Step 4. Obtain the states of EFSM model.

Algorithm 3 Obtain Web service state from EFSM

Input: Web services operation mode set $E = \{e_1, e_2...e_n\}$, corresponding set of value domain $V = \{V_1, V_2, ..., V_n\}$, operation set of Web services $O = \{o_1, o_2, ..., o_m\}$;

Output: EFSM state set Q and initial state q_0.

①By attributes of all mode values and according to conditions which constituting conflict mode value pair, set C of all conflict mode value pair (v, v') is calculated.

② Calculate the combinations of all mode value to form the possible state set Q,

$$Q = \prod_{i=1..n} V_i.$$

③For $\forall q \in Q$, let q_v be the set formed by mode values constructing q. If $v \in q_v$, $v' \in q_v$, and $(v, v') \in C$, then $Q = Q - \{q\}$.

④ Add initial state q_0.

⑤Return state set Q and the initial state q_0.

Step 5. Obtain the input and output sets of EFSM.

The set of input of all operations is modeled as the input set $\sum$ of EFSM. The set of output of all operations is modeled as the output set I of EFSM, where each input and output refers to one type of data.

Step 6. Obtain the processing function of EFSM: $\Phi : Q \times \Sigma \times QC \rightarrow Q$.

The constructed EFSM model is shown in Fig. 3, while the above process can be automated execution except the steps 1 and 7. Comparing with Web services testing modeling manually, the proposed approach saves test cost and avoids human errors.

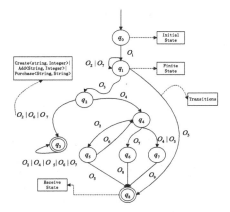

Fig. 3. Diagram of state transition for EFSM model

5 Data Generation Based on Operation Interface Contract Model

5.1 Test Data Generation Based on the Operation Interface Contract Model and Data Partition

The workflow proposed in the above chapter can acquire a stateful web service operation sequence test path automatically. Furthermore, operation sequences can be verified by test data for each operation sequence path one by one using conventional method. Nonetheless, there are still two shortcomings as follows:

(1) The test data for each operation sequence path have not considered the input/output dependencies between operations, as an example in a test path, the output message of previous operation may be the input message of next operation (where i and j said the index operation in the test path. $j > i$), so the test data for next operation can be derived from the output of previous operation. However, It will increase the workload of data generation while using conventional extraction methods;

(2) When obtaining the test data for an operation in test path, the appropriate input data should be taken into account to ensure that the test path can execute correctly.

Concerning on the above defects, we first design the test data using data partitioning method, divide test data into sub regions according to the parameters like input data and global variables [35, 36]. Through data partitioning analysis, the input/output data are verified the legitimacy, in order to guarantee the execution of the test path, improve the rationality of the design of test data. Besides, we match the input and output data of operation sequence according to the data dependencies described in operation interface contract model, finally reduce the unnecessary test data.

5.2 Test Suite Generation and Optimization Algorithm

Algorithm 4 Test suite generation algorithm

Input: Test paths set $O = \{P_1(o_1, o_2, o_5), P_2(), ..., P_n()\}$ in EFSM and interface contract model *Operation* $\diamondsuit$;

Output: Initial test data set *Testdata*$_0$.

For each set P_i in Set $O = \{P_1(o_1, o_2, o_5), P_2(), ..., P_n()\}$

  For each parameter o_i in set P_n

  $I = \varnothing$;

    if (o_i.pre==Null){

      Generate(o_i.input);

      execute(o_i.input,o_i.output);}

else if (o_i.input!=NULL) {   Dependency (o_i

.input,o_{i-1}.output)

      Generate($I - o_{j-1}$.output)}

      execute(o_i.input,o_i.output);}

    else {execute(o_i.input,o_i.output);}

  end for
end for

Algorithm 5 Test suite optimization algorithm

Input: Test suite set *Testdata*$_0$;
Output: Optimize test suite set *Testdata*.
While (o_i.next $\in P_n$)
{ GenerateDataFor(P_n)
  for each parameter o_i in set P_n:
    if (o_i.input $\notin Par_{valid}^{o_i}$){
    Break ;}
    end for }

6 Case Study

6.1 Coverage Analysis

To further validate the higher code and statement coverage of the generated test cases, 600 test cases are generated randomly. Here, we use business tool SoapUI to execute the test cases, the results show that some cases cannot return the results which lead to the invalid operation sequence path due to the blindness of data elements. Moreover, the generated test data are divided into 10 test sets with different selected test modules consisting of (50,100,150,200,250,300,350,400,450, 500) elements, respectively, then use software testing tool McCabe IQ (V8.0) to make instrument for these modules. The instrument source program is executed by different modules one by one while monitoring and obtaining service code coverage. Moreover, we compare our results with the code converge of those test data which are obtained randomly, the results confirm that our generated test suite perform well with higher statement and branch converge, as shown in Figs. 4 and 5.

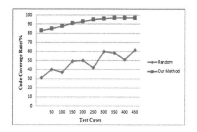

Fig. 4. Code coverage of each test suite   **Fig. 5.** Branch coverage of each test suite

According to the service requirement design document, the business process profile is constructed, and 18 paths are obtained for the executable operation sequence in the service of command execution module. Each operation sequence needs to establish multiple use case test paths according to the state transition of EFSM. In this paper, we analyze and calculate the coverage adequacy of service operation sequences for different number of test case sets, and compare them with randomly generated test cases. The coverage is shown in Table 1.

Table 1. Test cases and results

Number of test cases	Random		Our method	
	Coverage path	Path coverage/%	Coverage path	Path coverage/%
100	3	16.6	6	33.3
200	5	22.2	10	55.5
300	8	44.4	13	72.2
400	8	44.4	18	100
500	10	55.5	18	100

6.2 Analyze on Test Suite Error Detection Ability

To further validate the advantage of our proposed approach in error detection capability and test suite size, test cases are generated by existing methods for the operation sequence in tested service and compared the executed results with our proposed approach, as shown in Fig. 6. In addition, the plurality of operation are given in Table 2 for each existing methods during the process of execution: as we expected, our proposed method find more errors with fewer cases which show that the generated test cases have strong pertinence.

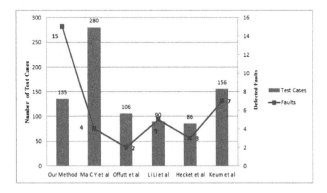

Fig. 6. Number of test cases and number of faults

The approaches presented in literature [13, 37] devote to the test data generation for single operation, but there are few errors that can be detected by single operation testing using boundary value method for stateful Web services. Although the approach proposed in literature [16, 18] also enhances the operation sequence testing using data flow, this approach only consider the relationship between a small amount of accidental operation, resulted in the number of cases is not enough, which reduce the cases of error detection ability. Besides, a model analysis approach is proposed in literature [7], because the model only relies on the generation of test personnel's experience, there is a serious imbalance on the generated data while reducing the testing efficiency, and the dependencies between data are not take into account simple for each operation which lead too large scale of the generated test data, cannot meet the requirement of testing. Therefore, our proposed method has the advantage on the test suite size and error detection ability while considering the interaction of complex sequences of operations.

In addition, according to the Table 2, some test cases cannot get the results of execution; this is reflected in the test data generation for test path without considering the feasibility of testing path. Some data may be illegal in the path which cause the path cannot be performed, unable to return the expected results. And these do not return the correct results case, the input parameters are often consistent with the data type of the demand, but submitted to the service, cannot return output result, it will be difficult to determine whether there is a false case design result or the Web services itself has defect. Successfully, the proposed method enhances the validity of test data according

Table 2. Test cases and results

Data generation method	Test cases	Detected faults	Fault description	No results	Time cost
Our method	135	15	Boundary exceptions, null value and operation interact exceptions faults etc.	2	120 s
Ma et al. [13]	280	4	Function faults for single operation	65	1000 s
Offutt et al. [37]	106	2	Partly boundary exceptions,	26	150 s
Li et al. [17]	90	5	Partly operation interact exceptions	10	180 s
Hecket [19]	86	3	Partly function faults	15	200 s
Keum [7]	156	7	Operation interact exceptions faults etc.	8	325 s

to the method of data partition and use the smallest time cost. In order to ensure the test path execution, achieve the design case is feasible, effective and efficiency while less returning no results.

7 Conclusion

In summary, we proposes a test data generation approach for stateful Web services, firstly build operation tree model and add semantic annotation based on standard WSDL, according to the information enhancement behavior, use finite state machine model (EFSM) to describe the dynamic behavior of the service, according to the test data generation interface contract model a single Web service operation sequence, and the superiority of the method in the test suite and error detection capability is verified by examples of previous studies cannot effectively solve the problem of automatic generation of operation sequence data, enhance the effectiveness of the degree of automation and test data path generation, so as to improve the automatic Web service the quality and efficiency of test data generation.

References

1. Mei, H., Zhang, L.: A framework for testing web services and its supporting tool. In: Proceedings of International Workshop on Service-Oriented System Engineering, pp. 199–206. IEEE Computer Society, Washington (2005)
2. Bartolini, C., Bertolino, A., Marchetti, E., et al.: WS-TAXI: a WSDL-based testing tool for web services. In: Proceedings of the International Conference on Software Testing Verification and Validation, pp. 326–335. IEEE Computer Society, Washington (2009)
3. Xu, L., Li, Y.H., Chen, L., et al.: A testing method for web services focusing on user requirements. Chin. J. Comput. **37**(3), 512–521 (2014)
4. Elia, I.A., Laranjeiro, N., Vieira, M.: A practical approach towards automatic testing of web services interoperability. Int. J. Web Serv. Res. **12**(3), 103–129 (2015)
5. Brenner, D., Atkinson, C., Hummel, O., et al.: Strategies for the run-time testing of third party web services. In: Proceedings of International Conference on Service-Oriented Computing an Applications, pp. 114–121. IEEE, Piscataway (2007)

6. Sinha, A., Paradkar, A.: Model based functional conformance testing of web services operating on persistent data. In: Proceeding of 2006 Workshop on Testing, Analysis, and Verification of Web Services and Application, pp. 17–22. ACM, New York (2006)

7. Keum, C., Kang, S., Ko, I.-Y., Baik, J., Choi, Y.-I.: Generating test cases for web services using extended finite state machine. In: Uyar, M.Ü., Duale, A.Y., Fecko, M.A. (eds.) TestCom 2006. LNCS, vol. 3964, pp. 103–117. Springer, Heidelberg (2006). https://doi.org/10.1007/11754008_7

8. Ma, C.Y., Zhou, Y., Lu, W.: Automatic test for web services. Comput. Sci. **39**(2), 162–169 (2012)

9. Li, Z., Jie, S., Wei, J., et al.: BPEL4WS unit testing: framework and implementation. In: Proceedings of the 2005 International Conference on Web Services (ICWS 2005), pp. 103–110. IEEE Computer Society, Washington (2005)

10. Tsai, W.T., Paul, R., Wang, Y., et al.: Extending WSDL to facilitate web services testing. In: Proceedings of the 7th IEEE International Symposium on High Assurance Systems Engineering, pp. 171–172. IEEE Computer Society, Washington (2002)

11. Xu, W.Z., Offutt, J., Luo, J.: Testing web services by XML perturbation. In: Proceedings of the 16th IEEE International Symposium on Software Reliability Engineering, pp. 256–266. IEEE Computer Society, Washington (2005)

12. Hanna, S., Munro, M.: An approach for specification-based test case generation for Web services. In: Proceedings of 2007 IEEE ACS International Conference on Computer Systems and Application, pp. 16–23. IEEE Computer Society, Washington (2007)

13. Ma, C.Y., Du, C.L., Zhang, T., et al.: WSDL-based automated test case generation for web service. In: Proceedings of the Computer Science and Software Engineering, pp. 731–737. IEEE Computer Society, Washington (2008)

14. Siblini, R., Mansour, N.: Testing web services. In: Proceedings of IEEE International Conference on Computer Systems and Applications, p. 135-vii. IEEE Computer Society, Washington (2005)

15. Jiang, Y., Xin, G.M., Shan, J.H., et al.: A method of automated test data generation for web service. Chin. J. Comput. **28**(4), 568–577 (2005)

16. Bai, X.Y., Dong, W.L., Tsai, W.T., et al.: WSDL-based automatic test case generation for web services testing. In: Proceedings of the 2005 IEEE International Workshop on Service-Oriented System Engineering, pp. 207–212. IEEE Computer Society, Washington (2005)

17. Li, L., Wu, C.: Automatic message flow analyses for web services based on WSDL. In: Proceedings of 2007 IEEE International Conference, pp. 25–28. IEEE Computer Society, Washington (2007)

18. Bertolino, A., Polini, A.: The audition framework for testing web services interoperability. In: Proceedings of the 31st EUROMICRO Conference on Software Engineering and Advanced Application, pp. 134–142. IEEE Computer Society, Washington (2005)

19. Heckel, R., Mariani, L.: Automatic conformance testing of web services. In: Cerioli, M. (ed.) FASE 2005. LNCS, vol. 3442, pp. 34–48. Springer, Heidelberg (2005). https://doi.org/10.1007/978-3-540-31984-9_4

20. Belli, F., Linschulte, M.: Event-driven modeling and testing of web services. In: Computer Software and Applications Conference, pp. 1163–1173. IEEE Computer Society, Washington (2008)

21. Paradkar, A., Sinha, A., Williams, C., et al.: Automated functional conformance test generation for semantic web services. In: Proceedings of IEEE International Conference on Web Services, pp. 110–117. IEEE Computer Society, Washington (2007)

22. Sinha, A., Paradkar, A.: Model-based functional conformance testing of web services operating on persistent data. In: Proceedings of the 2006 Workshop on Testing Analysis and Verification of Web Services and Applications, pp. 17–22. IEEE Computer Society, Washington (2006)
23. Paradkar, A.M.: Automated functional conformance test generation for semantic web services. In: Proceedings of 2007 IEEE International Conference on Web Services, pp. 110–117. IEEE Computer Society, Washington (2007)
24. Ma, C.Y., Wu, J.S., Zhang, T.: Web services sequence testing based on stream X-machine. In: Proceedings of the 10th International Conference on Quality Software, pp. 232–239. IEEE Computer Society, Washington (2010)
25. Bai, X.Y., Lu, H., Zhang, Y., et al.: Interface-based automated testing for open software architecture. In: Proceedings of the Computer and Applications Conference Workshops, pp. 149–154. IEEE Computer Society, Washington (2011)
26. Petrova, A., Dessislava, I., et al.: TASSA: testing framework for web service orchestrations. In: Proceedings of the 10th International Workshop on Automation of Software Test, pp. 8–12. IEEE Computer Society, Washington (2015)
27. Vanderveen, P., Janzen, M., Tappenden, A.F.: A web service test generator. In: Proceedings of 2014 IEEE International Conference on Software Maintenance and Evolution, pp. 516–520. IEEE Computer Society, Washington (2014)
28. W3C.Web service description language (WSDL) version 2.0 part1: core language [EB/OL], 26 June 2007. http://www.w3.org/TR/wsdl20/. Accessed 23 May 2016
29. Belhajjame, K., Embury, S.M.: Verification of semantic web service annotations using ontology-based partitioning. IEEE Trans. Serv. Comput. 7(3), 515–528 (2014)
30. He, L.J., Liu, L.C., Wu, C.: A modified operation similarity measure method based on WSDL description. Chin. J. Comput. 31(8), 1331–1339 (2008)
31. Kunal, M.: WSDL-S: Adding Semantics to WSDL- WhitePaper [EB/OL], 26 June 2007. http://www.w3.org/TR/2003/,2003-04-01John. Accessed 23 May 2016
32. Miller, J., Verma, K., Rajasekaran, P., et al.: WSDL-S: Adding semantics to WSDL - White paper [EB/OL], January 2004. http://lsdis.cs.uga.edu/library/download/wsdl-s.pdf. Accessed 23 May 2016
33. Horrocks, I.: SWRL: a semantic web rule language combining owland ruleML. W3C [EB/OL], May 2004. Accessed 23 May 2016
34. Hou, K.J., Bai, X.Y., Lu, H., et al.: Web service test data generation using interface semantic contract. J. Softw. 24(9), 2020–2041 (2013)
35. Ostrand, T.J., Baiter, M.J.: The category-partition method for specifying and generating functional tests. Commun. ACM 31(6), 676–686 (1988)
36. Chen, T.Y., Poon, P., Tse, T.H.: A choice relation framework for supporting category-partition test ease generation. IEEE Trans. Softw. Eng. 29(7), 577–593 (2003)
37. Xu, W., Offutt, J., Luo, J.: Testing web services by XML perturbation. In: International Symposium on Software Reliability Engineering, pp. 257–266. IEEE Computer Society, Washington (2005)

Transient Fault Detection and Recovery Mechanisms in μC/OS-II

Chengrui He[1], Li Zhang[1], Gang Wang[2], Ziqi Zhen[2],
and Lei Wang[2(✉)]

[1] School of Software, Beihang University, Beijing 100191, China
{hcr728,lily}@buaa.edu.cn
[2] School of Computer Science and Engineering, Beihang University,
Beijing 100191, China
{wanggang,zhnzq,wanglei}@buaa.edu.cn

Abstract. In avionics, satellites are widely used in meteorology, navigation and investigation. Satellites in space, however, are subject to radiation that causes transient fault. This often leads to single event upset on the logic state of device, undermining the stability and the correctness of the system. For example, transient fault can cause errors in the program execution flow, changing the state of or even crashing the system. In order to solve these problems, this paper puts forward a coarse-grained error detection scheme based on function-call relationships. We instrument signature codes at function entry and exit points at compile time to perform dynamic detection at runtime. We apply this method in the μC/OS-II kernel on a DSP platform. The coarse-grained error detection technology can reduce storage overhead effectively compared with basic block-based detection technology. For the moment, this method could be used in imbedded operating systems μC/OS-II, and it can simulate a program flow error caused by transient fault with the method of fault injection. With this method, it can help to detect the occurrence of an error and guarantee the normal running of the system using recovery mechanism. Finally, the result shows that technology of transient fault detection which is based on function call relationship could detect errors effectively, which guarantees the reliability and security of the running system.

Keywords: Transient fault · Static instrumentation · μC/OS-II

1 Introduction

In the aerospace industry, the enhancement of satellite systems increasingly relies on complex microelectronic devices [1, 2]. Transient errors such as single-event upsets (SEU) [3] in sensitive areas of semiconductor devices can happen [4], however, when large-scale integrated circuits in satellite systems are exposed to various high-energy particles and cosmic rays. An SEU may cause the program to run away and produce fatal errors in the system [5, 6]. Onboard operating systems are particularly vulnerable [7]. The research on software detection technology for control flow [8] is basically based on test evaluation. The test determines whether the system is running incorrectly by using a specific input data set on the system against the dynamic run value and the

© Springer Nature Switzerland AG 2018
L. Bu and Y. Xiong (Eds.): SATE 2018, LNCS 11293, pp. 202–218, 2018.
https://doi.org/10.1007/978-3-030-04272-1_13

preset value [9, 10]. However, the fault model of control flow has an uncertainty factor, and the different injection method lead to different result which generated from test data [11]. On the other hand, the software detection method for the control flow is based on fine-grained [12, 13]. If the inserted verification program is too large, it also affects the storage space of the real-time system.

Through the above analysis, we put forward a method for coarse-grained transient fault detection of program flow without changing the hardware environment of onboard computer, which enables the on-board operating system to detect transient faults. Meanwhile, we followed the fault analysis with a recovery mechanism to guarantee the normal operation of the onboard operating system. Finally, we implemented the method on a DSP platform. Applying the fault detection mechanism to the μC/OS-II operating system can capture system errors in time, which helps to further improve the security of the system and avoid unnecessary losses. Therefore, it has strong significance in detection method of transient fault.

The paper is organized as follows: Sect. 2 introduces the design of the fault detection scheme, mainly using the instrumentation algorithm for the function call relationship and instantiating the verification on the μC/OS-II system. Section 3 presents the design of the transient fault recovery mechanism. Section 4 describes the system implementation. Section 5 evaluates the scheme. Section 6 introduces related work. Section 7 concludes our work.

2 The Fault Detection Scheme

In this paper, we propose a coarse-grained fault detection method based on function call relationship. This method is built on the compilation technology. By compiling and processing the source code at the compile stage, the auxiliary analysis file would be generated, and then the plug-in tool is used to statically insert the source program. Finally, the instrumented program is verified in real-time experiment. Thus, we can determine the effectiveness of the system.

2.1 Framework

The design of the scheme is shown in Fig. 1.

Fig. 1. The system is divided into two parts, besides the front-end compilation processing part and the back-end code insertion module.

The system consists of two parts: the front-end compilation processing and the back-end code insertion. The front-end processes input source program and generates auxiliary analysis files. The output of the first stage is the input of the second. The back-end processes the auxiliary analysis files in order to determine the function call relationship graph. This stage imposes signature constraints based on attribute information of each function node in the function call graph.

With the knowledge of the function call graph, the code-insertion tool instruments the source program. Within this framework, the system deploys dynamic functions to validate the instrumented code.

2.2 Code Instrumentation Algorithm Based on Function Call Relationship

The instrumentation algorithm is built on the function call graph. Each function node is regarded as the most basic unit and each non-tail function node is assigned a unique signature attribute value Li. A function node corresponds to a bit in a binary number, e.g., for the jth function node, the jth bit is 1, and the remaining bits are 0, where j $\in$ (1, n). The variable Sin stores the value of the function attribute of the parent node, and the variable Lin holds the value of the signature attribute of the parent node. The relationship between function calls is represented by a numerical value, which is the function attribute. In the function call relationship, we regard function nodes other than root, leaf and tail nodes as ordinary nodes, and all nodes need to be detected. A function node with zero in-degree is called the root node. The in-degree of the function is zero means that there is no other function called it. Besides, a function node with zero out-degree is called the leaf node. If the out-degree of the function is zero, it means that the function did not call other function. We define a function node with zero out-degree and no definition in the source program as a tail node. For each ordinary node, a relationship attribute Si is assigned to record the calling relationships between functions. The value of Si is the logical OR of the attribute signature values of all non-tail nodes that can be directly called by this function node. Jump updates refer to using the global variable S to track the jump relationship of the function. Each time the function jumps, the value of S is updated once. A global runtime signature S is used to perform jump updates among functions. The global signature L holds the current node attribute value [14]. Whenever the function occurs exits, it is processed once with this code instrumentation algorithm. We have two rules for adding instructions at the entry and exit of a function:

$$Sin = S; \; Lin = L; \; L = Li; \; if \; (Li \; \& \; Sin == 0) \; error; \; S = Si; \tag{1}$$

$$If (Li \: ! = L) \: error; \; S = Sin; \; L = Lin; \tag{2}$$

We add rule (1) at the entrance of the function to validate whether the caller is legit. Rule (2) at the exit determines whether the function returns to the right callee. The global signature value is dynamically updated at runtime, and the initial value is the relationship attribute value $S1$ of the root node [15]. Since the root node is the program execution start function, we only need to update the global signature value at the root node entry, that is, when $S = S1$, and $L = L1$. Moreover, we compare the global signature value and $S1$ at the exit of the root node. When $((S\ != S1)\&\&(L\ != L1))$ we report error.

A leaf node calls none of other nodes. Therefore, it does not assign the relationship attribute Si, and the leaf node's entry verification instruction can be simplified as follows:

$$Sin = S;\ Lin = L;\ L = Li;\ if\ (Li\ \&\ Sin = = 0)\ error;\ S = 0; \tag{3}$$

$$If\,(Li\,! = L)\ error;\ S = Sin;\ L = Lin; \tag{4}$$

Figure 2 shows an abstract model of the program instrumented in accordance with the above-mentioned rules. The $S = Si$ statement is missing in the rules that insert at the leaf node's entry. The function of this statement is mainly reflected in the function nodes that have called other subroutines. This is to pass the attribute relationship of the current function node to the subroutine and so that error detection can be performed correctly when the function is nested. Meanwhile, the verification instructions inserted at the head and the end of function nodes are simple logic operations and assignments. In this article, we regard the instrumentation code as an atomic operation. The instrumentation code is much smaller than the function body itself.

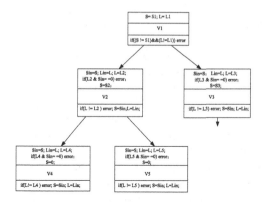

Fig. 2. This is the model after interpolation according to the above rules. Due to the particularity of leaf nodes, $S = Si$ is missing in the insertion rules.

In Fig. 3, each function node is assigned a signature attribute value Li and each ordinary function node is assigned a relationship attribute value Si. The signature values of $V1$, $V2$, and $V3$ are $L1$ (00000001), $L2$ (00000010), and $L3$ (00000100), respectively. The value of the relationship attribute value $S1$ is the result of logical OR of $L2$ and $L3$. The relationship attribute value of $S2$ is determined by the function relationship that is called by $V2$. In this function graph, we assume that the value of $S2$ is 1000 0000.

When the function of $V1$ runs correctly, it calls that of $V2$. Instructions from rule (1) execute at the entry of the $V2$ function and determine whether the call is from the right caller. Afterward, the value of *Sin* is updated to 00000110 which is logical AND with the attribute value of the current node. As shown in Fig. 4, since *Sin* has been updated to the relationship attribute value of the parent function, the result of the AND operation of *L2* and *Sin* is not NULL. Therefore, the verification code continues to execute to the end of rule (1). The running signature value *S* is updated to the relationship attribute value *S2* of the current function node. If other non-tail function nodes are called in *V2*, the relationship property value of *V2* is passed to the child function node. After the function node is correctly executed, it will use the rule (1) at the end to determine whether the current attribute value *Li* is equal to the global signature value *L*, thereby discovering runtime error and updating the running value signature *S* and *L* when the function exits.

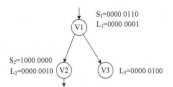

Fig. 3. This is the function call diagram. There are three function nodes, where *V1* and *V2* represent a common function node and *V3* represents a leaf node.

Fig. 4. This is runtime signature diagram. After executing the function head insert instruction, and then logically AND with the current node's attribute value, determine if the result is null.

When the function node *V2* returns, in *V1*, the runtime signature *S* is restored to the *S* value before *V1* was called, and *L* is also restored to the attribute value *L1*. So, when *V1* calls *V3*, according to the instruction rule (3), the system only needs to decide whether an error has occurred at the entrance of the leaf function node *V3*, and it is no longer necessary to update the value of the runtime signature *S*.

Our work is based on the function call relationship method. The code insertion is used by the import and export of modules which are based on functions. With the help of the def file in the auxiliary analysis files, the function's entry can be found and the line number information of functions can be found in the source file. On the other hand, it is necessary for the code instrumentation tool to scan the functions to determine their exits.

2.3   Fault Classification

During the operation of the system, external interference can easily cause errors in the execution of the program, e.g., a random jump to the wrong code. The system may not detect such an exception, but often the error has already affected the system itself. Such mistakes can often lead to catastrophic consequences. For these cases, analyzing calls or jumps for erroneous executions is valuable. This section divides the types of errors into two categories for analysis: jumping to the function entry and jumping to the function body.

(1) Illegal jump to the entry of another program:

According to the signature method, at the entrance of the function $V2$, the instrumented verification code is performed according to the instruction rule (1), $Sin = S$, and the value of Sin is updated to the relationship attribute value of the function $V1$, that is, $Sin = 0000\ 0110$.

Next, the call relationship between the functions $V1$ and $V2$ is examined, and the result of the logical AND of $L2$ and Sin is not zero. So, this call is legal. At the entrance of function $V2$, the value of real-time signature S is updated to the value represented by the child function, $0001\ 1000$. As shown in Fig. 5, the function $V2$ erroneously calls $V3$. At the entry of $V3$, first Sin is updated to the value of real-time signature S. As Sin should be the attribute relationship value of $S2$, i.e., $Sin = 0001\ 1000$. $L3$ is $0000\ 0100$ and the logical AND of Sin and $L3$, $Sin\ \&\ L3 ==0$. This means calling function $V3$ by $V2$ is illegal.

Fig. 5. Incorrect function call diagram, the function $V2$ erroneously calls $V3$.

Fig. 6. Schematic diagram of the jump in the faulty function body.

(2) Illegal jump to another function's body:

The solid line indicates a legal function call. The dotted line, however, represents the situation where executing the function $V2$, the program makes an illegal jump to the middle of the function $V3$ due to some error. As shown in Fig. 6.

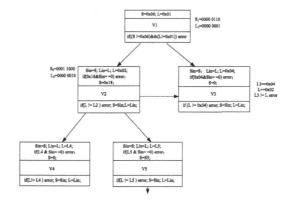

Fig. 7. Function error jump model diagram after instrumentation.

At the entry of the function *V2*, the signature information first updates the value of the real-time signature *S* to *S* = 0001 1000, and the global signature value *L* is updated to the value of *L2*, that is, *L* = 0000 0010. Jumping to the middle of function *V3* skips the entry verification. In *V3*, the value of real-time signature *S* stays 0001 1000. At the verification code at the exit of *V3*, since the global signature value *L* is not updated at *V3*'s entry and still the value of *L2*, the error is detected. Next, the system hands over the captured error to the error handler. The model after the insertion is as shown in the Fig. 7.

3 Error Recovery Mechanism

3.1 The Transparent Checkpoint Module

To ensure correct execution, a module's states should be kept consistent upon restarting [16]. To restart a module, the operating system must save and restore its runtime states transparently. Thus, we design a kernel module in the μC/OS-II kernel, called "the transparent checkpoint module".

The task of this module is to be responsible for the state information storage of these modules which in the kernel security points of other kernel modules. Once a kernel module errors while the system is running, the kernel is notified by the exception mechanism of μC/OS-II, and the kernel recovery the faulty module. In addition to overloading the kernel module, the kernel also restores the state information of the faulty module saved by the transparent checkpoint module to the kernel after a reboot, so that the kernel module can run correctly and continuously after restart. The transparent checkpoint needs to modify the μC/OS-II compilation configuration file, compiling the transparent checkpoint module into the system kernel image; Besides, it can modify the system kernel initialization code to enable the kernel start the transparent checkpoint module during initialization, and then run as a system task.

Since only one scheduling operation is performed in one operation, the status of the scheduling module in one running process can be divided into two types: a state before the execution of the scheduling operation (represented by state A) and a state after the execution of the scheduling operation (using state B). When the scheduling module running error in state A or B, the scheduling module could directly restore the statement before the error through the state information saved by the kernel security point, so that the scheduling module can continue running after a reboot.

As shown in Fig. 8. It processes notification messages sent by the kernel before modules are launched and saves the states including start addresses and lengths for the modules.

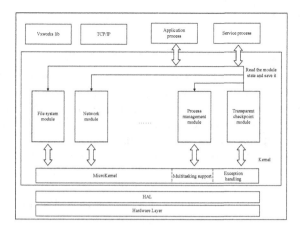

Fig. 8. The system structure diagram of adding the transparent checkpoint module.

3.2 The Kernel Security Point Module

The transparent checkpoint module must decide when, called a kernel security point [17], to save the state information of other kernel modules. It does this before and after the run of the scheduling module, as shown in Fig. 9.

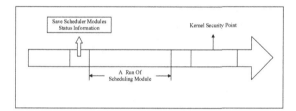

Fig. 9. The process of the transparent checkpoint module saving the status information of the scheduling module.

The timing has some major advantages. It is correct. The transparent checkpoint module will perform the two-core security point pair scheduling each time the scheduling module runs. The status information of the module is saved before an error occurs. The scheduling module runs only after a scheduling operation is completed and it generates an error at any time during a run. The most recently saved state information is the closest to the time of an error. Last, the scheme is simple, because the start and end of each operation of the scheduling module are fixed points. The transparent checkpoint module does not need to evaluate various conditions to determine the kernel security point and can relatively easily select the kernel security points.

4 System Implementation

4.1 μC/OS-II Experimental Environment Construction

The hardware platform we use is based on the Texas Instruments (TI) TMS320C6713 quad-core DSP processor, which is a 32-bit high-speed floating-point type DSP. The TMS320C6713 processor is based on the high-performance, advanced very-long-instruction-word (VLIW) architecture developed by TI, making this DSP an excellent choice for multifunction applications and real-time processing.

Our work is to sign and insert the μC/OS-II part of the source code and to run the compiled μC/OS-II kernel image on the DSP. The μC/OS-II image is compiled in WindowsXP.

We first need to modify and compile μC/OS-II on CCS. The image is then loaded onto the DSP through the emulator. Next the μC/OS-II operating system is kicked off. Code Composer Studio provides the functions of creating and compiling μC/OS-II kernel image, cutting μC/OS-II kernel [18], online debugging with target DSP development board, DSP status view, etc. The host machine construction includes:

(1) Installing the Code Composer Studio integrated development environment.
(2) Modifying the profile, including the BSP bootloader and CMD layout file.
(3) Compiling and downloading the program to the DSP development board through the emulator.

4.2 Generate a Secondary Analysis File

The open source static call graph generation tool Codeviz is used to modify GCC to obtain the auxiliary analysis file during compilation. This file contains information of each function including their relationships.

The function call sequence can be obtained by using the bt command under the gdb debugger. The function call sequence table is as shown in Table 1. The struct cgraph_node is produced after analyzing the abstract syntax tree and the call graph. We find the first function node called by node, and then finds each function node called by node according to the struct cgraph_edge, and finally gets all the calling relationships from the function node in the call graph.

Table 1. Function call sequence.

Calling sequence	Function name
1	main
2	toplev_main
3	c_common_parse_file
4	c_parse_file
5	yyparse
6	finish_funtion
7	cgraph_finalize_function
8	cgraph_alalyze_function

Using the above method, we obtain the auxiliary analysis file including the function definition (def file) and the function call relationship (call file). The def file contains for each function the name of the file and the line where the function is defined. The call file records the function call relationship, which contains the calling relationship of each pair of functions, and the name of the file where the function is called. Also, it contains the exact number of rows in the called functions.

4.3   Error Detection Under μC/OS-II

To combine error detection with recovery, we added a new module in the kernel which provides an interface for the task scheduler. Figure 10 shows the block diagram of the μC/OS-II kernel scheduling management modularization. We focus on function-based calling relationships in the module. Instrumentation and error recovery of the scheduling module are implemented.

As the scheduling module schedules tasks, if it receives an error trigger signal, it will pass a global identifier to a signature value. At runtime, the signature information at the function entry and exit is examined. When the condition is met, the system detects an error and analyzes the captured global identifier. If it indicates an exception, then an exception-causing instruction can be added to the task scheduling module for the captured information. After the exception is handled, the scheduling module is restored.

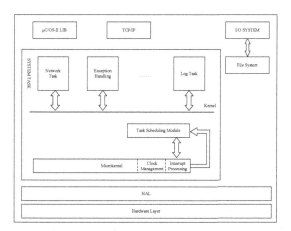

Fig. 10. System diagram of scheduling task modularity.

4.4   Error Recovery Under μC/OS-II

In this paper, we inject errors at runtime to conduct experiments. The method of error injection is to statically insert some instructions that cause errors in various areas of the scheduling module. And add a command in the kernel to determine whether to execute the instructions that caused the error. Besides providing a programming interface seterrnum() and geterrnum() to the upper layer to set and acquire the error number variable, so that the test program can inject errors into the scheduling module at run time, such as divide-by-zero errors, overflow errors and so on. In order to combine error detection and recovery technology, we add a bug repair module. The error repair module provides an interface to other kernel modules and application layer programs for call testing. To inject errors in program flows, a set of error test functions, testN_err (), are registered. The scheduling module calls the test functions.

The process is shown in Fig. 11. The activation program sends an error signal to the scheduling module; then the scheduling module changes the signature value of the function defined in the error repair module by the global variable according to the received error signal, and if the signature information is found during the function run, the signature statement is found. When an error occurs, the error flag is passed to the scheduling module itself. The scheduling module receives the error flag, triggering an exception. Finally, the exception handler will restore the task scheduling module.

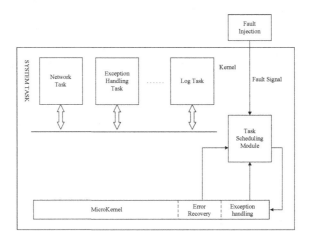

Fig. 11. The flowchart of fault injection and recovery.

5   Experimental Results and Analysis

In this paper, the error injection types are divided into two categories. One is the wrong function call relationship, that is, one function jumps by mistake to the entrance of another function. The error detection algorithm detects the error by executing the instrumented code at the function's entry. The other is when a function jumps to the middle of another function. At this time, the algorithm detects by executing the instrumented code exported by the function.

We insert a prompt to capture the wrong output statement in the exception handler to determine whether the system can capture the fault signal normally. When the scheduling module captures the fault signal, it will generate an exception and the fault would be processed by the exception handler. The prompt statement can be output, as shown in the following Fig. 12. First, this paper selects a set of one-way communication test cases. When the client sends a specific message value to the server, the client injects an error into the scheduling module. According to the output Information, therefore, we are able to determine that the injected error is captured normally.

This paper selects another set of test case to inject errors into the scheduling module, as shown in Fig. 13. In this case, the main program creates three concurrent execution processes. Two of the child processes serve as communication processes, and the other one injects an error into the scheduling module at set intervals. Figure 13 shows that each recovery of the scheduling module does not affect the execution of the upper-layer application. The final experimental results show that the errors are injected into the different parts of the scheduling module for 30 times, and the system can correctly capture errors.

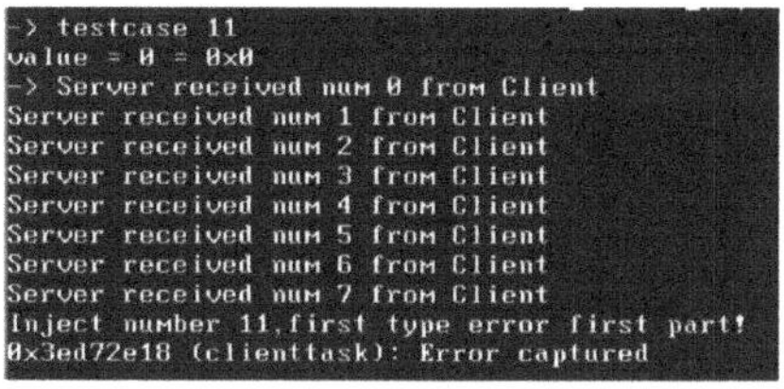

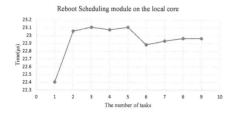

Fig. 12. Error capture schematic. 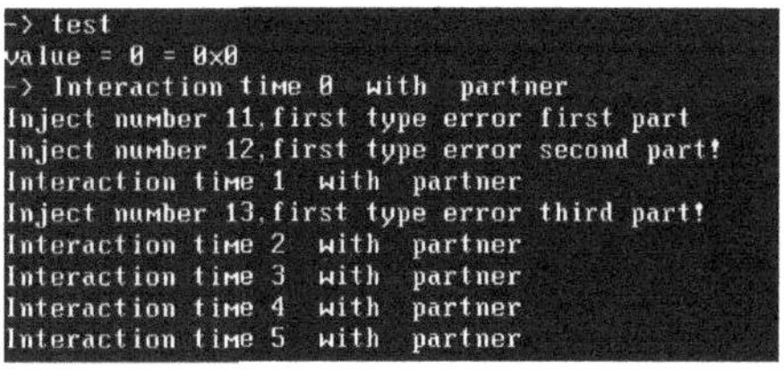   **Fig. 13.** Injecting errors & recovery.

In the case of the local core and other DSP cores, we separately perform the overhead time experiments that the scheduling module captured the fault and start recovery. The testing results are shown in the following Figs. 14 and 15.

Fig. 14. Reboot on the local core. 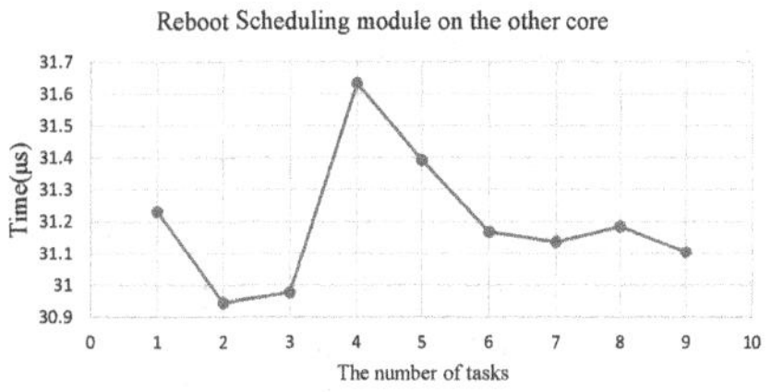   **Fig. 15.** Reboot on the other core.

These two figures show the time spent on restarting a task that does not require parameters in both the local core and other cores when the system detects an error under different loads. Among them, the following points can be seen:

Firstly, the time cost to restarting a task at the local core is lower than the time cost on other cores. It means that if the option exists, the task should be restarted at the local core as much as possible.

Second, the two figures show the relationship between the overhead time and the system load. Among them, the more tasks that are running at the same time, the higher load on the system. As can be seen from the Figs. 14 and 15, our method is not sensitive to the load of the system in this paper. In an embedded environment, this feature is the most feasible way to ensure maximum real-time, high stability and high availability of the system.

In addition, we also experimented with overhead time that to restart a task which requires parameters on the other DSP cores.

As can be seen from the Fig. 16, even if the parameters required by the task are small, but it will take more time to restart in the other cores. This is determined by the inter-core communication mechanism of the hardware. However, in the case where the parameters need to be passed, the time cost and the size of the passed parameters presents a relatively positive linear correlation. This method is in line with the expectations of this paper in terms of time overhead.

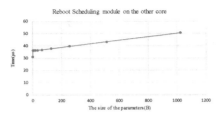

Fig. 16. Reboot on the other core (with parameters).

This would also show that in the case of parameters need to be passed. It is more efficient when task restart at the local core. This is due to the local core restart task does not need to send parameters, that is, the parameter is sent or not, and the parameter size has no effect on the restart cost of the task at the local core.

We test code coverage by using the Gcov tool in the fine-grained method which based on basic block signature. The gcov tool is used to count the 62 C programs currently tested, and the average of each plug-in statement takes 15B. If a fine-grained interpolation algorithm is applied to each basic block, then a total of at least 7374 * 15 = 110610B additional storage overhead will be generated, and the percentage of increased storage space will up to 31.4%. Such a large storage overhead can have a big impact on the real-time operating system. If the inserted verification program is too large, the storage overhead generated by the interpolation algorithm will be much larger than the coarse-grained interpolation algorithm proposed in this paper. Therefore, the coarse-grained method we proposed can save more time and space than the fine-grained method.

The coarse-grained detection method mainly focuses on jumps between functions, and cannot be detected for instruction errors inside functions. For example, a function jumps to a part of the middle of another function during execution, and returns to the original position after executing several statements. Then in this case, there is neither an entry detection point nor an exit detection point through the function. This kind of error is easily missed by the coarse-grained detection method. However, the fine-grained detection method divides the basic blocks inside the program, and there is a large possibility that an error instruction inside the function will appear in a basic block. Therefore, when the above error occurs, the fine-grained detection method is more advantageous, and the coarse-grained method cannot handle the problems that all fine-grained methods can handle.

By injecting errors into the scheduling module, we proved the reliability of the fault detection algorithm through experiments. Finally, the fault detection and recovery mechanism effectively ensure system safety and reliability.

6 Related Work

Single-event upset is a kind of transient error, also known as "soft error" [19], which can lead to misoperation of electronic systems [20]. Since the discovery of single-event upset [21] problems, domestic and foreign experts have been studying some mature transient error detection methods to prevent transient errors such as single-event upset [22, 23]. From the error detection method, it can be divided into hardware-based detection technology and software-based detection technology [24].

Hardware-based inspection is usually done by adding corresponding resources in exchange for reliability assurance. AAMER et al. proposed a method of error detection using a watchdog processor to perform concurrent system-level error detection by detecting the state of the main processor [25]. Zarandi et al. proposed an error detection and correction mechanism based on configuration bits in FPGAs [27]. Hardware redundancy is a technology that widely used in hardware detection methods. The most widely used is hardware three-mode redundancy TMR technology [28]. The three-mode redundancy technology uses three identical modules to perform operations in parallel, because of the three modules are mutually Independent. Therefore, to some extent the reliability of this system can be improved. TMR [30, 31] is a widely used fault-tolerant technology against the single-event upset for the FPGA platform.

Hardware-based fault-tolerant technology is based primarily on hardware redundancy, adding overhead to cable and hardware [32]. On the other hand, customized hardware systems have high hardware component overhead and poor commercial product flexibility. Software-based control flow detection reduces the design costs while providing greater flexibility than the previous one [33]. Alkhalifa et al. proposed the ECCA algorithm [34]. The ECCA signature algorithm implements the technology of hardware fault tolerance in software largely. However, this method also has certain disadvantages, that is, detection between high-level programming languages is not so flexible. In addition, compiler optimizations may also affect the instrumentation assertions.

Based on the Stanford ARGOS project, Oh et al. proposed a pure software-based CFCSS algorithm [14], which is an assembly language-based control flow detection method that performs detection in basic blocks. The CFCSS algorithm judges whether there is a control flow error by inserting the verification information and expands the multi-fan-in basic block through the real-time signature G and the correction signature D, which [36] greatly improves the error detection rate of the control flow.

For the watchdog detection method [26], there is too much initialization information of the watchdog detection method, that result in the high overhead and redundancy. Hamid R. Zarandi proposed an error detection and correction mechanism based on configuration bits in FPGAs [29]. Comparing with our method, the hardware overhead is costly more and the flexibility of custom hardware is weakly more. Thus, the software-based control flow detection has unique advantages that can significantly reduce costs. The ECCA algorithm and the CFCSS algorithm can determine whether there is a control flow error by inserting the verification information [35], and expand the multi-fan-in basic block through the real-time signature G and the correction signature D. But it can only perform at the entrance of the basic block cause of the signature technique. Then, the error cannot be detected when the program jumps from a part of a basic block to an entry of basic block which have a switch [37]. The method proposed in this paper is based on the function call relationship for static instrumentation. According to the auxiliary analysis file to determine the file name and the file start line number, thus the coverage of error detection is higher.

7   Conclusion

Satellites is sensitive to particle radiation in space, which causes high-energy particles to enter the sensitive area. That will cause transient errors and single-event flipping in the logic state of the device.

This paper presents transient fault detection and recovery methods. This transient fault detection technology is a coarse-grained fault detection method based on the function call relationship. It can ensure our scheme detect the program execution flow error caused by external errors with static instrumentation and dynamic runtime fault detection.

At the same time, applying this technology on the embedded operating system μC/OS-II and testing by injecting errors at runtime further validated the effectiveness of our methods.

Finally, we combine transient fault detection and recovery mechanism to develop a prototype system.

Acknowledgment. This work was supported by National Natural Science Foundation of China (No. 61672073 and 61272167).

References

1. James, B.F., Norton, O.W., Alexander, M.B.: The natural space environment: effects on spacecraft. NASA STI/Recon, Technical report N 95 (1994)
2. Boudjemai, A., Hocine, R., Guerionne, S.: Space environment effect on earth observation satellite instruments. In: International Conference on Recent Advances in Space Technologies, pp. 627–634. IEEE (2015)

3. Amrbar, M., Irom, F., Guertin, S.M., et al.: Heavy ion single event effects measurements of Xilinx Zynq-7000 FPGA. In: Radiation Effects Data Workshop, pp. 1–4. IEEE (2015)
4. Mccollum, M., James, B., Herr, J.: Operating in the space environment - a spacecraft charging study of the advanced X-ray astrophysics facility-spectroscopy. AIAA SPACE Forum (1994). https://doi.org/10.2514/6.1994-4471
5. Kimoto, Y., Yano, K., Ishizawa, J., et al.: Passive space-environment-effect measurement on the international space station. J. Spacecraft Rockets 46(1), 22–27 (2015)
6. Ciani, L., Catelani, M.: A fault tolerant architecture to avoid the effects of Single Event Upset (SEU) in avionics applications. Measurement 54(6), 256–263 (2014)
7. Hari, S.K.S., Adve, S.V., Naeimi, H., et al.: Relyzer: exploiting application-level fault equivalence to analyze application resiliency to transient faults. Comput. Archit. News 40(1), 123 (2015)
8. Nazarian, G., Rodrigues, D.G., Moreira, A., et al.: Bit-flip aware control-flow error detection. In: Euromicro International Conference on Parallel, Distributed and Network-Based Processing, pp. 215–221. IEEE (2015)
9. Jimenez, R.: Effects of natural environment charged particle heating on the design and performance of spacecraft cryogenic components. In: AIAA, 24th Thermophysics Conference (2013)
10. Nazarian, G., Nane, R., Gaydadjiev, G.N.: Low-cost software control-flow error recovery. In: Digital System Design, pp. 510–517. IEEE (2015)
11. Rhisheekesan, A.: Quantitative evaluation of control flow based soft error protection mechanisms. Dissertations & theses - Gradworks (2013)
12. Wolf, J., Fechner, B., Uhrig, S., et al.: Fine-grained timing and control flow error checking for hard real-time task execution. In: IEEE ISIE, pp. 257–266. IEEE (2012)
13. Ge, X., Talele, N., Payer, M., et al.: Fine-grained control-flow integrity for kernel software. In: IEEE European Symposium on Security and Privacy, pp. 179–194. IEEE (2016)
14. Oh, N., Shirvani, P.P., Mccluskey, E.J.: Control-flow checking by software signatures. IEEE Trans. Reliab. 51(1), 111–122 (2002)
15. Borin, E., Wang, C., Wu, Y., et al.: Software-based transparent and comprehensive control-flow error detection. In: International Symposium on Code Generation and Optimization, pp. 333–345. IEEE (2006)
16. Troiano, A., Corinto, F., Pasero, E.: A memristor circuit using basic elements with memory capability. In: Bassis, S., Esposito, A., Morabito, F.C. (eds.) Recent Advances of Neural Network Models and Applications. SIST, vol. 26, pp. 117–124. Springer, Cham (2014). https://doi.org/10.1007/978-3-319-04129-2_12
17. Lin, C.M., Dow, C.R.: Efficient checkpoint-based failure recovery techniques in mobile computing systems. J. Inf. Sci. Eng. 17(4), 549–573 (2011)
18. Wang, R., Li, Z.H.: A multiprocessor RTOS design of uC/OS. In: Advanced Materials Research, vol. 756, pp. 814–819. Trans Tech Publications (2013)
19. Mutuel, L.H.: Appreciating the effectiveness of single event effect mitigation techniques. In: Digital Avionics Systems Conference, pp. 5B1-1–5B1-11. IEEE (2014)
20. Beenamole, K.S.: Understanding single-event effects in FPGA for avionic system design. IETE Tech. Rev. 30(6), 497–505 (2013)
21. Ferlet-Cavrois, V., et al.: Single event transients in digital CMOS—a review. IEEE Trans. Nuclear Sci. 60(3), 1767–1790 (2013)
22. Hands, A., Fan, L., Ryden, K., et al.: New data and modelling for single event effects in the stratospheric radiation environment. IEEE Trans. Nucl. Sci. 64(1), 587–595 (2017)
23. Hayes, J.P., Polian, I., Becker, B.: An analysis framework for transient-error tolerance. In: IEEE VLSI Test Symposium, pp. 249–255. IEEE Computer Society (2007)

24. Rohani, A., Kerkhoff, H.G., Costenaro, E., et al.: Pulse-length determination techniques in the rectangular single event transient fault model. In: ICEC: Architectures, Modeling, and Simulation, pp. 213–218 (2015)
25. Mahmood, A., Mccluskey, E.J.: Concurrent error detection using watchdog processors-a survey. IEEE Trans. Comput. **37**(2), 160–174 (1988)
26. Chitsaz, B., Kirovski, D.: Watchdog processors in multicore systems: US, US7958396 (2011)
27. Zarandi, H.R., Miremadi, S.G., Argyrides, C., et al.: Fast SEU detection and correction in LUT configuration bits of SRAM-based FPGAs. In: IEEE IPDPS, pp. 1–6 (2007)
28. Nidhin, T.S., Bhattacharyya, A., Behera, R.P., et al.: SEU mitigation by golay code in the configuration memory of SRAM based FPGAs. In: ICCICCT. IEEE (2017)
29. Yin, P.Y., Chen, Y.H., Lu, C.W., et al.: A multi-stage fault-tolerant multiplier with triple module redundancy (TMR) technique. J. Circuits Syst. Comput. **23**(05), 725–735 (2013)
30. Almukhaizim, S., Sinanoglu, O.: A hazard-free majority voter for TMR-based fault tolerance in asynchronous circuits. In: International Design and Test Workshop, IDT 2007, pp. 93–98. IEEE (2008)
31. Mahatme, N.N., Chatterjee, I., Patki, A., et al.: An efficient technique to select logic nodes for single event transient pulse-width reduction. Microelectron. Reliab. **53**(1), 114–117 (2013)
32. Munk, P., et al.: A software fault-tolerance mechanism for real-time applications on many-core processors. In: The Workshop on Highly-Reliable Power-Efficient Embedded Designs (2016)
33. Zhu, X., Qin, X., Qiu, M.: QoS-aware fault-tolerant scheduling for real-time tasks on heterogeneous clusters. IEEE Trans. Comput. **60**(6), 800–812 (2011)
34. Alkhalifa, Z., Nair, V.S.S., et al.: Design and evaluation of system-level checks for on-line control flow error detection. IEEE Trans. Parallel Distrib. Syst. **10**(6), 627–641 (1999)
35. Jafari-Nodoushan, M., Miremadi, S.G., Ejlali, A.: Control-flow checking using branch instructions. In: IEEE/IFIP International Conference on Embedded and Ubiquitous Computing, pp. 66–72. IEEE (2009)
36. Ju, X., Zhang, H., Wang, A.: Error detection by software signatures based on control flow graph. In: International Conference on Future Computer and Information Technology, pp. 51–63 (2013)
37. Asghari, S.A., Taheri, H., et al.: Software-based control flow checking against transient faults in industrial environments. IEEE Trans. Industr. Inf. **10**(1), 481–490 (2013)

Author Index

Printed in the United States
By Bookmasters